Brief and Extended Interventions in Sexual Abuse

Second Edition

Robert H. Rencken

AMERICAN COUNSELING ASSOCIATION

American Counseling Association
5999 Stevenson Avenue, Alexandria, Virginia 22304

Brief and Extended Interventions in Sexual Abuse
Second Edition

10 9 8 7 6 5 4 3 2 1

American Counseling Association
5999 Stevenson Avenue
Alexandria, VA 22304

Director of Publications
Carolyn C. Baker

Cover design by Brian Gallagher

Library of Congress Cataloging-in-Publication Data

Rencken, Robert H.
Brief and extended interventions in sexual abuse/Robert H. Rencken.
p. cm.
Rev. ed. of: Intervention strategies for sexual abuse.
Includes bibliographical references and index.
ISBN 1-55620-178-8 (alk. paper)
1. Child sexual abuse—Treatment. 2. Sexually abused children—Rehabilitation. 3. Adult child sexual abuse victims—Rehabilitation.
I. Renken, Robert H. Intervention strategies for sexual abuse. II. Title

RC560.C46 R46 2000
616.85'836—dc21

To my children, their children, and our children . . .
and our grandchildren

CONTENTS

ACKNOWLEDGEMENTS

I greatly appreciate the influence and assistance of many people in my career, particularly as it shows in this book. In their professionalism, joy, caring, and concern, my colleagues in the counseling profession are always the best role models.

For *Intervention Strategies for Sexual Abuse,* I again thank Sara Welchert, Lizbeth Gray, Jacqueline Saltz, and Jean Wortman for their assistance. Their wisdom continues.

I thank and acknowledge the hard work and support of my colleagues in Sunnyside Unified School District and my partners in private practice, Charlie Lunden and Anne Serrano, as well as those involved in the ongoing struggle against sexual abuse.

I greatly appreciate the contribution of my clients to my knowledge. Your patience, courage, and love are the best rewards.

The pure joy and wonder of family fills me nowadays, and I thank all of my family members—David and Cindy, Kristin and David, C. J. and Lorca, and Stephen and Leanne, and, of course, the grandchildren.

Most of all, I acknowledge the love and patience of my wife and lover, Kay, who continues to be my role model in dealing with children, me included.

PREFACE

In traveling around the country doing workshops and seminars on the issues of sexual abuse, incest, and childhood sexuality, I have been consistently impressed with the range and diversity of professionals and other caregivers who are hungry for information. These are not people who want to specialize in the treatment of sexual abuse. In fact, many of them wish that it had never reared its head in their professional or personal lives and wish that it would simply go away. Although available information has exploded since the 1989 publication of the original volume, *Intervention Strategies for Sexual Abuse,* many questions still remain about the "big picture" of sexual abuse and how we as counselors can make a difference.

The information for which they hunger is basic and immediate: How should a known victim be treated in school? Why do "those perverts" do it? How does a history of abuse affect a college student's relationships? What strategies can be effective in intervening in a sexual abuse situation, even if I am not the primary counselor or therapist?

Many of the resources that have been recently published in the field of sexual abuse are directed toward the specialized treatment of one segment of the population affected (healing the survivor, behavioral treatment of the offender, play therapy with the young victim) or may add to the confusion of the consumer or clinician through unclear jargon and nonstandard categorization (e.g., pedophilia, molest, incest, deviant behavior, rape, sexaholism). For the average counselor or human development professional in the field, it might seem necessary to read a dozen books and attend two or three workshops to gain a basic understanding of the problem and to learn some basic intervention strategies.

The intent of this book is to provide a clear and basic framework for understanding the dimensions (scope, taxonomy, philosophy) and dynamics (individual, familial, societal) of pedosexual behavior, particularly child sexual abuse. The major focus is on the implementation of integrated intervention strategies for any professional who faces only one "piece of the puzzle."

Sexual abuse is a complex problem that is extremely taxing and challenging for the counselor/psychotherapist. The ideal counselor should be skilled in individual adult counseling, play therapy, marriage and relationship work, group process with children and adults, behavior modification, cognitive therapy, sexuality therapy, the criminal justice system, and family systems, among other areas. Many of us feel more comfortable and competent in some of these areas than in others. It is essential that we recognize this and focus our interventions within our area of competence and expertise. This book provides strategies for those interventions as well as a sense of the "big picture" that puts those interventions into an integrated perspective. The purpose of this book is to provide comprehensive yet understandable information to a range of counselors and mental health professionals who are not necessarily specialists in the arena of childhood sexual abuse. Evaluation, prevention, and treatment strategies for victims, survivors, offenders, and families are presented in an integrated context.

This revision of *Intervention Strategies for Sexual Abuse* adds a new dimension to the treatment of sexual abuse by providing options for brief interventions. This is a reflection of a perspective that has been increasingly important for our profession. In mental health settings, public or private, we are being challenged to use fewer and fewer sessions. In schools and agencies, we are faced with budgetary constraints that force us to limit the duration of our services. Although I still see sexual abuse in the category of long-term treatment, I put forth several brief interventions that can be both effective and helpful. These brief techniques are particularly helpful for counselors who are not specialists in the field.

These brief interventions are responsive to changing legal and political concerns, as well as economic factors. With an increasing emphasis and dependence on longer incarceration of offenders, the long-term goals of family reunification may not be realized and may be replaced by briefer or intermittent treatment, focussed on the victim/survivor. The implications of this are discussed.

The addition of brief options may provoke some new positive shifts away from the specialized, structured treatment of the past to a more free-flowing style, using more generalized techniques (and technicians). This is an area of major challenge for this book.

This revision is also important because of new, or newly emphasized, issues over these last 10 years:

- false accusations, an issue that has graced more afternoon talk shows than alien abductions;
- repressed and recovered memories, a related issue that has also drawn media attention;
- ritual and satanic abuse, a topic that has, perhaps, already waxed and waned, with its incredible tales of animal and human sacrifice;
- increased attention to female offenders, although this remains somewhat taboo;
- some increased attention to male victims; and
- counselors and therapists defending themselves against claims of malpractice, "planted" thoughts, and iatrogenic harm.

It will be tempting for the reader to flip directly to strategies applicable to his or her situation or population, for the school counselor to go to the "victims" section or the college dean to go to the "survivor" section. I believe, however, that this would deny the larger perspective and reinforce one of the problems we currently have—counselors working at cross-purposes and, sometimes, even adversarially. I do encourage rereading sections of particular interest. I also strongly encourage all professionals to ask themselves how they can be a part of the prevention of this major problem through treatment, advocacy, and research.

The treatment of individuals and families involved in sexual abuse has been the most rewarding part of my professional career. I hope that I can share some of that enthusiasm, encouragement, and empowerment.

About the Author

Bob Rencken has been a mental health counselor and clinical sexologist in private practice in Tucson, Arizona, for over 25 years. He is also a school psychologist with the Sunnyside Unified School District. His specialty in providing education and treatment around sexuality issues includes his longstanding interest in the topic of sexual abuse, being one of the pioneers in the field. He is the author of *Intervention Strategies in Sexual Abuse* and is a nationally recognized workshop presenter on these topics. He served as executive director of the Arizona Counselors Association for 14 years and served in various leadership positions, including the Governing Council of the American Counseling Association. He has been honored as "Outstanding Member" of the Arizona Counselors Association on two occasions, received the "Counselor of the Year" award from the American Mental Health Counselors Association, and received the prestigious Kitty Cole Human Rights Award from the American Counseling Association.

CHAPTER 1

Overview of the Problem

This chapter provides a perspective on the issues around sexual abuse and the importance of seeing the highly complex "big picture." I define and describe the problem and its impact; the use of a classification system; the pedosexual taxonomy; the societal, family, and individual dynamics that play the biggest part in the complexity of diagnostic and treatment interventions; important philosophical assumptions; and legal and criminal justice concerns. I discuss issues related to managed care and touch on a few controversial issues that have appeared in recent years.

It would be nice if somebody else had the problem. Not exactly "nice," but we could have the safety and luxury of sitting back and feeling sorry for "that poor kid." Maybe life was a little simpler before I knew very much about sexual abuse.

Counselors in all settings, however, are dealing with clients with a history of sexual abuse. Like it or not, prepared or not, counselors are hearing tales of abuse from many sources. We hear the 9-year-old tell about his neighbor forcing fellatio on him. We hear the 16-year-old tell about long-term coitus with her stepfather. We hear of the college student worrying about relationships because of her secret of abuse as a child. We hear the 30-year-old divorced woman tell of her generalized anger toward men. We hear about the tragic rape and murder of a 10-year-old boy. We hear, and hear about, the horror stories of sexual abuse.

When I ask counselors how they react to their clients' reports of sexual abuse, some common feelings surface: disgust, anger, sympathy, pity, rage. Many counselors also feel an accompanying sense of helplessness. What can I do to alleviate this devastating problem? Can I be more than an emotional Band-Aid? How can I find the time to deal with something this big? How can I erase what has happened? How can I deal with my own feelings and reactions?

The feelings and the questions are completely understandable. Most counselors, psychotherapists, social workers, psychologists, psychiatrists, and other helping professionals have had little or no academic training relating to sexually abused clients. Some have sought out workshops, seminars, or books that have possibly even added to the feeling of being overwhelmed. My intention in this volume is to unravel some of the complexity of the dynamics and treatment of sexual abuse so that you can make meaningful interventions in the lives of your clients, whether as a primary or supportive therapist. Although this book is not intended to train you as an expert or specialist in the field, it may be a helpful foundation and resource tool.

Can you visualize a snow-covered volcano? That's a fair metaphor for sexual abuse in several ways:

- Most of the time, to the casual observer, things look not only normal but better than normal, even pristine.
- Even when the volcano is dormant, the snow hides treacherous rocks and holes. The secret of sexual abuse covers up both the behavior and damage and may "successfully" cover them for years before the unsuspecting victim-survivor trips and falls.
- Volcanoes erupt forcefully. Victims of abuse store tremendous rage that may be unleashed.
- Just as the snow-covered volcano mixes elements—lava and snow, hot and cold—victims of abuse typically experience many conflicting emotions: love and hate, fear and guilt, power and weakness.
- After the eruption, lava also leaves scars, a new face on the mountain. This new face, like the old one, can be covered with snow. Again, on the surface, the scars may not be visible and may look "normal." We know, however, that another eruption is inevitable.
- The volcano eruption affects the surrounding area. When an individual is abused, family members and friends of the victim and the entire society are indirect victims.
- The potential for further eruption continues, unpredictable in time, intensity, and cause. Counselors of sexual abuse victims see the anger, rage, and pain years after abuse has ceased.

I return to this metaphor throughout the chapter. For now, suffice it to say that the issues of sexual abuse are among the most complicated, heterogeneous, and elusive that we as counselors and therapists face. As often as not, it seems that things are not what they seem because of denials, rationalizations, secrets, repression, fear, ambivalence, surface normality, and societal bias.

What do we know for sure? After 20 years of work and 10 years since the first edition of this book was published, the answer is still "not much." Although interest in the topic has certainly increased, most research still comes from clinical practice itself. We have done a surprisingly good job, in fact, of dealing with these issues through clinical networking rather than experimental, or even descriptive, research. The more recent research comes from sexology, sociology, psychology, and social work, including a new journal devoted to the topic, *Sexual Abuse: A Journal of Research and Treatment,* and several new support, advocacy, and resource organizations. Nevertheless, much of the research in this book is attributable to the clinical experience of dozens of therapists whose information is shared verbally as well as in writing.

Research in this area faces major obstacles: lack of data (sketchy data available only on reported cases), greatly varying terminology in both legal and scientific circles (e.g., *fondling, intercourse,* and *pederasty* each has varying definitions), differing legal statutes and punishments, the primary need to protect child victims, and strong societal biases.

What we do know about sexual abuse in terms of statistics is still summarized effectively in Finkelhor's (1984) research:

- Incidence research shows that between 8% to 38% of women and 5% to 9% of men in the United States have been victimized (Finkelhor, 1990; Freeman-Longo & Blanchard, 1998; Hunter, 1990; Li, West, & Woodhouse, 1993).
- Although specific statistics are not available, sexual abuse is an international concern.
- Sexual abuse is committed primarily by men (Bell & Weinberg, 1978; Finkelhor, 1979). Ninety-five percent of female victims and 80% of male victims are abused by men.
- By definition, sexual abuse is harmful.
- Most victims are between 8 and 12 years old, but many are younger.
- Stepfathers may be five times as likely to victimize a daughter sexually than fathers are, although other family members (brothers, uncles, grandfathers) could be offenders.

- Most female victimization occurs within the family.
- Boys are more likely to be abused outside the family than girls, but when abuse occurs, it is typically within the family.

Over the past 10 years, many attempts have been made to clarify the incidence research, especially in the light of popular media attention. In some recent research, the term *sexual abuse* has been changed to *unwanted sexual experiences,* but this has not really seemed to be helpful because it has blurred the line between child sexual abuse and forms of rape or other nonconsensual sexual contact. The incidence of sexual abuse has probably remained the same in the last 10 years, that is, too high. Despite media attention on the subject, particularly on the issue of false allegations (Althof, 1994; Loftus & Ketcham, 1994; Morfit, 1994; Spiegel, 1988; Wylie, 1993), incidence is underreported for the following reasons:

- Despite Finkelhor's (1984) attempts at gaining data from parent reports, much data are gathered from retrospective reports of previously unreported incidents or undergraduate psychology students.
- Increasingly severe penalties for offenders may discourage children from reporting or testifying against a family member. (However, data to support this contention are particularly difficult to obtain and interpret.)
- Adults are so uncomfortable with both sexuality and sexual abuse issues that they may have a tendency "not to get involved" in reporting.
- The victimization of boys is minimized because of our societal sexist beliefs that only girls are victims, only men are offenders, and boys can't cry (or tattle or feel or care) and should not only "take it" but, somehow, actually enjoy the sexual contact.
- Children are afraid to report.
- Abuse is masked by other behavior (running away, substance abuse, suicide, shyness, withdrawal).
- Despite growing awareness of the problem of abuse, children who report abuse often are not believed.

Regardless of the exact statistics, and even when using conservative estimates, there are hundreds of thousands of cases of sexual abuse each year. Clearly, our society abuses, exploits, and victimizes those who are less powerful—the children.

Impact

Measuring the impact of sexual abuse on children entails the same kind of obstacles as does incidence research. We can easily talk about the trauma of abuse, yet we know that children's reactions are neither predictable nor universal. We can talk about future difficulties with healthy sexual functioning and self-esteem (Herman, 1981; Maltz, 1991; Maltz & Holman, 1987), but we cannot predict how or when those effects may materialize. We also see a host of other effects: runaway behavior and delinquent and criminal activities (McCormack, 1986), binge eating (W. Jones & Emerson, 1994), and depression and anxiety (Murrey et al., 1993).

We can make some general statements about effects or potential effects which, although clearly not universal, are helpful for us in treating and supporting families, victims, and survivors of sexual abuse.

1. The process of sexualization that results from sexual abuse, discussed in chapter 2 on intervention strategies for the victim, is a developmental anomaly that affects the child's general adjustment by causing the child to skip the usual stages of psychosexual development.
2. The child loses trust, security, and, as a result, the essence of childhood.
3. The child experiences ambivalent feelings—love and hate, rage and guilt, stoicism and fear—that are difficult to manage.
4. The message is loud and clear that sex is exploitive, demanding, hurtful (and painful), and interwoven with power and manipulation, reinforcing our societal sex negativity and setting up the cycle of abuse.
5. Defenses are created that, although initially functional, become obstacles to treatment and successful adjustment: denial, repression, dissociation, anorgasmia, anorexia, obesity, substance use and abuse, running away, and the ultimate result:
6. Death, by overt or covert suicide or homicide.

The impact of sexual abuse is felt not only by the victim, as difficult as that may be—the victim's family, peers, and society are affected as well. Yet, the one person who is not often considered when we discuss impact is the offender. The most obvious consequences for sexual abuse are criminal prosecution or removal from the home. Issues relating to the criminal justice system are discussed later in this chapter, but clearly the threat of arrest, prison, probation, or mandated separation from the victim or the offender's family presents emotional, relational, financial, and employment burdens. This is not to discount the offender's responsibility or to imply that the offender doesn't "deserve" the consequences. Rather, it is necessary to acknowledge the pain, guilt (often at suicidal intensity), and confusion that *most* sexual abusers feel (the exceptions are discussed later). This pain may be present both before and after the report and, if untreated, continues indefinitely.

Probably the most persistent conflict on a day-to-day basis is experienced by the nonoffending spouse in intrafamilial abuse. The strained and dysfunctional marital relationship is often both the cause and effect of abuse. The mother is torn between loyalty toward, support of, and dependency on her husband on one side and protection and support of her child on the other. She is also burdened with the daily control, maintenance, and logistical support of the family, probably without the presence or assistance of her husband, placing tremendous time and energy constraints on her. Unfortunately, this conflict is too often resolved through denial, divorce, or abandonment, either physical or psychological.

Siblings may also be victims; they are not only fearful of being abused themselves but also may have been aware of the abuse and be unwitting keepers of the family "secret." In one case, a 22-year-old daughter had kept the family secret for 15 years and revealed it only when the parents were in prison on an unrelated charge. Siblings may defend against the fear and guilt by blaming the victim of abuse. If they can rationalize that the victim "asked for it" or "enjoyed it," then they can be less conflicted about loving the father.

Peers also may be affected and be torn between supporting and blaming the victim. Friends may even be involved in the report. Frequently, the victim admits the abuse to a friend, who tells her or his parent, who in turn reports to authorities. The most effective therapy group, not surprisingly, is the peer victim-survivor group.

The damage of sexual abuse to society is seen in several systems. Obviously, the damage to the family as the foundation of society affects basic affectional and relational systems. Sexualization affects societal concerns such as early pregnancy and sexually transmitted diseases (Fuller & Bartucci, 1991). Economic costs include direct costs (protection, prosecution, punishment), loss of productivity (loss of earning potential, long-term costs of disability, welfare support, underemployment), and structural costs (because the family foundation crumbles; Rencken, 1996a).

Freeman-Longo and Blanchard (1998) presented a compelling argument for viewing abuse and other sexual aggression as a public health problem as opposed to a criminal justice problem. They used the term *epidemic* as a health descriptor rather than as hyperbole to refer to incidence. They also emphasized the need for prevention more than prosecution, just as one would with any other health concerns. Their perspective is revisited in the discussion of prevention in chapter 6. They quoted Surgeon General C. Everett Koop in this regard:

> Identifying violence as a public health issue is a relatively new idea. Traditionally, when confronted by the circumstances of violence, the health professionals have deferred to the criminal justice system. Over the years we've tacitly and, I believe, mistakenly agreed that violence was the exclusive province of the police, the courts, and the penal system. To be sure, those agents of public safety and justice have served us well. But when we ask them to concentrate more on the prevention of violence and to provide additional services for victims, we may begin to burden the criminal system beyond reason. At that point, the professionals of medicine, nursing, and the health-related social services must come forward and recognize violence as their issue, also, one which profoundly affects the public health. (Freeman-Longo & Blanchard, 1998, pg. 17)

One must also acknowledge that recent research, including important longitudinal studies (Leitenberg, Greenwald, & Tarran, 1989; Li et al., 1993; Okami, Olmstead, & Abramson, 1997), raise the possibility that some children are not necessarily affected by early sexual experience and that such contact could even be positive. This research and other clinical anecdotal reports point to the possibility that some adults retrospectively report sexual contact with an adult during their childhood that was either pleasurable, nurturing, comforting, or exciting. It is presumed that these contacts probably were extrafamilial and were generally not reported as abusive. The number of children for whom this experience is neutral or positive can be assumed to be relatively small; we simply do not understand either the extent or the dynamics involved in such situations. Such research creates a dilemma for counselors between basic nonjudgmental acceptance as opposed to our more typical harm framework, and we must look carefully at the sexual interactions noted. (This is another reason for using the neutral term *pedosexual*, although I recognize the abusive results of most of these contacts.)

Finally, counselors should look at the impact of sexual abuse on the counseling profession and the practice of psychotherapy, regardless of professional affiliation. Until relatively recently, counselors and therapists were ignoring or actively denying the problem. In my view, we seemed to move to a stage of buck-passing where we became more aware of the problem, reported as we were required, but still wanted "others" (e.g., Child Protective Services, law enforcement, mental health system) to take care of it.

The therapeutic community has also been accused of being a part of the problem. The term *iatrogenic* has unfortunately been applied to counselors in the sexual abuse arena, mostly in the criticisms of "planted memories," leading questions, and some questionable tactics in diagnosis and treatment of Dissociative Identity Disorder (DID; formerly Multiple Personality Disorder). I address these concerns in the sections on victim and adult survivors treatment in chapter 4.

In the last 20 years, we have been making the transition to a more directly active role: probing for the possibility of abuse in child and adult clients; providing primary therapy for victims, offenders, and families; and taking an important supportive role with treatment teams and coordinating with various agencies. Counselors in all settings are on the "front line" in confronting this issue. We all have an ethical responsibility to be prepared.

Taxonomy

One of the biggest obstacles in research, education, and treatment of sexual abuse is the lack of common terminology and taxonomy (Waterman & Lusk, 1986). In fact, this is a significant problem in sexological research and writing in general. Understanding of the issues is confounded by philosophical differences (sexual behavior vs. abuse), ill-defined concepts (sexual abuse, incest, molestation), changing definitions, legal inconsistencies (intercourse, consensuality), and prejudicial labels (molester, pervert, promiscuous, deviate, baby-raper). Terms used in this book are defined in the Glossary; readers should note that there is no standard definition for terms, and these definitions may vary from one researcher or clinician to another.

A major challenge in classification or structure of sexual abuse (in fact, any sexual behavior) is the heterogeneity of the variables. The official nosological system of the American Psychiatric Association, currently the 4th edition of the *Diagnostic and Statistical Manual of Mental Disorders* (*DSM-IV;* American Psychiatric Association, 1994) addresses only three areas related to sexuality: Gender Identity (302.6, 302.8), Sexual Dysfunctions (302.7x), and a limited number of Paraphilias (e.g., Pedophilia , 302.2). With these few available categories, many clinicians, particularly clinical sexologists, frequently find themselves using "Other" diagnoses (e.g., "Other Sexual Disorder, 302.9," which may include other paraphilias or relationship problems).

The only two "official " diagnoses that may apply specifically to sexual abuse are Pedophilia (302.2) and Post-traumatic Stress Disorder (PTSD; 309.81), both of which are probably overused by clinicians. This is not to say, of course, that those affected (victim-survivor, offender, or collaterals) may not have diagnosable conditions, ranging from Adjustment to Affective to Personality Disorders.

All of this speaks to the difficulties of organizing and communicating a system for classifying sexual abuse. It is easy for us to say that each case has to be addressed individually. One must be aware of the generalizations that have been damaging (e.g., all offenders are incurable pedophiles, all victims suffer from PTSD or DID, all moms "really knew"). These have been used by legislators, the media, and the criminal justice system in a futile attempt to create concrete solutions to this muddy problem, making counselors' work that much more difficult. However, it is crucial to recognize commonalities, themes, and patterns in sexual abuse that allow more effective planning for treatment, recidivism risk reduction, and prevention.

The taxonomy presented here focuses on select criteria that I see as being the most crucial for decisions that are best for the child.

I have been using the term *pedosexual* as a generic term for any sexual contact involving a child or adolescent. Although this is stretching the typical usage of the prefix, *pedo-*, to include adolescents, it is helpful because of the overlapping of behaviors and issues. The term is reasonably objective and inclusive and provides us with the opportunity to classify behavior, dynamics, participants, level of coercion, and setting. It should be used as an adjective (e.g., pedosexual behavior) rather than as a noun (e.g., he is a pedosexual).

Attempts at taxonomy in this field have included bipolar classifications such as Groth and Birnbaum's (1978) concepts of fixated versus regressed offenders, Giaretto's (1982) focus on intrafamilial versus extrafamilial abuse, or Finkelhor's (1984) four preconditions. All of these dimensions need to be included in a taxonomy. Ryan (1999b) undertook the monumental task of describing the entire context of sexual abuse, from type of behavior to level of coercion to frequency and multiple other areas. Although this certainly is the most comprehensive description we have, it is probably too cumbersome for clinical work and includes variables that probably do not have much value for treatment. However, it remains an excellent research tool.

My pedosexual taxonomy has four axes: age of participants, setting (intrafamilial, extrafamilial), level of coercion, and offender dynamics (six categories; see Table 1). This type of taxonomy results in quite specific clinical and descriptive research and improved clinical communication.

These axes can be abbreviated as follows:

- The setting is either I (intrafamilial) or E (extrafamilial).
- The five possible age combinations become C/C (child-child), C/Ado (child-adolescent), C/Adu (child-adult), Ado/Ado (adolescent-adolescent), and Ado/Adu (adolescent-adult).
- The level of coercion is noted from L (low) to H (high); this is specified more in the section "Level of Coercion," which appears later in this chapter.
- The offender dynamics are R (regressed), P (pedophile), Ra (rapist), Ri (ritual) or S (symptomatic), and A (addictive/compulsive).

Thus, for example, "C/Adu, I, L, R" indicates the most common form of abuse, intrafamilial pedosexual contact between a regressed adult and a prepubertal child, with a low level of coercion.

Table 1. Pedosexual Taxonomy

Age group	Setting	Level of coercion	Offender dynamics
• Child-child	• Intrafamilial	• Verbal seduction	• Regressed
• Child-adolescent		• Indirect threats	• Pedophile
• Child-adult	• Extrafamilial, stranger	• Direct threats (without weapon)	• Rapist
• Adolescent-adolescent	• Extrafamilial, known to child	• Physical harm	• Ritualistic Symptomatic
• Adolescent-adult		• Threats with weapon	• Addictive/compulsive

It is also essential to describe behavior clearly and specifically. Instead of using words like fondling, we should specify whether or not there is digital penetration or clitoral stimulation and whether the behavior is active or receptive. Similarly, instead of oral sex, we need to specify fellatio or cunnilingus, and instead of intercourse, specify penile-vaginal, penile-femoral, and so forth. Specifying the behavior requires the correct use of basic anatomical terms. One of the most common errors is to refer to the vagina when really meaning labia. Using terms clearly and accurately helps us to understand the nature of the behavior and may be very important in dealing with the criminal justice system. Behavior does not, however, seem to have a clear prediction for the treatment of the child or adult. Some victims who are genitally touched once may have a stronger trauma reaction than one who is engaged in long-term coitus.

Age of Participants

The age of participants can be categorized by a matrix of child (prepubertal), adolescent (pubescent to age 18), and adult, yielding six possible combinations as noted in the table. Because the focus here is on pedosexual contact, I do not discuss the adult-adult combination even though sexual abuse does occur between adults and can be a criminal offense. The five remaining combinations are important in the taxonomy because they help to describe potential power imbalances.

Child–child. The frequency of child-child sexual contact has not been researched, although there is some indication that sibling incest may be the most frequent behavior (Wiehe, 1990). When one considers peer contact as well, the incidence is high. Although most cases probably are classified as "sex play" (e.g., "playing doctor"), this generalization may be less helpful than in the past. Because abuse (either physical or sexual) typically is described in terms of a power differential, a 5-year age difference has frequently been adopted as significant for that power difference (Finkelhor, 1984). However, therapists are more often seeing situations that involve clearly coercive (and probably abusive) behaviors involving children with little or no age difference. This seems to occur when one child has been powerfully sexualized. The assumption that either all child-child contacts are innocent or all are harmful is an oversimplification. The key factors in assessing actual or potential damage involve determining developmental appropriateness (Finkelhor & Dziuba-Leaterman, 1994; Yates, 1978) and coercion (Finkelhor, 1984), regardless of age difference.

Child–adolescent. In sexual contact between a child and an adolescent, the issue of power differential is much clearer although coercion may be more implicit, based on physical and cognitive differences. This area needs considerable research because the dynamics or motivation of an adolescent "offender" may be very different than those of an adult offender. This is further discussed in chapter 2 in the section on treating the adolescent offender.

Child–adult. Sexual contact between a child and an adult presents clear power differentials. Legally and psychologically, this age combination is most likely to be described as abusive.

Adolescent—adolescent. Contact between adolescents, like contact between children, does not typically raise concerns about abuse unless there is a power differential. (Note that this does not mean that we are not concerned with teenagers having sex with each other!) The 5-year age difference provides a helpful guideline but is even further complicated by size differential between sexes as well as consensus issues. Age of consensus is a significant societal quandary; I do not attempt to settle it here. Again, the extent of coercion is critical and determines whether behavior is labeled abusive, exploitive, or date-rape.

Adolescent–adult. Although popular wisdom has it that most pedosexual behavior occurs between adolescents and adults, it seems clear that most contact is in fact initiated when the victim is a child and may continue into his or her adolescence (Finkelhor, 1984). Some people entertain images of seductive "Lolitas" enticing men into sex; it simply doesn't happen that way.

Setting

The first axis the counselor should identify is setting, that is, whether the pedosexual behavior took place within or outside the family unit. In *intrafamilial abuse,* the living unit is the frame of reference. It includes those family members living together regardless of blood or legal relationship, including live-in boyfriends and stepparents. It does not typically include extended family members unless they are living with the family unit or are unusually emotionally close. The extrafamilial (i.e., outside the family) setting consists of two areas: contact with a stranger (the mythical man in the trench coat or "Chester the Molester") or contact with a person who is known to the child such as a friend of parents, baby sitter, a member of the extended family, or a neighbor. It is my experience that the "known" subcategory is much more likely than the "stranger" subcategory to be involved in sexual abuse and includes an element of violation of trust that adds to the trauma, similar to, but not as intense as, the issues that arise when parents are involved in abuse.

Level of Coercion

Level of coercion is an important axis in the pedosexual taxonomy; recent research emphasizes the impact of coercion on trauma and, therefore, treatment (Finkelhor, 1984; Hindman, 1989). The lowest level of coercion, probably most typical in childhood sexual abuse, is verbal seduction and includes flattery ("you're so cute/pretty/developing so well"), minimization ("this isn't so bad, no big thing"), normalization ("this feels good, everybody does this"), educational ("I'll teach you about your body, what boys will like"), or pseudoaffectional ("I love you so much"). This low level of coercion is frequently accompanied by vague threats (second level). These include emphasis on the secret ("you can't tell anyone," "this is our special time"), family consequences ("your mother won't understand," "your mother will punish you for telling"), or societal consequences ("you'll be taken away," "I'll go to jail").

The third level includes direct threats without a weapon ("I'll make you do it," "you might get hurt, cooperate or else") and finally, threats with a weapon. Trauma generally increases with each level of coercion, and the fear of physical danger may be more pervasive than the sexual contact.

Offender Dynamics

The fourth and most complex dimension of the pedosexual taxonomy is based on the dynamics of the offender. Clearly this is the most subjective component, and future research may make it possible to clarify this dimension. This dimension is critical when we see legislation enacted that is based on misinformation and miscategorization. The following proposed categories are not completely discrete.

Regressed. The regressed (as opposed to fixated) offender was identified by Groth and Birnbaum (1978) as one who has apparently not exhibited any predominant sexual attraction to significantly younger persons during his sexual development. More recently, the term "*situational*" (as opposed to "*preferential*") has been used with similar meaning (Freeman-Longo & Blanchard, 1998). Essentially, this type of offender is seen as "regressing" to a younger sex object. Although this category has been associated with intrafamilial abuse, it is also typical of the dynamics in much extrafamilial pedosexual contact. The exact etiology of the regression may be related to power issues, severe stress, substance abuse, marital dysfunction, history of physical or sexual abuse, or a combination of factors. Sexual arousal patterns vary, with some individuals not experiencing erection or other arousal, whereas others experience complex sexual fantasy through to orgasm. The presence of sexual arousal does *not* necessarily indicate a paraphilia or deviance from the norm, unless the individual has a predominant pattern of arousal by attraction to, or preference for, children. This regressed category includes the largest number of offenders.

Pedophile. The term *pedophilia* indicates a preferred pattern of sexual arousal to children and is one of the few terms that is defined in a standard way by the *DSM-IV* (American Psychiatric Association, 1994), although it is not always used with this standard definition. It is listed under the paraphilias. The criteria for a diagnosis of pedophilia include the following:

- The individual experiences recurrent intense sexually arousing fantasies, sexual urges, or behaviors involving sexual activity with a prepubescent child or children (generally age 13 or younger).
- These urges cause significant distress.
- The person is at least age 16 and at least 5 years older than the child.

The diagnosis also addresses whether the sexual attraction is to boys, girls, or both; whether it is limited to incest; and whether the pattern is exclusive (i.e., the individual is attracted only to children) or nonexclusive.

Two other paraphilias should be kept distinct from pedophilia: hebephilia (attraction to adolescent girls) and ephebophilia (attraction to adolescent boys). The dynamics of these latter two may be closer to those of adult attraction. Great caution is emphasized here.

Media outlets in particular tend to group all contact between adults and minors as pedophilia, leading to many false assumptions.

Pedophilia is linked with Groth and Birnbaum's (1978) category of the fixated offender (sexually attracted primarily or exclusively to significantly younger persons) or the preferential offender, as noted above. However, some pedophiles give at least surface indications of mature development but have retained the primary attraction to children. Although pedophiles may be a statistical minority, each is likely to have multiple victims, sometimes numbering into the hundreds. The prognosis for the treatment of pedophilia is very poor, as it is for most of the paraphilias, because it involves a set pattern of arousal over a long time.

Rapist. The primary pattern of the rapist is the use of sexual behavior as an expression of violence. Specific dynamics may include those of power, anger, or sadism, as described by Groth (1979). Precise legal and scientific criteria for defining rape may differ; in this book, I use *rape* to refer to forcible penetration or attempted penetration. The latter is included because the offender's intent and the victim's trauma are essentially the same whether or not penetration is actually achieved. Although pedosexual rape is relatively infrequent compared to either adult rape or other pedosexual contact, it understandably commands much public attention. Child rape tragically also may result in homicide or severe physical trauma, precipitating legislative or prosecutorial redress against all those vaguely labeled "child molesters." The issue of sexual arousal, particularly in the child rapist, is vague. The rapist tends to repeat his behavior with a high rate of recidivism, even if he has been convicted and incarcerated.

Ritualistic. Ritualistic abuse is characterized by the structured and repetitious nature of the behavior. These may include highly specific rules (no talking), verbal patterns (phrases or chants), objects (candles, costumes), temporal schedules (midnight), or prescribed sexual behavior (only masturbation or fellatio). This category includes satanic or other cult behavior and has garnered great media attention with tales of human or animal sacrifice and large numbers of victims. Very few cases have been objectively confirmed, but the possibility of ritualistic abuse at different levels, perhaps not as dramatic, is acknowledged.

Symptomatic. Symptomatic offenders are those whose pedosexual behavior is symptomatic of some other primary disorder.

Examples of such primary disorders include schizophrenia, mental retardation, substance abuse or dependence (use of alcohol as a disinhibitor would not make it a primary disorder), or major depression. It is important not to attribute causation to the disorder; that is, schizophrenia does not cause the pedosexual contact, but such contact may be one symptom of the disorder. Many offenders become depressed, anxious, or distressed after the pedosexual contact; again, such depression or distress would not be considered a primary disorder in this context. Symptomatic offenders constitute the smallest category of offenders, but they bear clinical attention because their primary disorder is sometimes overlooked in treatment or incarceration and probation decisions.

Addicted or compulsive. Much recent attention has been given to the concept of the sex addict (or sexaholic or sexually compulsive person; Carnes, 1983, 1985, 1988, 1991; Earle & Crow, 1989; Schneider, 1988; Schwartz, 1992). The label of *sex addict* still creates a stir of controversy within the sexological community, although there seems to be clinical agreement that some individuals are so driven and compulsive that they present a significant risk to themselves and, perhaps, others. Although researchers still have not clarified this phenomenon generally, there is much interest in the relationship between compulsive sexual behavior (however it is defined and interpreted) and other addictive or compulsive disorders as they relate to pedosexual contact.

Pedosexual behavior may be one of the behaviors that appear in a cluster along with other behaviors (usually one to three) that may include compulsive masturbation, voyeurism, exhibitionism, or dependence on prostitution or on sexually explicit media. Children, and most often adolescent girls, may become "targets of opportunity" for the sexually compulsive individual. In other words, children or adolescents may be more easily available than more typical adult partners. Although other pedosexual behavior patterns also may have compulsive or dependent elements, this pattern is converse; that is, the compulsion is primary and the child contact incidental.

Use of This Taxonomy

The taxonomy described in the preceding sections should help clinicians communicate more precisely and with a minimum of judgmental language. The *DSM* system addresses only one aspect of the problem of sexual abuse—pedophilia. Those affected by pedosexual contact, victim or offender, may well have one of a variety of diagnoses on the *DSM* Axis I (mental disorder) or Axis II (personality disorder), but these do not adequately relate to sexual abuse. All four dimensions of pedosexual taxonomy (setting, age group, level of coercion, and offender dynamics) should be used in describing pedosexual contact. When known, the duration or frequency of the behavior should also be noted (e.g., "one-time digital-anal penetration"or "weekly penile-vaginal coitus for 6 months.").

This taxonomy is used in discussion of dynamics and interventions in the rest of the book and in the case studies.

Approaching the Problem

One of the most important tasks of any counselor is to clearly identify philosophical assumptions, personal values, and the societal and environmental atmosphere surrounding any treatment situation. This is particularly true in working with sexual abuse. Counselors in the general area of sexuality have long been aware of the need for self-awareness regarding their own attitudes, values, and beliefs as well as sensitivity to others' values, belief systems, and decision-making processes. When the focus narrows to sex offenses, the need for sensitivity and awareness increases. In turn, when the focus narrows further to child sexual abuse, the counselor needs to be acutely aware of his or her assumptions, values, and societal and environmental milieu. In this section, I examine some of those areas. It is important to emphasize that this process of self-examination is not easy, and requires significant diligence and awareness. Most clinicians have not had a lot of experience in self-examination.

Most professionals who specialize in dealing with pedosexual issues have been asked, "How can you handle those perversions? Why do you deal with those slimeballs? How can you stand being in the same room with them? Why don't they just cut their balls off?" It is not unusual for people actually to question or impugn the motivation, ethics, or integrity of those working with the offender population or, indeed, with sexual abuse in general. Some critics will praise therapists working with children-victims-survivors but vilify those working with offenders. This kind of criticism is certainly difficult for the counselor to hear and reinforces the need to examine the personal agenda closely.

Societal prejudice against "molesters" has not been specifically investigated but may be based on one or more of the following:

1. outrage against the victimization of children;
2. general negativity about sex;
3. lack of knowledge about different forms of pedosexual contact including issues of arousal, behavior, and treatability;
4. images of the raincoat-clad "dirty old man";
5. association with other negative issues (valid or not) such as pornography and alcoholism;
6. assumptions of male sexual inadequacy (i.e., offenders aren't good enough for "real sex"); and
7. fear that "it could happen to me."

Societal prejudice could be tolerated were it not for the impact on the children and their families. Children's natural egocentricity leads them to conclude that they created the abuse situation by being "bad." The more negative society is, the more the child feels it. In intrafamilial abuse, it is typical for the child to blame herself or himself for all the disruption in the family. It is probably not too different from the well-documented magical thinking reactions of children in divorce—if they created the problem, then they can gain control and resolve it. This is a crucial dynamic to understand.

In talking with adult survivors of different forms of pedosexual contact, it becomes clear that they kept "the secret" for years not only to protect the offender and the rest of the family but also out of fear of being seen as tainted or culpable. The feelings of shame and (sometimes) blame that adult rape victims report are magnified in child victims by the distortions of normal child reactions. In the victim's mind, ambivalence and confusion may be more immediate and powerful than the rage and fear that one may expect. Societal prejudice frequently complicates this ambivalence and prevents the victim from recovery.

Sexual offenders must be held both accountable and totally responsible for their behavior. How can a counselor demand that accountability without condemning the offender? How can the counselor treat the victim without pity? How can the counselor maintain any sense of optimism? I believe that a set of philosophical assumptions may be necessary before we pursue issues of dynamics and treatment.

Basic Premises

1. The problem is treatable. Although some pedosexual offenders (particularly pedophiles, rapists, and addicts) may be very resistant to treatment, the majority of clients with whom counselors work can and do improve dramatically with treatment. This applies to victims, survivors, families, and offenders. Indeed, despite some of the negative issues described earlier, many therapists see their work with abusive families as extremely rewarding because of the changes that individuals and families show during treatment. This is certainly true when family units are able to proceed through the treatment process together.

Giaretto's (1982) reports of the low recidivism of offenders in his model family treatment program are corroborated by Tucson's experience of seeing only a handful of reoffenses in 20 years. That number is reduced even further if one uses Giaretto's criteria of a minimum of 10 sessions and successful termination. These are not isolated results; researchers and clinicians report very low recidivism rates (M. Alexander, 1999; Nagayama-Hall, 1995). Furthermore, anecdotal reports from families in treatment indicate that couples who do not divorce are not only functioning better than at the time of abuse but probably better than most families function. Of course, many couples do choose divorce early in the process, during treatment and after reunification. After a divorce, many spouses and families drop out of voluntary treatment, but others choose to continue in treatment and benefit remarkably.

There has been a major effort in attempting to define and quantify treatment efficacy. As would be expected, the research is hobbled by issues of definition, measurement, controls, survivor populations, and time limitations. Maletsky (1998) has done an excellent job of noting that the information that can be helpful in treating this problem is more important than meeting strict scientific criteria. There have been attempts to show efficacy with different techniques or different populations with varying success (Freeman-Longo, Bird, Stevenson, & Fiske, 1995; Hanson, 1997; Maletsky, 1996; Marshall & Anderson, 1996; Schlank & Shaw, 1996; Studer & Reddon, 1998).

2. *The child is the primary client.* The assumption that the child (victim) is the primary client is valid whether the counselor is treating the child directly, treating the offender, or any of the family. It is true even if the counselor acts as a consultant for the defense or never sees the child. The child (victim) and other children (potential victims) must remain the primary focus, with the question "What is best for the child?" as the bottom line. Answers to that question are neither easy nor unanimous and one must, in fact, refrain from the simple solutions such as supporting the child's removal from the home or the dissolution of the marriage. The question pervades

reporting, investigating, treatment planning, visitation, and, eventually, decisions regarding reunification or treatment termination of the victim or offender.

Assuming that the child is the primary client resolves the ethical dilemma of "Who is my client?" It places the counselor-therapist in a very different role from that of others in the adversarial system. It does not, however, prevent appropriate advocacy for the adult client (offender or spouse) either within the legal or mental health system. In fact, such advocacy may well result in significant benefit to the child. It is the counselor's advantage that she or he can step out of the adversarial process.

It is also important to add that the primacy of the child does not mean that the child gets to make important decisions, like whether to visit with the offender or whether to go to counseling. These clearly are adult decisions in which the child may be able to provide input. Any encouragement of the child to become a pseudoadult by making difficult treatment decisions is entirely inappropriate.

3. Treatment is prevention. Sexual abuse treatment is, almost by definition, "post facto" after the abuse and report have occurred. Sometimes months or years may have passed since the last incident. Treatment cannot erase what already has happened. It can, however, prevent reoccurrence for the victim and, by treating the offender, for future victims (Freeman-Longo & Blanchard, 1998; Studer & Reddon, 1998). By treating the victim, future abuse also may be prevented because many victims later become offenders (Ryan, 1999a). Treatment also acts as prevention for other problems for both victim and offender. The primary focus of treatment, then, is as much prevention as rehabilitation. Likewise, the focus of the criminal justice system could well be treatment and prevention as well as punishment.

4. The offender is 100% responsible for the abuse. The assumption that the offender is responsible is discussed in some detail in the treatment sections of the book. It is a basic assumption in dealing with any part of the sexual abuse problem and is possibly the single most important factor for the offender to accept. There are two facets to this assumption: (a) No one else can be responsible for the choice made by the offender (neither the "seductive" child nor the "nagging" spouse), and (b) nothing else can be blamed (alcohol, finances, abuse history, the "libido"). Even if a sophisticated rationale or etiology is discovered, the offender always bears the responsibility for making the choice to cross the line into pedosexual contact. The responsibility issue, therefore, is not one of blame, judgment, or guilt but rather a positive focus that initiates the change process, responsibility being emphasized as a positive, active focus.

5. *The offender is accountable to society.* The offender is responsible for the behavior and is accountable not only to the victim and victim's family but also to society at large. Because sexual abuse/assault/molestation are violations of the law, the offender may face prosecution, sentencing, probation, or incarceration depending on variables that the counselor typically cannot control. This is an unusual dimension for many counselors and distorts such standard practices as voluntary treatment and privileged communication. To some extent, the counselor also becomes accountable to society.

6. *Treatment requires an integrated team approach.* The nature of sexual abuse is complex, and treatment almost always involves multiple counselors or other therapists. Coordinated assessment and treatment planning may involve not only therapists but also Child Protective Services, probation departments, law enforcement, medical staff, school personnel, and others. The counselor, whether acting in a primary or supportive role, must be able to effectively communicate with and support the team while maintaining an appropriate advocacy and protection posture.

7. *The client is owed unconditional positive regard.* Treating an offender or victim may significantly test the most basic counseling tenet, that one must have unconditional positive regard for one's client. Feelings of anger, frustration, disgust, pity, or contempt can obviously color the objectivity and regard for the client (victim or offender). It is essential for the counselor to make a self-assessment, with unconditional positive regard as an important criterion. It may be better to withdraw from a case rather than to lose this focus.

8. *Sex positivism is necessary.* It is essential for the counselor to maintain a positive attitude regarding sexuality. Specifically, sexuality is best regarded as a positive force for the individual and society, even if it is sometimes used in negative ways.

I believe these assumptions not only allow but demand a positive approach to clients and to the problems of pedosexual contact and, particularly, abuse. This positive approach can be effective, if not perfect, regardless of a particular pathology or dysfunction.

Dynamics

The most consistent question—from victims, spouses, family, friends, judges, Child Protective Services, legislators, and, yes, offenders—is, "Why does sexual abuse occur?"

The most consistent answer—from victims, spouses, researchers, counselors, authors, and, yes, offenders—is, "I don't know."

You may be frustrated. You were hoping to get the answer to the "why" question by reading this book. Why isn't there a simple cause of sexual abuse?

We'd all like a relatively simple answer to the question, and we hope that researchers can identify a missing gene, a mutant virus, or a hormone imbalance. Barring such a physiological breakthrough, we would like a simple psychosocial explanation—history of abuse, lack of oral gratification, contingency reinforcement—but the problem is too complex and the variables too heterogeneous. As reflected in the taxonomy (which intentionally reduces the number of variables), there are hundreds of possible combinations of behaviors, participants, settings, and dynamics.

Perhaps we may even be asking the wrong question. Rather than looking for the "why," which implies causation, we need to look at the "how." How was the abuse set up? How did disinhibiting factors work? How was the secret kept? How can we protect the child?

"How did this happen?" becomes a question of description rather than causation, and therefore infinitely easier to handle. It may also be equally effective in the treatment process because it leads to the end goal, "How can we make sure it doesn't happen again?"

Knowledge of individual, familial, and societal dynamics, both general and case-specific, leads to a much clearer picture of past, present, and future functioning.

A metaphor that I typically use with clients is to picture their abuse situation as a jigsaw puzzle without the box cover, total confusion without a sense of what the puzzle is going to look like when completed. At first, there is a sense of despair—the task seems overwhelming and a lot of hard work is spent in sorting out pieces and colors with no obvious matches. The counselor hasn't seen this particular puzzle either but has seen other puzzles like it (understands dynamics) and knows some ways of dealing with them by finding straight edges and like colors (intervention strategies). With those strategies, a match is found, then another, and another. There is a glimmer of encouragement as correct matches lead to patterns, which accelerates the process. Sometimes the counselor makes a match or points one out, but, mostly, the client has to see the matches. Finally, the picture emerges. Most of the time, this happens even if all the pieces do not fit and are not in place. The puzzle solution does not have to be 100% perfect.

Clearly, understanding dynamics can help with seeing *how* things fit. (Did you ever try to figure out, the *why* of a jigsaw puzzle?) Exploring the dynamics, beginning at the societal level, may provide some clues.

Societal Dynamics. It is difficult for many of us to look at societal issues because they imply some responsibility on our part for the existence of the problem of sexual abuse. How does this fit with the philosophical assumption that the offender is 100% responsible for the abuse?

Society and its microcosm, the family, create the environment for abuse, just as they create the environment for healthy functioning, growth, and development. Issues at the societal level may be pervasive and, at the same time, subtle and resistant to change. The following are some issues to consider:

1. We remain a male-controlled society. It is no coincidence that pedosexual contact (especially pedophilia and rape) is essentially a male phenomenon (Finkelhor, 1984). Although the number of female offenders may be underreported for a number of reasons (to be discussed later), men clearly predominate (so much so that masculine pronouns are used in this book to refer to offenders). As long as a control and power imbalance exists, women and children risk being seen as available for, submissive to, or dependent on men or, at the extreme, as the chattel of men. Under these conditions, even at their most benign level, the man can feel a sense of permission to engage in sexual behavior. These are the same conditions that contribute to spousal rape, battering, physical child abuse, neglect, and lack of support. There can certainly be an argument that women's power and sense of control have increased, even over these last 10 years. In some men, this has created a backlash; men feel an even greater need to be in control of this perceived threat.

2. Despite the surface value we place on precocity and pseudoadult behavior, children are at the lower point of the control-power ladder. Their lack of power (physical, verbal, role) increases the chance of exploitation, manipulation, and abuse. Despite media attention to these issues, we continue to be a society that devalues children and does not believe them. Also, with some intention, we keep children powerless in the sexual arena by not providing enough information on

sexuality in general and abuse prevention in particular.

3. We also remain a sex-negative society (Rencken, 1996b). We acknowledge sexuality as positive in the context of reproduction and marriage but label other expressions of sexuality as negative to one extent or another. Sex is used exploitively to sell products, people, and programs. Sex becomes a powerful tool and weapon rather than an expression of intimacy. I sometimes refer to sexuality as a magnifying glass—it can make good things outstanding and bad things horrible. This is true of our societal dynamics. Penalties for sexual abuse generally are much more severe than they are for physical abuse.

4. We are a society that believes in punishment as problem resolution. We think that longer prison sentences (or execution or castration) reduces crime. We think that nations that offend us should be "nuked." We think children should be physically punished at school (Maurer, 1972–1994) and at home (Dobson, 1970). We believe that might makes right.

Family Dynamics. There is little empirical research on family style, that is, how the abusive family unit functions. Families in which sexual abuse occurs tend to be isolative, rigid, and conservative-traditional in style (Finkelhor, 1979; Herman, 1981). Courtois (1988) discussed a whole list of characteristics, emphasizing the family systems perspective: denial, poor tolerance for differences, overly moralistic, no positive touching, and a low tolerance for humor. Abusive families tend to devalue or discount communication and depend on clear power structures. They are seen as less cohesive and adaptable (P. Alexander & Lupfer, 1987) than are healthy families. Although there is a common belief that marital and sexual functioning is poor (Courtois, 1988; Maltz, 1991; Pawlak, Boulet, & Bradford, 1991), in fact my experience with these families suggests that there is not more sexual dysfunction than in most couples, which is, of course, quite high.

Probably more significant as a contributing factor than specific sexual arousal or satisfaction issues in such families is the issue of role confusion. In healthy families, an intergenerational boundary exists between adults and children. This boundary may be explicit (parents draw the rules and that's that) or more implicit (family meetings and logical consequences). The boundary is clear regardless of whether parental style is authoritarian, permissive, or democratic.

One characteristic of dysfunctional families is a lack, or distortion, of that boundary. Specifically, abusive families show three patterns of boundary breakdown:

1. *Dictatorial or possessive father.* In this pattern, the father figure is in a position of ultimate control. This is more than an authoritar-

ian style; it is one in which the spouse and children are seen equally as possessions or objects. Once the spouse is pushed over the boundary into the status of false equality with the children, the possibility is set up for the father to sexually abuse any (or all) of the children. He clearly sees this as his right and frequently finds it difficult to see any harm in the situation. The secrecy factor is very strong in the family, and sexual contact between father and children may be of long duration. The biological father rather than the stepfather is typically the offender. This pattern is illustrated in Case Study A (see chapter 5).

2. *Immature or irresponsible father.* In this pattern, the father figure is typically a rather dependent person who has difficulty with responsible adult behavior. Diagnostically, he may or may not fit the criteria for Dependent Personality Disorder but frequently has elements of one or more personality disorders. There may be a pattern of work instability, substance abuse or dependence, relationship difficulties, and general lack of appropriate control over his own life. The spouse may either be a strong woman who has shown independent survival patterns, or she may match the dependent patterns of her partner. Passive-aggressive patterns are typical in either partner. Here, the father crosses the boundary and becomes like an irresponsible child. Again, a false equality is set up and father sees "permission" to have sexual contact with a child, most frequently the oldest daughter, who is probably closest in psychological age to him. This pattern is reinforced in a blended family where the incest taboo is weaker. The first sexual contact may precipitate other symptoms, such as increased substance abuse or significant depression in the father and withdrawal or runaway behavior in the child. This symptomatology increases the possibility of a report. The intensity of the secret in these families is variable. It is far less likely that the abuse will be of an extended duration. There are probably one or two victims in the family.

3. *Pseudoadult child.* This pattern may well exist in combination with the above, but it is unique in that it is the child who crosses the boundary with pseudoadult behavior. Beyond typical "oldest child" patterns, the child (again generally the oldest daughter) goes past the role of "assistant mother" to become substitute mother and spouse. In some of the literature, this child is described as *parentified.* It is essential to emphasize that this does not mean that she has any responsibility for somehow creating the abuse. She has been drawn over that boundary in a way that seems both important and essential at the time. This role may be enhanced by an actual or presumed absence or disability on the mother's part such as illness, injury, or irresponsibility. The child takes on the family chores

(cooking, cleaning, laundry, child care of siblings) and, implicitly, the role of pleasing the father. This may initially include cooking his favorite meal (at least as well as Mom) and progress to neck massage, leg or back massage, and "accidental" genital contact. Because this is a powerful role, the child frequently experiences strong emotional conflict and guilt around the report of the abuse. The report may well happen when this maternal child sees actual or potential sexual contact between the father and a sibling. The child in this role may almost completely lose the opportunity to go through the developmental stages of childhood and may show great resistance to reporting and treatment.

Each of these patterns sets up a false equality and sets the stage for abusive behavior. Because the whole family has been involved in setting up these patterns, the question of family, rather than offender, responsibility is sometimes raised. Statements like "mom pushed him to do it with her nagging," "Susie liked the attention and encouraged it," or "everybody knew about it and nobody did anything about it" frequently are used as rationalizations or minimizations by the offender and the whole family. So, will the real bad guy please stand up?

It may be helpful to look at two different kinds of responsibility. First and foremost, the offender assumes 100% of the responsibility for the sexual contact. As the adult, he is the one who crosses the line, regardless of the reaction of the child. This is important to emphasize—100%!

There is a separate responsibility that the entire family has in establishing the patterns and atmosphere that existed at the time of abuse. They are responsible for those patterns, whether or not abuse actually occurs. The parents bear responsibility for their marital relationship and their parenting behaviors. Each bears responsibility for his or her share of the family financial and household management. The children, to an appropriately lesser degree, have their own responsibility for their share of family functioning. Accepting this notion of family (corporate) responsibility allows the counselor to enlist the whole family in mutual empowerment and responsibility for changing the maladaptive patterns. This responsibility is in fact a major positive force rather than an issue of fault or blame. It can provoke significant systemic change. Responsibility (as opposed to guilt) is a clear positive activator.

Individual Dynamics. The one area that consistently begs for more research is the understanding of individual dynamics of the offender. Attempts have made to look at characteristics like cognitive distortions and lack of empathy (McGrath, Cann, & Konopasky,

1998); adverse development (Marshall & Barbaree, 1990); difficulty with self-regulation (Ward, Hudson, & Keenan, 1998); physiological disorders, such as alcohol-induced brain dysfunction (Williams, 1999); and, finally, metatheoretical integration (Ward & Hudson, 1998).

The need for this information in treatment is overshadowed by the need for objective information that would be useful in investigations, prosecution, sentencing and, generally, risk management. Prosecutors and judges need clear, objective information that indicates that Offender A is a high-risk rapist who should go to prison for 40 years, but Offender B is a low-risk intrafamilial abuser who should be given probation with treatment. This information has not been available, and the judicial response has been, rather predictably, on the conservative side, with long sentences more likely.

To the casual observer of an offenders' group, there are frequently occurring stereotypes. Regressed and dependent offenders (those most likely to be in such a group) may exhibit marked appearance dichotomies from "macho" tattoo-bearing, loud individuals to meek, "mousy," short men with glasses. Clearly, stereotypes are not helpful in terms of the evaluative and diagnostic decisions but have to be seen as a reality factor. Educated, compliant, and economically resourceful individuals are not only able to navigate the criminal justice system better but may be seen as less of a risk, an assumption certainly not validated in research and clinical experience.

Thus far, the criminal justice system has used evaluations performed by court personnel, independent contractors, or evaluator-consultants hired by one side or the other in an adversarial style. The typical expectations of these evaluations may range from evidentiary (does the accused fit a "profile" of offenders), to risk of recidivism, to risk on probation, to "benefit" from incarceration. There are also more typical forensic evaluations for determination of whether an individual is competent to stand trial, knew right from wrong, and related issues, which are not seen very often in these cases. Typical evaluations include a clinical evaluation, completion of the Minnesota Multiphasic Personality Inventory (MMPI; Hathaway & McKinley, 1943) and other personality questionnaires, sex history, psychophysiological measures, and other assorted psychodiagnostic tools. Whether any of these instruments validly measures complex situations like abuse remains a controversial topic.

Psychophysiological assessment has been a strongly touted addition. An instrument called a *plethysmograph* can record even small changes in the penis that, theoretically, are small enough that they cannot be consciously controlled by the man. There have also been interesting approaches using polygraphy (Blasingame, 1998). Although there are many questions about the predictive value of the information derived from these techniques, they have been used successfully to assess treatment effectiveness (Freund & Blanchard, 1989; Howes, 1998).

One would think that by this time clinicians would have amassed a vast database to enable accurate predictions regarding recidivism. Although data are available, we are hampered by a lack of consistent taxonomy or even agreement on variables. Levin and Stava (1987) reviewed MMPI research and reported that "given the amount of MMPI research performed, the yield regarding knowledge of the personality of the sex offender seems rather sparse. In general negative or inconsistent findings outweigh those of a positive nature" (p. 68). They reported that rapists and forceful pedophiles show similar profiles of social alienation, hostility, and peculiarities of thought and that pedophiliac tendencies may somehow be associated with a "strong and rather rigid superego" (p. 68). They also concluded from both MMPI and non-MMPI research that "rapists and pedophiles are guilt-ridden individuals who attempt to inhibit expressions of aggression" (p. 68). There has also been some progress in the use of the MMPI to pinpoint deniers, although this work is preliminary (Baldwin & Roys, 1998). There were no clear conclusions regarding other pedosexual offenders. There is some hope that the revision of the MMPI, the MMPI-2 (Butcher, Dahlstrom, Graham, Tallegen, & Kremmer, 1989), may be an improved source of data.

Clinical experience with regressed offenders shows little consistency regarding *DSM-IV* Axis I diagnoses except for depressive symptoms that may be reactive to the report and the legal process. Axis II disorders seem to focus on dependent and passive-aggressive personalities with immaturity and, to a lesser extent, antisocial tendencies. Borderline personality disorders also may be seen. Occupationally, these offenders range from clergy to cowboy, from truckers to police, from military to mechanics, and from teachers to (yes) counselors.

Given current limitations, professionals must accept pedosexual offenders as a remarkably discordant group with few similarities. We cannot at this time defend a single "profile." We are forced to put this part of the jigsaw puzzle together uniquely each time.

Legal Issues and the Criminal Justice System

Like everything else in the pedosexual arena, the legal system is usually a complex obstacle for the counselor. Most counselors' thoughts about becoming a part of the legal labyrinth range from cautious curiosity to paranoia. Counselors trained in conflict resolution, mediation, and a "win-win" or "I'm OK, you're OK" philosophy are uncomfortable dealing with the adversarial judicial system. The focus of courts is not directly the protection of the child but rather the prosecution and (one hopes just) punishment of a criminal. We are not used to that concept. Treatment may not be available in the correctional system, so it is not likely that offenders will, in fact, be rehabilitated. Freeman-Longo and Blanchard (1998) summarized the ineffectiveness of criminal punishment.

Many states have revised their laws on statutes of limitations so that the limitations start at the point that the victim/survivor becomes aware of the abuse. This has implications for the repressed/recovered memories controversy (to be addressed later). More adult children are pursuing civil or criminal retribution against an offender, typically a parent, who is alleged to have abused her or him 20, 30, or 40 years earlier. Another issue is mandatory sentencing, in which the judge has very little latitude or discretion regarding the terms of sentence. These sentences are typically very harsh for sex offenders, including sex offender registration laws and, possibly, public notice of sex offenses, including Megan's law, as discussed in Freeman-Longo and Blanchard (1998).

I am frequently asked about privileged communication in sexual abuse cases, particularly those involved in the criminal justice system. The mandatory reporting statutes are clear and must be obeyed. In some jurisdictions, report is mandated only if the information comes directly from the child. In other words, information volunteered by an offender that he committed abuse would be treated like any other crime. We would have to ask ourselves if we had a "duty to warn." In many cases we clearly do have such a duty, because we have to protect a victim or potential victim, but, in cases where there is no clear threat, we may not have to report. The best way to handle these situations is to obtain a release from the client, which may require skilled negotiating by the counselor. There is an assumption that because child protective investigations are reported, there is no longer any confidentiality; generally, that is true only as regards to the report that you made, not to other information that the client may have divulged. You may be subpoenaed for this information, and you may have to testify under court order, just as you might in other cases.

In most treatment programs or integrated teams there are highly explicit agreements or contracts about privileged communication. For example, the offender knows that if he reveals new abusive behavior or certain violations of probation, this information will be reported to the probation department or Child Protective Services. Other information may be protected, unless the therapist sees a clear and significant threat. Most of the time, clients want the counselor to be cooperative with the treatment team so that progress can be documented, presumably improving the chance of release from probation or parole, restoration of rights (if convicted of a felony), and possible family reunification.

Counselors who are confronted with sexual abuse have to deal with at least some elements of the system. It is helpful, and in some cases essential, to have a general understanding of the roles the counselor may play in a given setting and what a typical chronology might look like. This information should be general enough to be accurate regardless of jurisdiction, but procedures and statutes do vary, and the reader is certainly encouraged to obtain legal consultation. The reader is also referred to other resource books regarding strategies for testimony, record keeping, and privileged communication.

Roles

When working with sexual abuse victims and offenders, the counselor may play one or more roles. The most frequent task is to provide information, either formally or informally. There are two occasions for formal information: making the report (more about that later) and serving as a witness. Essentially, in these two formal areas, the counselor is like any other citizen and may be called on to report what he or she has directly observed or heard from a student or client. Privileged communication or confidentiality may not be applicable. Information may be presented in a taped interview, written report, deposition, or court testimony. In fact, many mandatory reporting laws require a written report as a component of the process.

Informal information sharing may include cooperating with an investigation or providing ongoing progress reports on victims or offenders in treatment. As noted above, the client should be informed as to what information will be shared and with whom. Whenever possible, a release form should be signed. It is usually to the client's advantage to do so.

Another role that counselors, particularly child counselors, must assume is that of advocate. Some jurisdictions may appoint individuals or panels as advocates. Beyond being a witness, this person ensures that the client's interests are addressed appropriately in both the legal and treatment systems, including foster care. This appointed advocate may be (should request to be) invited to attend staffings, hearings, trials, and the like. In addition, courts may appoint a legal advocate (attorney) for the child(ren).

The counselor may also be called to testify as an expert witness. The expert witness may have different rules regarding testimony. For example, the expert witness is generally the only one who is permitted to express an opinion and can report hearsay evidence. The expert has to be stipulated as such by the court (with possible challenge by one of the "sides"). The expert witness may either be seen as "independent" (all sides agreeing to accept the information) or as a consultant to one or more parties, in which the information probably will be viewed as helpful to the side that hires the consultant. In the latter situation, the counselor/consultant is bound by the highest standards of ethical conduct regarding objectivity and concern about the current and potential victims. The expert may testify regarding an evaluation, treatment, or more general information, sometimes even without having seen the party involved. In some circumstances, the expert may be asked to provide a written report in lieu of, or in addition to, testimony.

Settings

There are generally four different settings or forums in which the counselor may appear: criminal, juvenile, family, or civil court. If the offender is being prosecuted for a criminal offense, the case is heard in criminal (or superior) court. The counselor could be asked for information during investigation, preliminary hearing or grand jury, trial, or sentencing mitigation hearing. The victim may also have to testify at any or all of those, although the courts have been moving toward keeping such appearances to a minimum.

Juvenile court may be involved in several ways. If the offender is a juvenile, the case may be prosecuted and go to trial in the offender's jurisdiction. Juvenile court may have different rules of evidence and, generally, more latitude may be given to the counselor who is testifying, particularly in the area of recommendations. The counselor may report on evaluations or the progress of treatment of either the child or the parents. A typical case for juvenile court originates through a dependency petition in which the state, working through Child Protective Services, may ask for custody of a victim and, possibly, siblings. This custody may be physical (the state removes the child from the home and places her or him into a shelter or foster care) or nonphysical (the child remains at home, but the state can mandate treatment, control visits, etc.). Rules are specified for judicial review (e.g., at 30- or 90-day intervals). Families are advised of their rights and have the right to be legally represented, as does the child. In some cases, juvenile court may be asked to rule on severance, the relinquishment or termination of parental rights that gives the state permanent custody and enables an adoption process.

More and more sexual abuse cases are being heard in family, conciliation, or divorce court. The phenomenon of allegations of abuse during custody fights is not new. Even though criminal charges may not be filed, custody and visitation decisions may be based on allegations made by the children. This arena is often the most difficult for the counselor because it produces the largest number of false allegations by children (MacFarlane, 1986; Spiegel, 1988). One parent also may attempt to alienate the children from the other parent (Gardner, 1987).

The least likely setting for the disposition of sexual abuse cases is in civil court. Based on the increasing amount of litigation being heard, however, there could well be an increase in this arena. There is also, of course, the possibility that the number of these suits may have leveled off. It has somewhat increased the likelihood that a person who is not charged criminally for one reason or another could be sued for damages. In a recent case in which I consulted, the parents of a victim sued the parents of a juvenile offender for damages, resulting in a financial settlement.

The Process

It may be helpful to put the information presented in the preceding sections into a chronology of a typical case to clarify the critical points for intervention or advocacy.

1. *The initial report.* All states have mandatory reporting laws regarding child abuse, particularly for school and health-related personnel. There is typically a waiver of liability for those who make a report in good faith, and increasingly severe penalties for failure to report even suspected abuse. Mandatory reporting transcends any client–patient confidentiality. For a discussion of therapeutic issues regarding the report, see chapter 2. If the counselor works for a system or agency that has specific procedures for reporting abuse to others in the system, like a supervisor or principal, it still remains the ethical and, probably, the legal duty of the counselor to ensure that the report is made. Counselors cannot rely on others to make a report; they may not. The report may either be made to a child protective agency or to law enforcement. In many jurisdictions, the report is automatically shared between those two agencies.

2. *The investigation.* Child Protective Services or the appropriate law enforcement agency investigate the report, typically conjointly. Frequently, cases are handled on a priority basis. Sexual abuse cases are lower on the priority list than cases where there is an immediate risk of death or injury, but usually sexual abuse is relatively high on the list. Some states have mandated time frames in which a report must be investigated. Investigators want information about the abuse, but they also may ask questions about general adjustment regarding the child or family. Let the investigators investigate! Investigation is not the counselor's job.

3A. *Prosecution.* The prosecution (county, district or state attorney) decides whether to formally charge an alleged offender. There also may be a discussion of a plea bargain at this point. The plea bargain is an agreement where the offender pleads guilty or no contest to one or more charges in return for dismissal of other charges, expecting a reduced sentence.

B. *Child Protective Services.* While the prosecution decision is being made, Child Protective Services personnel decide (with court approval) whether or not to remove a child. In many cases, it will encourage the offender to leave the home (it may or may not be able to order that) in order to leave the child there. The agency is frequently forced to make critical decisions for the protection of the child in a short period of time.

4. *Pretrial.* If there is a decision to prosecute, the offender is arraigned. He pleads innocent, even if he has already acknowledged guilt, to allow the process to officially start. A decision is made whether to release him and, if he is released, whether he must post bond. An attorney is appointed if necessary. A preliminary hearing or grand jury decide whether there is enough evidence to proceed to trial, and an indictment, or formal charges, is filed.

5. *Trial.* If there is no plea bargain, the case proceeds to trial. Unfortunately, this is often a lengthy process. It may well be to everyone's benefit to plea bargain to avoid trial. Physical evidence may be sparse, and conviction for sexual abuse, particularly with young children, may be difficult. As mandatory sentences have increased, many defense attorneys have taken advantage of this and preferred to go to trial, where antagonism replaces healing and is a guaranteed losing proposition.

6. *Sentencing.* Whether sentencing results from conviction by trial or plea bargaining, it is usually another critical point for the counselor. Typically, a presentencing investigation is held to determine appropriateness of probation versus incarceration. The victim may well be asked for input at this time. In some states with manda-

tory sentencing laws, the judge may have limited discretion. Jurisdictions vary in their sentencing from straight probation (usually with mandatory treatment) to a combination of probation and jail (maybe in a work release program) to prison incarceration with or without chance of parole.

7. *Probation.* Adult and juvenile offenders may be placed on probation. Generally, probation is an alternative to prison, whereas parole is a monitoring process after release from prison. Probation requirements may vary considerably regarding frequency of reports, treatment mandates, restrictions on visitation or contact with minors, alcohol consumption, and other issues. Whether the counselor is in a primary or supportive role, he or she must coordinate closely with the probation officer regarding mutual expectations and roles. The counselor also should clearly communicate these expectations and roles to the client. There should be a written agreement indicating the limits of confidentiality. The counselor probably needs to report attendance, general progress, risk assessment, family progress, fee payment, and violations of probation conditions. The probation officer may be on the treatment team and attend staffings or meetings of the treatment team. Additionally, he or she may require periodic written or verbal reports for significant decisions like visitation, termination of treatment, or family reunification. The probation officer usually also maintains contact with the victim and the victim's counselor or therapist, even though she or he may not be legally mandated to do that.

The legal process and criminal justice system present a real challenge for many counselors. Clients often look to their counselors for support and, answers to the understandable feelings of confusion they experience, and, although counselors should emphasize that they are not offering the services or expertise of an attorney, their knowledge of the system benefits their clients. This knowledge also is important so that appropriate therapeutic interventions can be made.

Navigating Managed Care

It may be helpful at this point to discuss some strategies for dealing with insurance and managed care. I call this *playing with the system.* By *play* I do not mean to suggest that this is an easy or fun concept or that ethics are sacrificed. What I mean is that the best advocacy for you and the client is accomplished when you know the rules, the process, and the expectations of third-party payment.

Experienced mental health and rehabilitation counselors are familiar with the use and pitfalls of the *DSM-IV*. Some diagnoses (e.g., V-codes, Adjustment Disorders, Sexual Disorders, School Problems) may not be covered, and this discrimination is not always consistent or predictable. A special consideration for abuse cases is that insurance companies may also specifically deny any court-mandated treatment or evaluation and certainly do not pay for staffings, meetings, or court testimony.

We have learned to do our homework, ascertaining what diagnoses may be excluded and keeping our eyes and minds open to other diagnostic possibilities, including the use of "rule out" diagnoses. Again, this does not have to create ethical dilemmas—we are just paying attention to our client's options.

Managed care typically requires full *DSM* diagnosis but usually goes beyond that to some level of assessment, treatment plan, and ongoing measure of progress toward goals. This is typically done in writing (notably now, with faxes), although there may be telephonic authorizations. Although these requirements are not difficult for most of us, they certainly can be time consuming.

Many counselors and therapists underutilize managed care because they neglect their advocacy roles. They are automatically intimidated by session restrictions and corporate style. They may be used to the client taking full responsibility for insurance and resist "outside control." The key to dealing with these frequently valid concerns is in clarifying the client's coverage. We may, for example, be told that we are authorized for three sessions, but the coverage is actually 20 sessions per year. We may have to persistently advocate and account for those added sessions. It also is important to know when the contract year begins, when authorizations may automatically expire, and also when new authorization may give an additional cluster of sessions.

Sexual abuse counselors, whether generalists or specialists, also typically have concerns about restrictions on treatment modalities, with less or no coverage for collateral parent visits, family therapy, sex/marital therapy or groups, particularly if they are psychoeducationally oriented. These restrictions may actually be more of a frustrating and complicated issue than the number of allowed sessions because the multimodal team treatment approach is so critical in this arena. Some of these approaches can be "coded" under the generic rubric of "psychotherapy," but some will not and may require fee-for-service payment by the client family. Perhaps that expense can be minimized.

These possible restrictions, limitations, and requirements really emphasize the need for multiple funding sources in dealing with the complexities and realities of treating clients with sexual abuse. (It also means that not many counselors are going to get rich with these cases—that's why we write books!) Coordination with an integrated and comprehensive treatment program that may be able to solicit community funding (donations, United Way, state contracts), children's funding (Child Protective Services, mental health), or correctional/rehabilitation funding (probation, disability) is incredibly helpful. These resources may be virtually impossible to access for the individual or small group practice. Such a treatment program may specifically be able to offer groups that are crucial to the treatment process (see Giaretto, 1982).

New, Renewed, and Controversial Issues

Or, sometimes, a flash in the pan can set a house on fire.

Several issues have received remarkable attention both within the professional literature and dialogue and also in the public media, an area of little experience for most of us. I have actually witnessed an "educational presentation" on repressed memory at a convention that ended up with a literal shouting match between academicians and researchers on one "side" and clinicians on the other. Here I attempt to summarize the cogent ideas and suggest ways of dealing with each in a sensitive and positive way.

1. *The increased attention on sexual abuse and proliferation of victims/survivors, experts and books.* In the early days of sexual abuse treatment, those of us in the field would be grateful for any attention given to the problem. We learned from every survivor who spoke out, every family that successfully reunited, and every therapist who shared her or his findings, frequently on what I called the "Xerox network." Most bookstores couldn't spell "sexual abuse," but now they have entire sections on "Abuse" or "Abuse/Recovery" or "Self-help and Recovery" that promote volumes on the subject, written primarily for the general public. Best sellers include *The Courage to Heal* (Bass & Davis, 1988), *The Courage to Heal Workbook* (Davis, 1990), *Allies in Healing* (Davis, 1991), *Healing the Incest Wound* (Courtois, 1988), *The Sexual Healing Journey* (Maltz, 1991) and *Victims No Longer* (Lew, 1988).

Despite their biases, these (and many other) books have contributed to the awareness, acknowledgement, validation, and treatment of sexual abuse. Unfortunately, the proliferation of expert opinions, particularly on the sensational TV talk shows, has created a backlash of desensitization and lack of credibility among the public. Most people are so uncomfortable about and afraid of sexual abuse that they rationalize and minimize the problem.

The "solution" for this public reaction is simple and complex. We must continue to deliver the message that sexual abuse is a pervasive, ongoing problem that affects much of the population, especially children. Much sexual abuse is neither sensational, sexsational, nor even exceedingly traumatic. We need to emphasize that our treatment is productive, effective, and responsible. We may not have mass media exposure, so we have the responsibility to deliver this message to whoever will hear us in the general and professional communities.

2. *False allegations.* The next two issues certainly overlap but should be treated separately. False allegations may be leveled by the young child, the adolescent, and the adult survivor. It is only the latter that overlaps with the recovered memory concerns.

In the young child, we are likely to see confusion over events, chronology, and time frames of a normal developmental nature. It simply is difficult for the child to articulate an abusive situation using adult concepts (e.g., inappropriate touch, genital contact). There is also a normal memory warp regarding details, adding to the confusion. The McMartin preschool case demonstrated the futility of prosecuting a case with 4-year-old victims and witnesses. The McMartin case was the center of the sexual abuse controversy, with young children alleging ritual sexual, emotional, and physical abuse that included sacrifice and extremely scary threats of retribution, power, and control. After a very long and dramatic trial, virtually all charges against the accused adults were either dropped or ended in acquittal because the children's stories were so incredulous. The investigation process became the identified weakness in the case, with allegations of leading questions and "planting" information. The unfortunate loser in that case was "the truth." We will never know what actually happened.

Clues to the sexual abuse of young children come from adult sexual behavior, fear and mistrust of adults, and unusual difficulties in interactive relationships. These are crucial clinically but may be inadmissible in the legal system or inadequate as reasons to involve Child Protective Services.

Already noted is the category of false allegation as a result of custody or visitation disputes. This issue certainly continues.

Adolescents may accuse one parent in custody situations or as a revenge for actual or perceived punishment. They are frequently able to lie well and present a real challenge to the counselor and the system. Although most abuse begins in the prepubescent period, some may occur in adolescence.

As noted, false allegations from adults overlap with the memory issues. The attention created by reports of major trauma in survivors led to the "discovery" of hundreds of adults who "remembered" abuse. These reports became more bizarre, grotesque, and incredible. We, as a society, were faced with traumatic intrafamilial civil litigation and, in some cases, criminal prosecution. Jurisdictions changed statutes of limitations to relate to the time frame after the event was recalled, rather than when the alleged abuse occurred. Many adults were frustrated with the court system because proving these cases was next to impossible. As counselors and therapists (particularly as specialists), we were also put on trial; initially seen as saviors or rescuers, we were now only vilified as dupes, charlatans, and self-serving "experts." Our credibility took a significant blow as we were accused of "planting" memories, using leading questions, and overdiagnosing conditions like DID.

Again, we lost the truth in the process. We know, of course, that adults do recall events from the past with different levels of clarity. The major error for many therapists, in my opinions, was in assuming the role of investigator or rescuer and dealing with the lurid details of abuse and confrontation with the alleged offender rather than the emotional health of the survivor. The promise of "closure" by confrontation and litigation was more fantasy than reality and resulted in even more pain for our clients.

Although some authorities (Loftus & Ketcham, 1994; Morfit, 1994) cautioned counselors against leading questions and total belief, others pointed out the processes of memory in physiology (Knopp & Benson, 1996) and the ambiguity of the victim's accommodation (Summit, 1983). The important strategy is truly focussing on the here and now, dealing with feelings and resultant action rather than details and coping strategies rather than litigation. As discussed previously, it is essential for the counselor to focus on these positive approaches rather than getting into lurid details and investigatory glory. Specific treatment issues are discussed in chapter 4.

3. *Repressed and recovered memories.* The pioneering work of Loftus and Ketcham (1994) initially focused on Loftus's area of expertise, the neurophysiology and psychology of memory. She has testified about the fallacies of memory in court as well as in the research field. Although not discounting the harmful effects of sexual abuse, she was also moved by reports of false allegations or allegations of abuse, physical trauma and rape that had occurred many years or decades previously. She counted herself as a "cynic" rather than a "true believer" (most of whom were clinicians). Although not a clinician, she began hearing repetitive stories of women being

coaxed out of "denial" and confronting both memories and the people that were supposedly to blame for tremendous pain, pain that had not been perceived before entering therapy. Her critical observations of the therapy process with abuse victims/survivors led to criticism from clinicians that she just did not understand the emotional state of these individuals. She has been particularly skeptical of symptom checklists, group process, and quick diagnostic conclusions of sexual abuse. Her descriptions of therapist interactions with individuals and groups were both scary and accurate for many therapists whom I have known in the field, who became crusaders, rescuers, and healing zealots.

Morfit (1994) was even more critical of the whole process of psychotherapy, beyond the possible errors of individual therapists. The works of these two self-proclaimed "cynics" had created doubt, defensiveness, and our own level of denial. It is our responsibility to restore that integrity and, simply, do our job.

4. *Ritual and satanic abuse.* The McMartin case was a major contributor to national fear of the possibility of ritual, specifically satanic, abuses. *Ritual abuse* refers to a prescribed structure and pattern of behavior (perhaps including certain clothing, times, or images); *satanic or cult abuse* provided dramatic images of animal abuse or sacrifice, human infant sacrifice, and orgiastic sexual behavior. At one point, there was a claim that 100,000 babies had been killed in these groups. Independent investigators, however, uncovered almost no evidence or validation of the existence of these groups. Clearly, we do sometimes deal with ritual abuse with its highly defined behaviors, but the existence of cult abuse is speculative at best. When we deal with survivors, perhaps with major disorders like psychosis, Borderline Personality, or DID, we must remain supportive, accepting, and nonjudgmental in our perceptions while, at the same time, gently confronting the reality just as we would with nonabuse cases. When ritual abuse does happen, it tends to create highly idiopathic survivors and presents a challenge on many levels, leading to the addition of this area in the pedosexual taxonomy.

5. *Female offenders.* Offenses by female individuals have been seen as rare and probably rooted in psychosis. More recently, however, female offenders have received more attention in both the professional and popular literature (Davin, Hislop, & Dunbar, 1999; Rosencrans, 1997). This new attention has created some interesting tangential effects. This behavior is seen as the "last taboo" (Elliott, 1993; Miletski, 1995). We know that in the past, this contact has been underreported because of the seriousness of the damage, denial, repression, and women not being seen as capable of abuse

(Sgroi & Sargent, 1993). We are probably now getting a more realistic picture.

Female offenders tend to have weak ego development, low self-esteem, poor social skills, and interpersonal problems but are probably not psychotic or substance abusers as had been previously reported (Mathews, Mathews, & Speltz, 1989; Matthews, 1993). Remarkably, in my practice I have seen relatively few of these cases, and they did, in fact, fit the stereotype of psychotic or heavy substance abuse scenarios. In one case, a collaborative mom was sentenced to 25 years (over the objection of her children) and released in 10 years. The others either were not prosecuted or plea-bargained to a non-sexual offense, a double standard that is usually not challenged. More information focused on treatment will be presented later.

6. *Male victims and mother-son incest.* The attention to male victims has increased somewhat although the concerns have been around for a long time, typically with the assumption that there still was a male perpetrator. Two major books on boy victims (Hunter, 1990; Lew, 1988) drew more discussion and some more concerns although incidence probably remains underreported.

As I discuss in the treatment section, the issues of denial, underreporting, and double standards present difficult challenges for the counselor. Our knowledge in this area is clearly still expanding.

7. *Severe reactions, including DID.* Part of the legitimate drama, as well as the histrionics, in false accusations and recovered memories was in the number of cases diagnosed as PTSD and DID. Experienced professionals questioned the frequency of these diagnoses, probably because the professionals had been taught that they were rare, even in high-risk groups like combat veterans, but also because they were, in fact, overused. My experience with many treatment providers is that any hint of sexual abuse triggered the PTSD classification, whereas any dissociative incident was seen as DID without regard to the criteria of *DSM-IV.* Lay and professional reports played into the old stereotypes and prejudices about "hysterical" (now called *histrionic*) women with severe emotional and behavioral problems. This also led to a myriad of unorthodox or idiopathic treatment techniques that drew even more criticism (e.g., bonding exercises including simulated nursing, hypnotic regression, and simulated physical aggression).

Certainly, many adults with severe disorders have sexual abuse or other early trauma as a factor in their histories, but it is very seldom the sole factor. As with so many other problems, the sexual component provides a magnifying effect, making problems into crises and major disorders whenever sex is involved.

8. *Counselors' and therapists' role in societal sex negativity.* One of the assumptions noted early in this chapter was that of sex positivism, an approach that validates the pleasure, intimacy, and healing of sexuality. Marty Klein and Leanor Tiefor (1997) did a stirring presentation on the role of sex therapists and researchers in societal negativity including issues that specifically apply to sexual abuse by both generalists and specialists.

Although abuse is clearly an issue of power and control, it is too easy to jump to the conclusion that sex is out of control and that "excessive" sex drive is responsible for much of our woes. Offenders are seen as sex maniacs or addicts when sexual desire is typically a small part of the problem. Consensual contact is automatically seen as coercive. Sexually explicit media is labeled as pornography and, usually falsely, linked to child sexual abuse. Even sexuality education is absurdly attacked, as it has been for years, with the axiom that it leads to greater sexual experimentation and activity. Like fear about HIV/AIDS and, historically, teen pregnancy, we must actively struggle to maintain a proactive, healthy approach to the very real problems.

The complexities of child sexual abuse and pedosexual contact have been emphasized in this chapter. The multiple combinations of dynamics, behavior, and level of trauma present severe challenges in trying to comprehend the "puzzle." Counselors, as professionals, and related professionals have the opportunity to confront this major problem with a positive perspective. The results of 20 years of clinical experience show us that we can all make a significant difference in the lives of all those affected by sexual abuse, whether children or adults. We have been able to put together puzzles, one at a time, and not always perfectly, but we are dramatically improving our capabilities by expanding research and continuing clinical communication.

CHAPTER 2

Intervention Strategies With Victims of Abuse

One might think that making a diagnosis and treatment planning are fairly straightforward processes—gather symptoms, check out hypotheses, make a diagnosis, plan treatment to deal with symptoms or underlying problems, and reevaluate. Counselors know how tricky the process can be when dealing with children and their short attention spans, limited verbal ability, and unique perceptions of the world. Complicate that picture with sexual abuse and the counselor faces a real challenge.

In this section, I focus on the sexually abused child at three age periods: younger than 7 years old, 7 to puberty, and puberty to 18 years old (adolescence). I present intervention strategies appropriate to each of those periods. Unless noted, the strategies apply to either sex. In the first two age categories, I assume that the intervention is taking place within 1 year of the last abusive incident. In the adolescent period, I discuss delayed intervention as well.

The counselor working with the child may be in either a primary or supportive role. The interventions discussed can be used in both situations, but the supportive counselor also has the responsibility for coordinating with the primary counselor/therapist.

Treating the Young Child (Less Than Age 7)

Perhaps the most important viewpoint in dealing with young children is a developmental one. It is essential for counselors to have a good understanding of normal psychosexual development as well as cognitive and social development. This is particularly essential with young children because of their verbal limitations.

Young children are eager to please and inappropriately answer "yes" to many questions. Answers may not be organized and may seem tangential or, in fact, may be lies, especially to avoid punishment. Children also are egocentric and may have difficulty dealing with strangers (Waterman, 1986).

Yates (1978) provided an in-depth treatment of early childhood psychosexual development, and the National Guidelines Task Force (1991) provided the most comprehensive structure for understanding childhood development. Gordon and Schroeder (1995) attempted to look at developmental approaches to issues like sexual abuse. Children are curious about male-female physical and gender role differences. Masturbation is typical and may be more overt in girls at this age. Although "humping" behavior is not unusual, the exact nature of coitus (penile penetration) is only rarely known. In fact, if there is any notion of penetration, anal intercourse seems much more logical to the young child.

Two general qualities are important in considering the typical sexually abused young child: fear and adult-type sexual knowledge. Fear may be shown directly in terms of withdrawal or indirectly in the form of nightmares and night terrors. Withdrawal may be expressed indiscriminantly against any person, strangers, or men in general. The trauma may come from a wide variety of sources and, at this age, some sexual abuse actually may not be very traumatic. Because young children do not, almost by definition, know that sexual behavior is "bad," the physical sensations may feel good, particularly in a nurturing situation like bathing or play. It may well be that physical pain or discomfort may be more traumatic, whether or not it is associated with sexual contact.

The issue of a child's fear of, or withdrawal from, strangers may be an obstacle for the counselor, and establishing trust is critical in evaluating or treating the child. The counselor must provide a sense of warmth, caring, and respect for the child while still assuming a clearly adult role. Fortunately, most counselors dealing with this age group are experienced with these issues and need only give extra attention to trust if there is an indication of abuse.

The presence of atypical knowledge of sex is another less-than-perfect indicator of abuse. In making an assessment, the counselor should look for adult-type behavior or knowledge. Typical child behaviors include giggling about toileting, anatomical curiosity (playing doctor or "have you got what I've got," touching of others' genitals), and masturbation. Language is simple and, perhaps, repetitive (e.g., ca-ca, pee-pee, weenie, poo-poo, gina, boobies, tinkle). These behaviors become marginal when adult activity, motivation, or language is indicated—digital penetration, extended stroking of genitals, coercion or persuasion, or genital kissing. As mentioned earlier, nonabused children do engage in "humping" either with or without clothing, perhaps influenced by their exposure to such sources as cable TV and the Internet, but generally they are not aware that penetration is involved. Marginal language includes *fuck* (as a verb form rather than expletive), *lay, cock, pussy, suck, bang.* Any display of these types of behavior or use of such language would certainly warrant added attention and concern.

Evidence of adult behavior should really raise some red flags. Included in this category would be oral-genital contact, penile penetration (or clear attempt at penetration), oral-breast contact, and open-mouth kissing. Language includes use of such words as *screw, butt-fuck, rimming, fisting, eat out, blowjob.* Chances are that these behaviors were learned by either close observations of adults, extended exposure to sexually explicit media, or sexual abuse.

The Report

Dealing with children younger than 7 years old poses some unique problems regarding the report to authorities and legal process in general. The basic premise, of course, is that a report is necessary for the protection of the child. Because a report is usually mandated for suspicion of abuse as well as clear evidence, the counselor may be obligated to report with only a minimal level of certainty regarding actual abuse.

The temptation is perhaps strongest with this age range to continue to push for more information either before or after the report—in other words, to become part of the investigation. This temptation should be resisted for two reasons: Such activity by the counselor can easily create confusion for the child and seriously jeopardize or sabotage the prosecutor's case. The latter occurs if there is any hint of leading questions, evaluator bias, or, even, encouragement for the child to talk about abuse. If the counselor needs to pursue an assessment or evaluation (perhaps if asked to do so by the investigation team), extra preparation is necessary through reading, workshops, or video training. The reader is specifically referred to MacFarlane and Waterman (1986. The fact that Kee MacFarlane's interviews were so scrutinized during the McMartin preschool case emphasizes how tricky this arena can be.)

A sense of frustration frequently pervades the investigation phase. Even if the child gives some clear signals of former abuse during an assessment, prosecutors may be reluctant to go to trial without physical evidence (and typically there isn't any). They have to rely on the testimony of a young child, whose credibility can easily be challenged. Some relatively new legal developments, including the increased acceptance of videotaped evidence, may be helpful, but the system has not undergone any major changes.

In the assessment process, an ethical issue arises when the counselor assumes the role of both evaluator and ongoing therapist. Although it may seem to make sense at the time, this does set up the possibility of a conflict of interest or lack of objectivity. The roles should be separated.

Early Treatment Phase

With 6- to 7-year-old children, the early treatment phase should be focused on crisis intervention. With this age group, however, the primary concern is trust and building rapport.

Whenever possible, the counselor should use the child's mother as a bridge in helping to build trust. This may be a slight deviation from the way the counselor would treat a nonabused child. Clearly, the counselor would not be able to use the mother in cases where she is suspected of involvement in the abuse. Caution should be taken in a case where the mother is still in a stage of denial regarding the veracity of the report or is blaming the child. The mother can help by taking the following steps.

1. *Preparing the child.* The child can be told that she or he is going to a nice, pleasant place to meet a new grownup who talks and plays with kids. Ideally, the mother has had a chance previously to meet the counselor so she can describe this new grownup with one or two specifics (e.g., this grownup has a nice smile or talks softly or has a soft rug). This can be done in a rather factual way, without trying to convince the child. If the child asks why they are visiting, the mother may simply say that they are going to talk about how things are going in the family. If asked directly, the mother should not lie about the abuse concerns.

2. *Accompanying the child.* The mother can encourage the child to bring a favorite toy or object (teddy bear, doll). She can stay with the child through the first session and as many of the subsequent sessions as the counselor deems helpful.

3. *Supporting the child.* It seems almost silly to think that a mother would not support her child. It would not be unusual, how-

ever, for a highly stressed mother in the beginning stages of the abuse crisis to meet her own needs first, whether intentionally or not. One way this is manifested is for the mother to get into the role of investigator (asking the famous "why" questions) or feeling caught in the trap between spouse and children, a major drainer of emotional and physical energy. As a result, the child may get some protection, but he or she also is likely to perceive the chaos in the family and may feel a lot of the mother's ambivalence or rage toward the father. The essence of support is to give the child permission to feel—that it is OK for the child to act like a child and to be frightened, confused, and ambivalent. The mother also should resist the temptation to act as therapist, that is, to get involved in the details of the abuse and to draw conclusions from play activities or verbal cues. If the mother is in denial, showing support becomes more difficult but, perhaps, even more important.

4. *Being there.* During a crisis like abuse, the child's biggest fear is abandonment. The message the child perceives is that because there is so much chaos, either or both parents might just leave to escape the problems. This fear is obviously aggravated if there has been, or may be, a divorce; if the father has moved out; or if there have been loud or violent arguments.

5. *Participating in therapy.* The mother might also help the child, and herself, by agreeing to individual therapy if indicated. Frequently, she will have many issues and feelings that would be more appropriately addressed outside her child's counseling sessions.

The Therapeutic Atmosphere

In both the early and ongoing phases of treatment with the young child, the counselor's most important task may be in creating an atmosphere for trust building. This effort involves the physical environment as well as the counselor's behavior.

The physical environment should be simple but clearly focused on the young child. It could be an office or playroom as long as it provides warmth and comfort for the child and includes child-sized furniture, pillows, or a clean, comfortable carpet that the counselor feels comfortable sitting on. There should be a small selection of simple toys available: blocks, puppets, soft dolls (anatomically correct are preferable), a doll house (or other ways to portray a family), paper of various sizes with large crayons or markers, and clay or play dough. A sand tray or box may be beneficial if the room allows. A larger selection than this will shorten the attention span, diffuse the play, and reduce contact with the counselor. It there is a large space, the "kid's special area" should be clearly defined.

The counselor's behavior is more critical than the physical environment. The young child should be approached with gentleness but without condescending baby talk. Several minutes should be spent with the mother and child together in the waiting area. The counselor can bring an object (stuffed animal, puppet) to meet the child or can acknowledge an object the child has brought. Initial focus should be on anything "special" about the child (the toy, colorful clothing, big smile, etc.). This allows the child's egocentricity to be experienced as OK. The child should be approached from a basically equal height; the counselor should sit next to the child and squat or sit while the child stands, in order to avoid the rather threatening posture of looming over the child. Above all, the child can relate to a gentle humor focusing on the "child" part of the counselor ("sometimes adults like to do things like play with blocks or sit on the floor," "that's a silly looking horse I drew, it looks like a hippopotamus") and, at the same time, acknowledging the child's achievements ("that's a great block tower," "what neat colors"). Both approaches emphasize the equality and basic OK-ness of both the child and adult without a false front.

Ongoing Treatment

Whether the duration of treatment is short term (less than 6 months) or longer term (over a year) depends on the level of trust achieved and the overall stability in the child's life (foster placement, stability of parents, etc.; Long, 1986).

Issues. Long (1986) has done a good job of adapting Porter, Blick, and Sgroi's (1982) treatment issues for victims of sexual abuse to the younger population. These are summarized in the following list:

1. *"Damaged goods" syndrome.* This refers to self-, familial, and societal perception of the child as different, used, pitiful, vulnerable, and maybe partly to blame. Young children see the sexual contact as so dissonant or incongruous that they ask even more than the usual number of unproductive "why" questions.

2. *Guilt.* Although the young child does not feel the same guilt or shame as an older child would, egocentricity leads to the conclusion that she or he is the cause of all the chaos and confusion in the home, absence of father, and "strange" reactions of mother.

3. *Fear.* Fear of abandonment is the primary fear for this age group.

4. *Depression.* Although withdrawal is usually related to anxiety, it can also be an indication of depression, as can somatic complaints (particularly stomach pain), listlessness, and "spacey" behavior.

5. *Low self-esteem and poor social skills.* I would modify this slightly to focus more on perceived powerlessness and helplessness. The child can either go into withdrawal behavior or become an extremely powerful child in the sense of bossiness or highly controlling behavior in dealing with peers or adults.

6. *Repressed anger and hostility.* Although some young children do not experience anger because of the context of the abuse, some do experience and repress anger. Anger may be directed at the mother as well as the offender.

7. *Inability to trust.* This may well be the most important issue, particularly in intrafamilial abuse. It may be aggravated by the duration of the contact and the amount of physical pain or discomfort experienced.

8. *Blurred role boundaries and role confusion.* As mentioned in the previous discussion of family dynamics, the child can perceive significant problems as to who is in charge of the family and who is responsible for protection. This also reemphasizes the importance of the mother in the recovery process as a strong, protective person.

9. *Pseudomaturity and failure to complete developmental tasks.* This is a very common effect that can fool an inexperienced counselor. The child can look almost supernormal, with advanced language and mannerisms. This is related to the power issues noted previously. The child is put into an inappropriately powerful role and does not move through developmental stages in sequence. This includes not only sexualization but also physical, cognitive, and affective development.

10. *Self-mastery and control.* The child feels no sense of control or options. Regaining these options is an important goal of treatment.

In addition to these 10 areas, Long (1986) identified 5 more issues specific to treating the young abused child: importance of teaming with the child's mother, inappropriate attachment behavior, infantile regressive behavior, need for body contact and body awareness, and need for education about feelings. The importance of teaming with the mother has already been discussed; for the importance of appropriate attachment, see Lindstrom (1999).

The issue of inappropriate attachment is particularly important in this stage of ongoing treatment. Once the issues of trust in the early stage of treatment are successfully handled, it is easy for the child to become extremely attached to the counselor. The counselor may be one of the few people who has really listened to and respected the child and the child's feelings. Even when the child expresses considerable anger, fear, or sadness in a session, the child comes to value the time with the counselor and sees the counselor as nurturing. The counselor can become an important model for appropriate, nonexploitive, and fully consensual touching. Pats on the shoulder and back and hugs of greeting consistently emphasize positive physical contact during conversation or play. Counselors should be aware of this and establish a comfortable limit; for example, permitting lap-sitting only briefly, if at all, and encouraging the child to play independently and creatively with more verbal interactions from the counselor. The counselor also should be aware of the child's natural tendency to test limits and to move rather quickly from "affectionate" attachment to powerful testing behaviors such as hitting, drawing on the wall instead of the paper, or wanting to use "adult toys" such as the telephone or an answering machine. Whereas it is good modeling for the counselor to care for his or her property, the more important result is the child's knowledge, perhaps for the first time, that limits may be set out of caring.

The tendency toward infantile regression is important to observe. Young children frequently regress, not only in response to a fearful situation but, more indirectly, to express their need for nurturance, comfort, and security. The counselor's office or playroom may be a safe place to "act like a baby" and cuddle up for hugs and protection, perhaps with some thumb-sucking. The child can be permitted to engage in this behavior and also be encouraged to move on to more developmentally appropriate interaction.

Affective awareness is a major issue at any age within this age group. The child should be aware of basic feelings and be able to label them. There are many techniques for teaching this, and children react quite well to simple happy face drawings or to illustrations of children and adults in child-oriented books.

It may seem that this stage of treatment deals only indirectly with the abuse issues. Remember that one philosophical assumption is that treatment is prevention. That is particularly true at this age. Overemphasis on details of the abuse may be counterproductive because it may focus on the child's vulnerability and weakness rather than on an appropriate sense of power and control. It may also seem illogical to the young child who has repressed the abuse in order to move on to several new developmental tasks and concerns.

Group work, specifically a young child's playgroup, may be a helpful adjunct to treatment. Children develop trust with other children and find out that they aren't different. (Obviously, this option may not even be available to some counselors, depending on the number and age of their clients.) Playgroups can be positive in terms of appropriate social skill development, particularly if sexualization has resulted in significant sexual acting out. They can also resolve the typical problem of isolation in sexual abuse victims. Power issues also can be addressed. Playgroups may even become the primary treatment modality in a longer range plan. Playgroups should consist of a small group of boys and girls of a homogeneous age. Placement should be continually reevaluated. It is also possible to use group contexts that are not, by design, therapeutic in order to expose the child to developmentally normal children.

The participation of a parent, particularly the mother, in the playgroup process is crucial at this age. Some models include the mother directly in the group itself on a continuing basis, and others use an alternate group format (the child is seen for 2 or 3 weeks, then the mother is seen in a group). Damon and Waterman (1986) presented a parallel play group model in which children and mothers meet in separate groups at the same time, each dealing with a predetermined, structured task (e.g., saying "no," body awareness). These approaches strongly emphasize the mother–child bonding process.

Empowerment and Termination. Although empowerment was mentioned in the list of treatment issues during the ongoing phase, it should be clearly reemphasized during the last stage of treatment. Even when the child has successfully resolved the major issues of treatment, whether they be fear, withdrawal, anger, or sexualization, he or she remains more vulnerable to further abuse or exploitation than the nonabused child. Before termination is complete, an educational or therapeutic approach can be used to improve the child's appropriate sense of power and, therefore, self-defense. The following behaviors indicate empowerment:

1. *The ability to seek help.* This includes asking the mother, teachers, siblings, or adult relatives for help in any situation, not just sexual or abuse situations in which the child feels helpless. It also includes asking for help from the counselor and, as part of the termination process, agreeing to return for more sessions when necessary. The child can be given a business card to put in a special place and encouraged to call the counselor in the future, "just to say hi." It is amazing how often children respond to this suggestion.
2. *The ability to say "no."* Even the most well-intentioned parent cringes when facing the possibility of his or her 4-year-old actually

being more negative than he or she already is. Of course, the ability to say "no" to inappropriate touching is specific and does not usually result in the child becoming more generally negative. In fact, the child with strong self-esteem is less likely to engage in limit-testing and more likely to sense the power in accepting responsibility. Protection should be taught regarding people within the family as well as "stranger danger."

3. *The ability to express feelings.* The child should be able to identify feelings more clearly and have a sense of permission that expressing feelings will be accepted by the adults the child knows.

The presence of these behaviors in the child will certainly help the counselor to feel more comfortable about the termination process, but it still may be a difficult time for the counselor. Counselors, particularly those who are relatively inexperienced in this area, may well have a more difficult time in letting go than the child. Having seen themselves as the rescuers and protectors of the child, they fear the child may be vulnerable in their absence. Because children form strong attachments, the counselors also feel significant and understandable loss. This sense of loss may interfere with clinical decisions regarding the option of brief interventions—counselors may be reluctant to "let go" of children and may easily create or rationalize the need for extended treatment.

The goodbye process should focus on reassurances that the counselor will "be there." Other counselors or staff who have related with the child should also reassure the child that they will be there as well (or in case the primary counselor is unavailable). An exchange of small gifts or tokens (a drawing or card) is helpful in reassuring the child.

In general, the young victim clearly influences counselors' emotions and motivation as healers. Counselors want to make all victims better and do it quickly; they have to recognize that children do not work on the same timetable. Fortunately, there is a good chance for a significant positive interaction at this young age. Because the treatment of sexual abuse is such a new phenomenon in many ways, it may take some time for counselors to see the role that they have played in preventing further abuse.

The Young Male Victim. As noted earlier, the observations and strategies for the young child are appropriate for both male and female victims. A few additional comments on the young male victim may be helpful.

More than any other age group, the young boy is seen as similar to the girl. Offenders report seeing the young child as attractive because there is a nonspecific sexuality; that is, both sexes look very much the same. There is also less fear of homosexuality for the offender because he can rationalize that the young boy doesn't look at all like an adult male. The *DSM-IV* (American Psychiatric Association, 1994), no longer uses the terms *homosexual* and *heterosexual* as descriptors of pedophiles, because those terms apply only to adult orientation rather than the gender of the child victim.

The male victim presents himself for therapy much like the girl. There may be a somewhat greater tendency for acting-out, limit-testing, or overactive behavior. There also may be more extreme swings or exaggerations during treatment—more overt affection as well as more rebellion.

At this age, there is frequently a question of preference for the sex of the counselor in relation to abused boys. Although a male counselor may well be effective as a role model to show that men can be sensitive and nonabusive, the boy may still feel more comfortable with a female counselor, particularly in the early stages of treatment. Hunter (1990) disagreed with the prevailing opinion that male therapists cannot be effective. He emphasized that this decision should be made on a case-by-case basis. If at all possible, the child should have contact with at least one male counselor who is on the treatment team. This may be the parents' counselor or a colleague of the primary counselor. The play group is an especially valuable opportunity for appropriate male models.

Brief Interventions. Short-term treatment can be effective with young children. In a brief intervention, trust-building is still essential and desired, and treatment goals and issues are the same as those outlined throughout the book. There is simply more responsibility on the counselor to control the timing and duration of treatment in a more aggressive manner. There are no guidelines regarding the use of brief interventions. The plan must be individualized but can be attempted in most cases.

Generally, brief interventions include one or more of following:

1. fewer total sessions;
2. less frequent sessions, therefore extending overall duration;
3. seeing more than one person (dyads, triads and families);
4. adjunct group approaches;
5. a more active treatment style, including the increased chance of confrontation or challenge by the counselor; and
6. clear treatment plans, accountability, and advocacy with third-party payers, whether insurance or governmental.

Again, generally, counselors may have to work harder to be as creative, flexible, and yet accountable as the case allows.

Brief interventions with the young child are particularly problematic because the child's verbal skills and trust are limited. The use of mother-child dyads, noted earlier, is more important with perhaps only one or two individual child sessions. This is only possible when the mother is clearly supportive.

An initial three sessions may be held weekly but then expanded to biweekly for 2–3 sessions and then monthly. The mother or both parents can be seen separately. Sessions may be scheduled at points of possible crisis rather than regularly; for example, at the time of offender arrest or sentencing, removal from the home (this situation almost totally rules out brief approaches), visitation, and reunification. With the young child, time is required to stabilize, normalize, and (here's a new word) developmentalize the child. Less frequent contacts over a long period of time may be an answer.

As noted earlier, counselors must be more active when treatment is brief. Many of us who deal with children can document the shift away from laissez-faire styles (free, unstructured play), with an occasional insightful comment on our part. We have been forced to reevaluate this approach with abused and nonabused children (and adults). Counselor activity does not mean that the counselor either directs or commands the sessions. However, guiding the content and process makes sense ("I'm happy you're playing with the dolls. How are the dolls feeling? What are you feeling?"). This cannot be forced because the child is still allowed to initiate play behavior and, usually, verbal interactions. It is appropriate to "touch bases" on particular problems that the mother may introduce (tantrums, toileting, aggression), but many of these can be kept in a developmental, rather than traumatic, context.

Adjunct groups include child play and parenting education groups, both of which need not be specifically therapeutically focused. Child play groups may be formed by parents who are all in a treatment program or who may not have abused children; in fact, such groups may be a normal part of a general early childhood setting (preschool, day care, school). Parent education should be general and developmental and include what to expect from children and consistent strategies. Problems specific to the abuse can then be addressed in the treatment setting. Both types of adjunct groups are available in the community; managed care and governmental funding need not be involved.

Treating the Victim Age 7 to Puberty

Counselors who work with sexually abused children most likely deal with children age 7 to puberty. As efforts at prevention and education improve, the elapsed time between incident and report may be shortened. Because the largest number of cases are initiated in this prepubertal age group, the number of children whom counselors will be seeing may significantly increase. However, we have not yet seen that happen.

Why is this age group so "popular" among offenders? Why don't offenders prefer the adolescent "nubile" bodies that are so strongly associated with arousal in movies and TV? Why aren't they more aroused by adult development and turned off by the lack of it? (I caught you asking "why" questions again.)

The questions are, of course, puzzling, especially if one thinks logically about arousal. These issues are explored in more depth in chapter 3. Suffice it to say at this point that issues of power and control may be much stronger issues than sexual arousal. The "attractiveness" of the 7 to puberty group may be a combination of their being mature enough to interact verbally and, therefore, present a false image of consensuality and, yet, having very little real power in relationship to adults, particularly within the family. The child usually assumes that the parent is "right" and, at least initially, accepts the abuse, despite pain, discomfort, or a clear sense that it is "wrong." Some of the best examples of this are shown in how many children react to the first attempt at inappropriate touching: silence, feigning sleep, or denial that the touch happened.

How is the 7 to puberty age group different from the younger group discussed above? Perhaps the most identifiable difference for the counselor is the dramatically improved verbal communication. The older child is more fluent and understandable, is able to order syntax, and generally is able to correctly order events and objects in time and space. There is also an improved ability to articulate affect, although this may be an area of concern for the abused child.

The child in this age group is more in touch with the self in relationship to others and has lost some, but not all, of the earlier egocentricity. The sense of security has broadened to accommodate increased independence. There is a better sense of family beyond the mother-child bond and a better sense of bonding with the father or father-figure. There is also a sense of loyalty and (critical to the problem of sexual abuse) the ability to keep a secret.

The Report

The clearest signs of sexual abuse in this age group are physical signs not usually seen in others: genital irritation, bruising, or swelling; urinary burning; recurrent or sudden-onset encopresis or enuresis; and vaginal or rectal bleeding or discharge. Most abuse, of course, causes little visible harm. As prosecutors note, there is typically little physical evidence.

Psychological and behavioral signs and symptoms include behavioral acting-out, poor academics, withdrawal, running away, substance use/abuse, peer problems, difficulty relating to men, and wanting to stay away from home. Unfortunately, these are similar to the indicators for learning disabilities, depression, substance abuse, and a host of other difficulties. What are some behaviors that are unique to the abused child? Two specific areas stand out: the pressure to keep the secret, and sexual or sexually related behavior.

If you ask most children what their parents do for a living, how many are in their family, or how many rooms that are in their home, you'll probably get a quick, if sometimes inaccurate, answer. If you ask the abused child (in this case, a victim of any form of abuse) the same question, he or she will look at you with a slightly glazed look and either stammer out a response or ask you why you want to know. Although "the secret" is not always so obvious, we should not underestimate the amount of energy it takes to keep it. The child may well become more distractable, lose interest in school, and move away from peers who might have been considered friends. Peers, in fact, may be an important part of the picture because they notice significant behavioral changes before adults do. As noted earlier, peers frequently become the source of a report because they either detect a problem or elicit the truth from the victim and then report it either to their parents or to a teacher.

Sexual behavior remains a significant part of the picture, although we may be led astray by sexual language. Whereas language gives some of the best clues in the case of the younger child, the slightly older child is likely to use rather explicit language, both as expletive and in reference to sexual relationships. Behavior, however, may still remain a primary clue. Although exploratory behavior is still common, children in this age group are more likely to look for information from peers or from sexually explicit media rather than from physical contact. When physical contact does happen, it is again most likely to be touching, with little likelihood of either oral or vaginal penetration. Clearly sexual behavior is a strong indicator of sexualization. (Note, however, that it is possible for sexualization to occur in the absence of abuse, if, for example, there has been extended exposure to sexually explicit media.)

In female victims, one of the major indicators of sexual abuse is a sudden interest in boyfriends, and particularly an interest in boys who are 4–5 years older. Behavior in these pairs is remarkably inappropriate; 7- and 8-year-olds kiss and hold hands, and 11- and 12-year-olds engage in extended kissing, genital stroking, and oral-genital contact.

Whether the counselor is the first to notice these signs or whether the report is received unexpectedly, the counselor may be one of the first adults to hear a report of sexual abuse. The counselor's tasks are basic: report the abuse and support the victim. Some counselors have expressed concern that the two tasks are antithetical, that the report to authorities destroys a counseling relationship. The report is necessary for many reasons:

1. It is the law. As mentioned previously, even if counselors are obliged to report to another person in a school or agency, they are still responsible for ensuring that the report is made. The child must see that the adults around him or her will follow the law.
2. The child can seek out other support but needs the protection of Child Protective Services or law enforcement first. Some counselors develop a rather egocentric position that only they can help, understand, or communicate with a specific child.
3. With honesty and the focus on feelings, the counseling relationship can survive the report.

During the session in which the child divulges the abuse, support takes precedence over interrogation. There is a tendency to press for details, but they may be neither necessary nor helpful. The most essential details are the identity of the offender and clear time, date, and behavior involved in one incident. Further interrogation may simply be confusing and put the child on the defensive. Let the investigators investigate! It is far more important to reassure the child of having done the right thing and to accept the child's feelings of fear, anger, guilt, ambivalence, and confusion.

Protection, the primary focus of the time period around the report, is the role of the Child Protective Service or law enforcement, and not the counselor's role. Regardless of the process used or the efficacy of "the system," it has the task of and resources for protecting the child.

How can the counselor assist the system in protecting the child? Primarily, the counselor's report should be an accurate description of the child's report. The counselor also may be present in a supportive role when the investigators question the child. The counselor may provide helpful information regarding the child's behavior, peer relations, emotional adjustment, and family relationships. If the child remains in contact with the counselor after the report, the counselor then becomes a member of the treatment team and may even be identified as the primary therapist.

During the time of the report, there is a strong possibility that the counselor will be asked to deal with the veracity of the report. This will happen because the offender, at least initially, will almost certainly deny the allegation. Many adults choose to believe an adult over a child. The counselor may be one of the few adults that the child trusts, and it is essential that the child be believed until there is a clear reason not to do so. This is not to say that children never lie—that is clearly an oversimplification. It implies rather that the role of the counselor is to support the child, not investigate the allegations. (Do you have the message clear, yet?) Without denying the possible harm from false allegations, there is an even more pressing danger in allowing unreported abuse to continue. There is even reason to believe that the report alone may be one of the most important factors in the prevention of new abuse. Given that caveat, some guidelines relevant to veracity may be helpful.

1. Although children are not normally adept at describing sexual encounters that are fantasies, they can repeat things that they have been told in a very literal way. They do not, however, have the ability to describe behavior fully unless they have actually experienced it. Therefore, asking a child to describe a behavior in different words may be a helpful check against the possibility that the child may have read about or seen sexually explicit behavior. These media exposures may be superimposed on the actual abuse.
2. Children may lie if they fear punishment, especially if they feel, correctly or not, that they have done something wrong. They may, in fact, be more likely to deny an actual abuse than to create a fantasy abuse.
3. Because children have a strong need to please, it is essential for the counselor to avoid leading questions such as "did Daddy touch you in your private parts?" for reasons of accuracy and legal evidence.
4. Older children and adolescents may have power or revenge motivations for making a report, but these motivations are relatively rare and are usually dropped or changed dramati-

cally once the consequences are clear. These are some of the most difficult cases to sort out.

The role of the counselor during the report period is to provide support regardless of the specific veracity or accuracy of the child's report. The child needs support, whether the report is totally or partially true, an exaggeration, misunderstanding, or fantasy.

Crisis Intervention

It is difficult to put a precise time frame on the crisis intervention phase. In fact, crises should be expected throughout the process.

It would not be a mistake to assume that every victim and every offender is a suicide risk. That risk should be explicitly evaluated during the crisis stage. The more emotional conflict involved, the higher the suicide risk. It is not unusual to see the child swing between report, recantation, and change because of this conflict, which leads to perceptions of rejection by parents or other adults. With the child's typical egocentricity, the child perceives that the family's problems are caused by the report rather than the molestation and thinks of suicide as a solution.

The suicide risk dramatically emphasizes the conflict the victim experiences, with alternating (and simultaneous) feelings of fear, guilt, and rage magnified by basic ambivalence. Rage is the easiest feeling for most adults to understand, but the most difficult for the child to express. We can empathize with the sense of violation, betrayal of trust, and secrecy. We expect and encourage the expression of rage, and we are surprised when it doesn't occur. For many children, it is extremely difficult to reconcile their rage with the affection they may otherwise have felt and with strong societal messages that children are supposed to obey their parents, even when they would prefer not to. The rage may not truly surface for years. This ambivalence is one of the most important features in understanding the unique qualities of sexual abuse and is easily misunderstood.

The difficulty in reconciling rage overlaps with the guilt factor. The child initially is likely to feel that he or she is the one who did something "bad" or was a part of something bad. This is complicated in children who, at some level or on some occasions, enjoyed the attention, affection, or physical sensations of the sexual contact. The guilt may even intensify once the child experiences the upset subsequent to the report—his or her removal or the father's removal, the mother's surprising incongruity, the siblings' blame, and peers' questioning and curiosity. It may be easier for the child to express anger toward the mother than the offender.

Children may exhibit a range of fear behaviors. They may fear physical punishment from either parent, reinforced by direct or implied threat from the offender during the sexual contact. That threat also may induce fear of parental divorce ("If Mom finds out, she'll leave us") or maternal rejection ("Mom won't like you for doing this") and may be accompanied by the all-too-truthful statement that "Nobody will believe anyway." This is compounded by the fear of the legal system (court appearance) and, later, fear of losing the father to prison. For the victim of extrafamilial contact, the fear of physical retribution may be more of an issue.

The key to dealing with the fear, guilt, and rage, particularly during the crisis stage, is to focus on the child. All of these feelings are totally acceptable. When children develop an appropriate sense of relative powerlessness, they are better able to understand their lack of blame, fault, and so forth while still leaving open the option that they can become more powerful. The theme of returning the victim's "normal" childhood is repeated throughout the treatment process. At this point, the "permission" to feel is critical.

Ongoing Treatment

Issues. A framework for this longest phase of treatment is provided by examining Porter et al.'s (1982) 10 "impact issues" as they apply to the 7- to 12-year-old age group and then proceeding with some specific intervention strategies. I focus particularly on the victims of intrafamilial abuse and then discuss separately any issues that apply specifically to other forms of pedosexual contact. The 10 impact and treatment issues are as follows:

1. *"Damaged goods" syndrome.* This applies whether there has been any physical damage or not. In the past, it was possible to take some small comfort in the fact that most cases of sexual abuse did not result in major physical damage. Unfortunately, we may not be able to protect our children from the impact of HIV/AIDS. Although the percentage of AIDS cases attributable to abuse has been small, the seriousness of the consequences compels us to remain concerned (Fuller & Bartucci, 1991). Regardless of physical injury, society and the child both label the sexualization experience as creating an oddity to be both pitied and feared. It is a typical cri-

sis point, for example, when a victim/survivor reveals the experience to a serious boyfriend or girlfriend or, later, a spouse.

2. *Guilt.* Children see themselves as responsible for the sexual behavior itself (especially if they enjoyed it and the offender reinforced that), responsible for the report (whether or not it came from them directly), and responsible for the chaos in the family as a result of the report. This is a recurring theme in treatment. It surfaces in the crisis intervention phase, and it continues to be a topic through individual and family work.

3. *Fear.* Like the young child, the 7- to 12-year-old continues to feel a significant fear of abandonment, particularly if there has been a foster placement. The child has a realistic fear that the mother may choose the father over her or him. The fear of punishment or retribution mentioned during the crisis intervention phase may continue for some time into treatment. It should be emphasized that this fear may take the form of acting-out, aggressive, or "power" behaviors rather than the more typical withdrawal that one might expect.

4. *Depression.* During the crisis intervention phase there is a suicide risk in many cases, and depression will continue, particularly if there is a sense of rejection from either parent, which is quite likely. The counselor needs to refocus continually on the child's feelings of need for self-affirmation and worth.

5. *Low self-esteem and poor social skills.* Again, I prefer to focus on the child's feeling of powerlessness and lack of control. This feeling may be even more apparent in the 7- to 12-year-old child than it is in younger children. Verbal and physical limit-testing may be more severe and may include aggressive as well as sexual behavior. Although this behavior also may be linked to anger, there is a good chance it has more to do with compensating for a perceived lack of power and control. This type of behavior is frequently described as being unprovoked and may be directed at peers or siblings toward whom the child previously had related in a friendly manner.

6. *Repressed anger and hostility.* The child's anger tends to build up over a period of time; the child may initially accept the behavior but then experience a sense of violated rage. This buildup may be one of the factors most closely related to the duration of the sexual contact. Much of this anger may be vented and handled more easily if there is an early report. On the other hand, if the report is never made, as is the case with adult survivors (to be discussed in detail later), the anger and rage may well be debilitating and highly resistant to treatment. It is also important to note that much, sometimes most, of the anger is directed at the mother for failing to protect the child or report the abuse. The child frequently assumes that the

mother knew, or must have known, or should have known, about what was happening.

7. *Inability to trust.* At this age, it may be hard for the child to regain the sense of trust. Again, there may be considerable lack of trust in the mother, and this relationship must be rebonded as soon as possible. There also may be greater difficulty with trust issues if the offender was the natural father or a stepfather of long duration. This lack of trust frequently is generalized to all men and may continue into adulthood, interfering with normal, positive relationships.

8. *Blurred role boundaries and role confusion.* This issue was described in the section on family dynamics and receives additional attention as we look at the family treatment modality. If the child is not able to deal with role boundaries in the family context, the counselor will have to deal with it using role-play and other forms of substitutes.

9. *Pseudomaturity and failure to complete developmental tasks.* The abused child, particularly the oldest child, will easily assume a pseudoadult role in the family either as a cause or effect of the abuse. There may well be a parentification of one or more of the children. It would not be unusual for a 9-year-old to look behaviorally like a 15-, 18-, 25-, or 39-year-old at various times and to be expected to move among those ages at the demand of the offender or the rest of the family. This is both a reflection of the sexualization (as it applies specifically to sexual roles and behavior) and the more general pseudomaturity.

A special note on sexualization issues is important here. As noted previously, sexualization is essentially a developmental issue. The extent of this developmental skip may be hard to predict. It is apparently not directly related to age, type of sexual behavior, or duration of the abuse. The only exception to this unpredictability may be a relationship between the occurrence of penile-vaginal coitus and the extent of sexualization. Sexualization may include flirting, seductiveness, increased masturbation, exhibitionism, sexual contact with older (or much younger) partners, or prostitution. These behaviors create obstacles to treatment for the following reasons:

a. Crises are created that distract from the treatment.
b. Responsibility issues are clouded by the rationalization that the victim must have been "enjoying the sex" or that the victim seduced the offender in some way.
c. The victim becomes the negative focus of the family, frequently while the offender is "getting better."
d. The family's resistance increases as it finds ways to blame the problems on "the system."
e. Siblings revert to blaming the victim.

f. The victim may defend herself or himself by running away or by opposing reunification.

10. *Self-mastery and control.* The abused child does not have the same sense of choice and control over everyday life as the healthy, nonabused child. As a result, the abused child also lacks the advantages of learning from consequences because the logical connection between choice and consequence is not clear. Despite the pseudomaturity and false sense of power, the child actually remains overly dependent and lacks the opportunity for responsible independence.

Intervention Strategies. By the end of the crisis intervention phase, much, if not most, of the legal process may have been completed. Although this eliminates some of the need for teamwork, it shifts the focus to treatment planning and integration. Probably several counselors and therapists will be involved in the treatment process, especially if the whole family is participating. It is essential that there be close coordination among those involved. This certainly speaks to the advantage of having one coordinated treatment program, although treatment planning and integration are still workable in other situations.

1. *Peer support and therapy groups.* As soon as the crisis issues seem controlled or stabilized, consideration should be given to group involvement. This may take the form of creating a play group for the younger children or a peer support group for the older children in order to focus on social skills, interaction, appropriate development, and a supportive environment for expression of feelings and self-mastery. Some children may have a special need for group therapy to focus more intensively on feelings. This is a particularly good environment for dealing with issues of responsibility, anger, fear, and guilt. The presence of, and feedback from, peers can be tremendously validating and provide a continuing reality contact that may be more effective than one provided by the adult counselor. Peers also can be extremely validating of the treatment process. (Of course, there's always the risk that the children may express the negative experiences of treatment or "the system.") Groups should be as homogeneous as possible with respect to age and, at the older end of this age group, in grouping by sex. Older children and adolescents can act as peer facilitators, with significant advantages to both the facilitator and the younger children. Groups should certainly be small enough to ensure appropriate control and supervision and allow time and space for expression (maximum of 6–8 children if supervisory help is available).

2. *Apology sessions.* If the family is moving in the direction of reunification, the major events in this treatment phase may well be the apology sessions. If there is not going to be a reunification, or if the contact was extrafamilial, modifications will have to be made to allow the victim psychologically to confront the offender. Whether the apology sessions involve direct or indirect confrontation, the counselor should encourage venting, exploration of past patterns, and option-building for future patterns.

The apology sessions are a series of structured confrontations between the victim and offender and also may include the nonoffending spouse and other family members. These are called *clarification sessions* by Hindman (1989), because there is an emphasis on clarification of responsibilities, later leading to "restitution." The importance of communication between victim and offender is addressed by Yokley and McGuire (1990) and Hindman and Hutchens (1990). The first of these sessions may come early in the process, depending on the child's readiness, with the bulk of the sessions coming in the middle stage of treatment. The timing is flexible, but the earlier the initial session occurs, the less the anxiety. The specific goals of these sessions are apology, responsibility acceptance, report acceptance, and mutual commitment to treatment, regardless of the likelihood of reunification. The offender also will accept responsibility for any consequences to him, such as incarceration.

Preparation for the apology and confrontation session. The child must have a good sense of being protected before attempting an actual or psychological confrontation. This includes having been able to talk about the details of the abuse with the counselor and acknowledging the various feelings involved such as fear, rage, and guilt. Although these feelings do not need to have been resolved at this point, they need to have been expressed and, as best as possible, understood. It should be clear to the child that the responsibility for the abuse rests with the offender and that there is a support system available (mother, counselor, school personnel, "the system") that believes her or him and will provide protection from future harm. It is not necessary that the child "want" to see the offender, although many children do at this point. It is important, however, that the child feel a sense of control over the timing and content of the session. The child can practice for the sessions through role-playing with the counselor or by writing letters or drawing pictures for the offender, whether sent or not. The offender will have been similarly prepared.

The first session. The initial apology session should include the child, the offender, the spouse, the child's counselor, and the offender's counselor. The child should be the first to arrive, if possible, in order to meet the offender's counselor, see the room that will be used, and perhaps even arrange the chairs to be comfortable (children frequently place themselves between their counselor and their mother). The child should be reassured that any reactions, thoughts, or feelings are permitted. The initial contact between child and offender may be anything from an icy lack of eye contact to a cheerful hug. The offender has to apologize for the abuse very specifically, as well as for other problems such as abusive language, physical abuse, or general disruption of the family. Responsibility issues are clarified, and the report is acknowledged as a positive and necessary action that facilitates change in the family. Any reaction on the child's part should be met with reassurance from all those present. The responses of any of the participants in this session are not predictable. Details of the abuse may be given at this session or may be more appropriate at a future session.

Further sessions. The number and spacing of further apology sessions are determined by the treatment team. The sessions should deal with the specific details of the abuse so that minimization is avoided and all those in protecting roles have a clear picture. They also have to address the setup used by the offender, including progressive patterns of seduction and substance use or abuse. The family should be aware of marital, communication, and parenting issues, although these may be better addressed in more detail in future family sessions. One or more of the apology sessions should include all family members to ensure that the other children are aware of who is responsible for the abuse, because at that point they are quite likely to still blame the victim for causing all this difficulty. Involving all family members also helps expose and break the "family secret" pattern. Special attention should be given to the siblings, who also have been victimized by fear, confusion, and stress within the family. It is also important to note that even though the victim is the primary beneficiary of the apology session, it is also usually a very important positive step for the offender, despite the discomfort of the confrontation. Most offenders feel quite guilty and want to express this, and they also have real concerns about the welfare of the child.

Indirect confrontation. The use of indirect confrontation may help either to prepare the child for a direct confrontation, process information from a direct session, or provide the child with an opportunity for expression when a direct session is not possible (e.g., the offender is incarcerated, under a no-contact order, is extrafamilial or even unknown). The same basic goals apply: expressing feelings, clarifying responsibility, and creating protection. This can be facilitated through techniques like role-play with the counselor or with dolls, writing or dictating letters that may or may not be sent, drawing, or or other expressive play (clay, paints, etc.)

The apology sessions are often the most challenging and rewarding for the counselor. They are frequently unpredictable, eliciting emotions ranging from rage to tears. They are productive in that they may provide significant insight for both the family and counselors into the intra- and interpersonal dynamics and provide material for future individual and dyad sessions. The apology sessions also serve as important benchmarks when the treatment team makes decisions about visitation and possible reunification.

3. *Clarification of roles and responsibilities.* This stage of treatment involves both individual and family modalities. Specific strategies related to family systems are addressed in connection with family treatment. This may be a stage of long duration and overlap with earlier and later stages. Whereas the apology process focuses on the responsibility issues, this stage goes one step further to focus on the appropriate role of the child, a difficult task for the victim and family.

A major issue to tackle is the previously mentioned corporate family responsibility for the condition of the family system before, during, and after the abuse. Again, to emphasize, even though the offender assumes 100% of the responsibility for the incident(s), the family also assumes its own accountability. Acceptance of this accountability is not easy for many families, and it is during this stage of treatment that major issues of resistance may arise. Having weathered the initial crises and, perhaps, the legal process, families are quick to see the problem as resolved and wish to forget the whole thing and put it behind them. This understandable but dangerous wish may cause the family to revert to the same dysfunctional patterns that existed prior to the abuse. It is also an easy trap for the counselor to embrace because the victim frequently will cooperate in this resistance. The family will rebel against the involvement of the "system" without any acknowledgment of their dependency needs and their lack of skills for independent healthy functioning.

Dealing with the victim individually during this phase also may mean focusing on resistance in the form of conflict over future roles and responsibilities. The child may well have significant difficulty in resuming appropriate child-level roles. The child may both enjoy and resent the pseudoadult power and the accompanying lack of real control. The counselor must set up the atmosphere for the child to be accepted as a child and set reasonable and appropriate limits for the child, in and out of the office.

The child can make most of the decisions regarding the activities during these sessions within a set of options that the counselor provides. Usually the child can bring a toy or game from home or play with the toys in the counselor's office or playroom. Like any other play therapy environment, the toys should be enjoyable and potentially expressive but also allow conversation and interaction with the counselor. Although expression of feelings is always an appropriate goal, during this phase there should also be an opportunity to set family roles and activities.

a. Family drawings are extremely useful on an ongoing basis to literally obtain a picture of past, current, or future structure. The drawings can be static or kinetic and are useful at different stages of treatment. Different components can be requested (child and siblings, child and parents, whole nuclear or extended family, pets, etc.).
b. Small figures (dolls, play or action figures, clay) can represent the family or family members and can be moved to different structural or activity positions.
c. The counselor can role-play situations, roles, or interactions either directly or through the use of dolls, stuffed animals, or puppets; for example, "Here's the big doll coming into the little doll's room. How does the little doll feel? What can he or she say?"
d. Limits should be clear regarding behavior that is not acceptable in the sessions including hitting the counselor, self-harm, actual (as opposed to symbolic) destruction, and noise levels inappropriate to the setting.
e. Limits should also be clear regarding physical and psychological space/distance in the room. The counselor should determine whether either arm's distance or lap-sitting feels comfortable and when hugs are OK.
f. Roles can be clarified through appropriate responsibility. The parents can be encouraged to determine reasonable jobs or chores for the child and apply principles of encouragement and consequences to support doing these jobs. The counselor can reinforce the importance of these jobs to the child and discuss ways to do the jobs either more quickly or easily. The victim needs to be able to return to the appropriate child role in the family, expressing feelings, receiving

nurturance and protection, and taking on an age-appropriate share of responsibility within the family.

4. *Empowerment.* Empowerment is a primary issue at this, somewhat later, point in the treatment process. The empowerment process includes:

a. reinforcement of the report,
b. rebonding with the mother,
c. assertiveness and self-protection,
d. redefining the relationship with the father,
e. resumption of age-appropriate roles wherever possible, and
f. positive control and attitudes regarding sexuality.

One of the key elements in any form of sexual abuse is a power imbalance. Whether coercion, seduction, or force is used, the child is powerless against the physical, verbal, or affectional power tools of the adult. Victims may react in seemingly opposite ways. Whereas one child may assume the withdrawn, isolated, helpless stance, another may act out sexually, engage in aggressive activity, and rebel at school. Other children may react in other ways.

Regardless of the behavior, the root is the same: powerlessness and anxiety. These effects are sometimes doubly traumatic when one considers the family dynamics, where children often have been given unusually powerful and pseudoadult roles before the abuse.

The child is likely to use inappropriate power techniques in an attempt to regain some of the perceived lost power. The attempt, of course, backfires as the adults tend to either "fight fire with fire" or "give up," either pattern accelerating the power issues.

Parents can use typically suggested techniques for dealing with the power issues: set limits, clarify consequences, or withdraw from power struggles. They also can use positive approaches to encourage appropriate empowerment, thereby reducing the child's need for unproductive power.

The first point in the recovery process for empowerment possibilities is the report. The report can be an extremely scary time for the child because it is such a powerful weapon; it is necessary for protection and affects the rest of the family. The child needs strong reinforcement to view the report as a perfectly reasonable and appropriate step to "make things better" in order to stop dwelling on its devastating and traumatic aspects. Once the report has been made, the child should be reassured that the adults will take the responsibility for protecting the child.

Because the mother in a typical abuse case is torn between protecting her child(ren) and supporting her husband, her behavior is of critical importance to the child. The mother should initiate a sense of protection, which can then progress to a rebonding. The importance of this is suggested by the mother–child dyad being the first dyad to be brought into focus during treatment. This dyad will meet at various points throughout the treatment process to clarify and solidify the bond.

When trying to provide the child with a sense of empowerment, one of the most difficult tasks is striking a balance between assertiveness and self-protection on the one hand and aggressiveness and dictatorial power on the other. The child is capable of self-protection while maintaining his or her role as child in the family. The basic message is similar to what we would give to an abused adult—taking care of oneself does not infringe on the rights of others or relieve one of social or familial responsibilities. This focus on assertiveness is facilitated greatly through the peer group work described earlier.

It seems obvious that the child's relationship with the father-offender must be redefined. Many would redefine the relationship by separating the two—by either incarcerating the offender or removing the child from the home. Other options are available, however. Through individual, dyad, triad, and group treatment as well as carefully monitored visitation, a major shift in the relationship can be facilitated.

One frequent question lay and professional people often ask is how the victim or any of those involved can possibly "forgive and forget." The truth is that they don't. They probably shouldn't! An analogy may be helpful: The abuse, like other traumatic events, is eventually "filed away"; it continues to exist as a memory but, with time, is integrated as part of experience and removed from everyday life. There may be times, of course, when the files are pulled back out so that some issues can be handled. By "filing" the experience, victims and families are able to get on with their lives while still acknowledging the event and responsibility. Although many variables may affect the child's ability to file things away, this method is clearly healthier than the denial and minimization that exemplifies the pathology.

The redefined relationship is accomplished by the offender's assumption of an appropriate set of roles as adult, parent, and spouse and the child's resumption of the child role. These roles are achieved through individual effort, including treatment, and the mutual support of the whole family.

The last focus in the empowerment phase is on positive attitudes and control regarding sexual issues. One of the typical rationalizations of the pedosexual offender is that he has provided sex education to the child. The obvious problem with this is that the "education" provided is almost all negative, emphasizing exploitation over consensus, coercion over communication, and physical sensation over intimacy. The task of the treatment process, therefore, is to emphasize sex positivism—the concept that we can all maintain a positive attitude about our sexuality regardless of our experiences.

Sex positivism revolves around three principles (Rencken, 1996b): knowledge, consensuality, and lack of harm. All three should be addressed consistently during treatment. Sexual abuse is essentially and functionally defined by the absence of these three components, despite the possibility that some cases may have one or two of these things present. The child needs to receive correct and complete sexual information. This is sometimes resisted by the family, who would almost like to psychologically "revirginize" the child and deny the sexualization. Information should include anatomy and physiology, human sexual responses (this can validate their own responses to the abuse), contraception, values, psychosexual development, relationships, and societal attitudes. Obviously, this information has to be set in an age-appropriate context. The child also should receive strong messages about consensuality, lack of harm, and self-protection and be helped to realize that being in positive control over self also includes a positive control over one's sexuality.

Empowerment, then, includes the concepts of positive, assertive control, and responsibility. Positive control, in turn, goes along with appropriate power, both individually and in the family and society.

5. *Termination.* Although the duration of treatment may be highly variable, the child will probably be the first of the key people in the abuse situation to complete treatment. This will certainly be true in brief interventions (to be discussed in the last section of this chapter). This, generally, has a lot to do with children's resilience and the normal healing process of development. If the treatment process involves the whole family, there is also the bonus that the child's progress can be monitored through longer duration modalities of marital and family contact. Readiness for termination can be assessed with the following conditions:

a. The child has successfully addressed all of the 10 treatment issues noted previously. The issues do not all need to be "resolved" perfectly; healing is a continuing process. Particular emphasis should be placed on the empowerment and control issues because they are necessary for the child's healing and protection.

b. The child is at minimal risk for revictimization, either by the original offender or another offender. I do not use the phrase *no risk* in referring to either victim or offender. Part of risk management lies in obtaining a strong commitment from the child to report new incidents or seek help from responsible adults who will believe and support the child. This may include building a solid adult support network. It also includes a firm agreement to return to the counselor for further sessions if there are any problems, whether or not they seem related to the abuse issues. The counselor may wish to schedule a phone date in the not-too-distant future to cement that agreement.

c. The child has established a peer support system either independently or through the treatment program. The child is no longer isolated although most children will not become outgoing or totally change their interactive styles.

d. The child has established and is maintaining an independent and age-appropriate lifestyle. As termination approaches, the counselor will observe the child's increased ability to handle problems and decreased need to deal with them in treatment. The most effective treatment will have given the child the tools to be able to deal with these issues. One way of looking at this is for the counselor to monitor her or his own reactions to the child. If the counselor is having fun with the child during sessions rather than dealing with treatment issues, it is probably time to examine the possibility of termination.

As noted in the section on child victims younger than age 7, the termination session(s) should include some appropriate goodbye ritual, such as an exchange of small gifts, pictures, or drawings. There also should be a focus on the concept of the counselor "being there" and, certainly, a business card or other reminder of the counselor's address and phone number. Children frequently keep this in a "special place" for a long time after termination as a reminder of the support available.

Warning Signs. The counselor involved with a sexual abuse victim, whether as the primary therapist or as a team member, has an obligation to watch for warning signs. These may be signs of danger to the child or indicators of potential difficulties in the family or in the treatment process. The first of these dangers, of course, is the risk of suicide discussed earlier. The counselor should be alert to severe depression, enduring guilt, and suicidal ideation (e.g., "They would all be better off without me"). Self-destructive tendencies can manifest as withdrawal or as high-risk behaviors, not necessarily of a sexual nature. For example, one 9-year-old I treated stole a golf cart, drove it down a main street, and then crashed it into a riverbed.

Another major problem lies in the risk of victims dissociating. Although there is still much need for research (especially as this applies to children), dissociation in sexual abuse victims may lead to the development of Dissociative Identity Disorder, a severe consequence. Most of the adult survivors who do develop DID apparently have not had treatment as children, leading to some optimism that it can be averted through treatment. Particular attention should be paid to victims' statements that they "tuned out" during the sexual contact or that they felt like they were somebody else watching the contact take place. The possibility of DID should not be taken lightly or impulsively used as a diagnosis.

The rage factor, which is a very reasonable reaction and is present in most victims, also should be monitored. Rage infrequently can lead to a decompensation and psychotic reaction. Early emphasis on rage ventilation and reduction is critical.

Although the inappropriate power behavior mentioned earlier is to be expected, some children accelerate this behavior to the point of rejecting all authority in the family or society. Clearly, this rejection, frequently accompanied by resistance to therapy, leads to major problems and acting-out behaviors. The counselor consistently has to reinforce the advantages of positive control and responsibility without becoming another authority figure to the child. There may be occasions, however, where the counselor may need to set limits.

Counselors should beware black-and-white solutions or rosy reports by the child or the family. The very pathology that helped set up the abuse will lead to a "quick fix" if counselors go strictly by the child's or the family's reports that everything is wonderful. The counselor must remain accountable throughout the process.

Victims of Other Pedosexual Behavior

Although most of the treatment process above applies to any victim of pedosexual contact with an adult, it focuses mostly on the intrafamilial setting with the regressed offender. In this section, I discuss other specific pedosexual situations.

The pedophile. Because the pedophile typically caters to the pleasure of the child, seducing the child with games, food, or other nurturing behavior, the victim is liable to express significant confusion. Victims may even be puzzled to learn that the pedophile is associated with harm. This is confounded when the victim learns that the pedophile was reported by another victim. Even after describing the pedophile's behavior, victims may, at most, acknowledge that they themselves (and not the adult) did something "dirty." Only after the involvement of police and, perhaps, an arrest, will some children acknowledge the seriousness of the problem and feel significant guilt or embarrassment. The responsibility issues should be clarified quickly. Because this form of contact is generally extrafamilial, there is a risk that treatment will not be mandated or monitored by Child Protective Services. In addition, parents might hope that the problem will "blow over" and are not likely to risk embarrassment by initiating treatment voluntarily.

Another issue of concern for the victim of the pedophile is that other children who are known to the victim have been involved, either concurrently or serially. The child will have to cope with the joint victimization and be reassured that none of the children was responsible for the behavior. The child may also have to be reassured that he or she can provide the names of other children involved to protect them, not because the child did something bad (i.e., the victim is not "tattling"). Because there is a strong probability that the pedophile will not admit to his behavior or its illegality, the victim may have to testify or, at least, give a taped statement or deposition. The child also may have to receive special attention if photographs, movies, or videotapes were taken. Because victims of pedophiles are more likely to be boys than victims of other forms of abuse, the section on the male victim should be consulted.

Rape. The rape victim consistently seems to be the most traumatized of the pedosexual victims in the following ways:

a. *Physical trauma.* Victims of rape experience more physical injury than any other victims of sexual abuse to the point that physical injury should be anticipated. Serious physical injury (unless it is unrelated physical abuse) is almost always related to the violence of rape. The trauma can also include homicide; rape is typically the only deadly point on the sexual abuse spectrum. The more common injuries are the result of actual or attempted forced penetration of the vagina or anus resulting in fissures, muscle tears, or internal damage from bruises to hemorrhage. Some damage can be permanent, particularly when it affects the female reproductive system.

b. *Emotional trauma.* The force, and threat of force, in the rape situation represents the ultimate coercion and creates the worst negative effects of coercion (Finkelhor, 1984). Trauma for the child is similar to that in adult rape victims, with two possible areas of increased vulnerability: the physical size and power differential are greater, leading to an even greater feeling of helplessness, and the child is less aware of the sexual context, focusing even more on the pain and violence of the situation. This is the area that generally requires the most intensive therapeutic intervention. If the offender is known to the victim, confrontation and apology sessions may be appropriate after careful preparation and planning.

c. *Need for long-term care.* Rape victims generally require long-term care because of the high levels of physical and emotional trauma and their inability to confront the offender. There is also the frustration that the offender will not be caught or that they may have to handle the strain of trial testimony. There are likely to be very strong defensive mechanisms, including denial and dissociation, that may be resistant to treatment.

Sexual addiction/compulsivity. The victim of this form of pedosexual contact is more likely to be an adolescent than otherwise and is also more likely to be one of several victims. The victimization may occur either within or outside the family. Although there may well be a diffusion of energy or focus, the child still may experience the same full range of emotions as other pedosexual victims. The only mitigation is that the responsibility may more clearly rest on the offender, and it is more likely that the offender will be seen as "sick" or disordered. In communities with treatment programs geared specifically to this issue, the victim may be able to receive some additional support and, in some situations, benefit from some codependency exploration.

Symptomatic. The victim of the symptomatic offender may have different reactions depending on his or her closeness to the offender. One who is closely related, or has seen the offender for a long period of time, may be able to see the sexual contact as similar to other strange or bizarre symptoms and accept it as such but, for the child whose age ranges from 7 to 12, even this view may be difficult and confusing. A victim of an unknown offender faces issues similar to those of other extrafamilial victims. Again, there may be some small benefit to knowing "the reason" for the contact and some decrease in fear if it is seen as treatable.

The Male Victim

The specific plight of the male victim is one of the least understood in the whole arena of pedosexual behavior despite valiant attempts at clinical research (Finkelhor, 1990; Hindman, 1989; Hunter, 1990; Lew, 1988; Nyman & Svensson, 1997). Both the causes and effects of male victimization are less known than those of female victimization. As noted previously, the number and percentage of male victims are probably significantly underreported compared to those of girls. Finkelhor estimated that 33 to 50% of all victims of sexual abuse are boys, and Hunter reported that between 2.5 and 16% of victims are male. This underreporting seems to be related to a societal belief that boys are not seen as "attractive" to adult men and that if there were any sexual contact, boys would enjoy it and would not consider it abusive. This is particularly true in the case of a female offender. Hindman noted that male individuals do not perceive themselves as victims and that disclosure is difficult because they are usually not encouraged to seek help or protection, whether as a child victim or an adult survivor. Hunter emphasized that unless therapists create an unusually safe environment, victims may not report sexual abuse. As we have found in female victimization, we are gaining more knowledge by talking with adult male survivors about their experiences, including the men who continue to feel that their experience was not, in fact, harmful or traumatic (Bauserman & Davis, 1996; Li et al., 1993).

From the reported cases available to date, one concludes that it is likely that the boy will be victimized by a male adult. Boys who are victimized also are more likely to be younger than girls, to be abused in extrafamilial settings, and to be victimized in conjunction with other children (Finkelhor, 1984). This may be true in the pedophile situation or in other extrafamilial contacts (e.g., coaches, baby sitters, youth leaders, and other trusted adults). This same-sex involvement is critical for the victim because for some time after the contact, there will be a concern about homosexuality (more of a concern with increased age). The male victim will question whether this has "made him" a homosexual or whether, in fact, he already was a homosexual and somehow set up the offense. This will be a concern for the victim even though the offender may not have a preference for male adults. In fact, gay adults may have a lower incidence of same-sex contact with children than do heterosexual men. Particularly in the pedophile population, the offender's sexual orientation is largely irrelevant and response to either sex is asexual. The *DSM-IV* (American Psychiatric Association, 1994) reflects this change by no longer referring to "homosexual" contact, changing to the more accurate description of "same-sex."

The male victim, therefore, even more than the female victim, will probably have more "why" questions: "Why me? Why a boy?

Aren't you supposed to do that stuff with girls? Why pick me? Nothing fits anywhere. Why did I get hard? Why do the other kids call me queer when they did the same things?" The answers are even more elusive.

We know very little about arousal patterns in same-sex pedosexual contact. Although there is some indication from offender reports of a history of sexual abuse, these data are incomplete and inconclusive. Stevenson and Gajarsky (1991), for example, noted that although both male and female individuals who were victimized as children reported other unwanted experiences as adults, the men were more likely to become sexually aggressive. If there is a history of abuse, there may or may not be a connection between the age of the victim-offender when he was abused and the age of the new victim. Little information is available regarding behavioral specifics or duration of contacts.

The counselor should deal directly with homophobic concerns, even if the victim does not initiate discussion of the issue. The topic can be approached in a fairly routine way as a typical concern of children who have been put in this situation. Reassurance should be given that this incident will not cause homosexuality. The sex of the counselor may or may not be significant depending on the child's needs; however, male counselors may have to pay extra attention to both the possible homophobic concerns and the importance of male role modeling (Hunter, 1990). The boy will need to receive strong messages that validate warmth and sensitive nurturing as well as strength and power.

Brief Interventions

Are brief interventions possible when priority must be given to developing trust and building rapport? We may have to do some creative thinking.

Managed care has had a significant negative effect on treatment of both victims and offenders, but providers who treat victims are more likely to be affected by the system constraints. Problems include documentation, reduction in sessions, and poor confidentiality, with about 75% of participants in one study reporting that managed care had at least a moderate impact on their practice (Berliner & New, 1999). Similar concerns have been raised by Huber (1997) and Iglehart (1996), and those of us who are affected hear one horror story after another related to "mangled care."

As previously noted, however, the need for briefer interventions is advocated by several sources, not only managed care. Instead of approaching treatment with the notion that we may be involved in 2–3 years of weekly therapy, we can consider either time-specific or phase-specific counseling. Although we may need 4–5 weekly sessions early in the process, we may be able to space them out, depending on the phase of treatment. In other words, we may need concentrated attention on the crisis intervention phase but then reduce the ongoing phase until it is time for family therapies and the final empowerment stage. We may well be able to save dozens of sessions by focusing in on the specific phase. (However, we must remain flexible enough to see the child quickly if there is some unusual or untoward event.)

The variation on this plan is to create a time sequence of weekly, then biweekly, then monthly sessions and adjusting the frequency of sessions as necessary. Essentially, this enables us to provide concentrated help when the child really needs it (as best as we can define that) and maintain a fairly predictable schedule. This can be combined with the episodic or phase-specific intervention. It should be emphasized that it will remain important for the same counselor to be available even if there are periods of time when there is less face-to-face contact. This provides reassurance that the child will not be abandoned. If necessary, other counselors could assist in the process (school counselors, group facilitators, activity leaders), but the primary therapist should remain available.

The most promising way of reducing sessions and perhaps even reducing the overall duration of treatment is through the increased use of family sessions—dyads, triads, and whole families. Family treatment can be instituted much earlier than has been done in the past, using the apology sessions as a springboard for directing focus to the family. This approach may prevent the child from being pushed even further into the identified victim role. A cognitive-behavioral model, long advocated in offender treatment (Hanson, 1997; Maletzky, 1998; Marshall & Anderson, 1996), is a good base for working with families. McCarthy (1990) has noted that this approach leads to establishing communication and guidelines to prevent further abuse, revitalizing the marriage relationship, and, ultimately, keeping the family together. Family members are able to see themselves as survivors rather than as victims. This is an effective approach, especially when compared with removal of the child, and one that I have replicated with modifications with many clients.

Another approach that has been helpful in the arena of brief family interventions has been Solution-Focused Brief Therapy (Fleming & Rickord, 1997), which again focuses more on present and future behavior rather than on reliving or attempting to fix history. (Unfortunately, many victim and survivor counselors have focused on the past rather than the present or future.)

Introducing the family approaches early (or earlier) in the treatment process also has the effect of normalizing the child's life. This should not be equated with either denial or minimization; in fact, it acknowledges that the abuse is a very serious problem that has to be addressed rather than emphasizing the pathology of any family member. When there is even a chance of reunification, the family will be the instrument that will have to solve problems and create options well after treatment is complete. It makes sense to accentuate that process; after all, family dynamics probably played a great part in creating or sustaining the abuse.

The initial family treatment may involve two counselors (one treating the child and one treating the adult), but one counselor may be sufficient after roles and responsibilities have been clarified. Usually this is the child's counselor. If it is not, the child certainly should be involved in that decision. This shift to one counselor may also be a big help with managed care and other funding sources where the concept of conjoint or even collateral therapy is virtually prohibited.

Brief interventions can prove to be helpful and may reduce the stigma experienced by the victim and family. These concerns must always be balanced with consideration of the child's needs.

The victim between the ages of 7 and puberty provides a complex series of challenges for the counselor who is either in the primary or supportive role. For most children, prognosis can be optimistic, with the natural healing process working in a positive, parallel track with treatment. This should not, however, in any way call the need for treatment into question. The scars created by sexual abuse do not heal on their own, either while the behavior is occurring or in the aftermath. The victim does not get better without the active support and involvement of parents, whether the abuse occurred within or outside the home. The child has a right to treatment and recovery.

Treating the Adolescent Victim

Treating adolescents is different than treating children in several important ways, both in terms of issues and in terms of intervention strategies. One major difference is that the adolescent is more likely to be a "survivor" as well as a victim. In other words, the pedosexual behavior may have happened years before the counselor encounters this troubled client. For the purpose of this discussion, I define an *immediate intervention* as one that occurs within 1 year of the last pedosexual contact and a *delayed intervention* as one that occurs more than 1 year after the last pedosexual contact. There may even be some benefit in defining an even longer delayed intervention, but that raises more questions than it answers.

Thus far I have used the term *victim* to refer to child clients in order to emphasize the child's total lack of responsibility for the contact and also the child's helplessness within the situation. Several of the treatment issues and goals previously noted address the movement away from that helplessness to a feeling of appropriate power and control. It could certainly be said that the treatment process helps to move the child from the victim role to the survivor role. Many victims, of course, become survivors even without treatment, although with more difficulty or less efficiency. The adolescent in need of delayed intervention is presumably a survivor who still experiences significant pain and suffering. In this section, I identify differences, when they exist, between immediate (victim) and delayed (survivor) intervention. I also may refer to the *victim/survivor* as an inclusive category.

How does adolescence differ from the previously described age groups in terms of normal developmental issues? The major issues during adolescence revolve around the establishment of identity and independence, clearly evolving a sense of self as opposed to family (Salkind & Ambron, 1987).

Erikson (1968) identified the task of this age group as the struggle with "identity versus role diffusion." This normal task is of obvious interest to counselors when examining the adolescent victim/ survivor with inherent and considerable role confusion. Elkind (1967) also wrote about adolescent egocentrism; adolescents become self-absorbed and self-conscious, acknowledging others' thoughts and opinions but imagining these thoughts to be centered on themselves. As a society, we reinforce this sense by assigning a great value to the fashions, lifestyle, and spirit of the adolescent, with many adults maintaining an adolescent outlook, including a significant egocentrism and lack of responsibility. A great value is placed on independence and rebellion (witness the large number of movie plots based on teenage themes that could be subtitled "Teen knows best" or "Adults really are hopeless geeks").

There may also be a strong emphasis on fantasy or role rehearsal during adolescence and young adulthood. Many teenagers create a fantasy of themselves (as rock stars, actors, NBA players, valedictorians) and risk frustration at not being able to accomplish this while they are still teenagers, if at all. This fantasy may have played a part in the recent murders at Columbine High School in Littleton, Colorado, where the main issue seemed to be the establishment of a unique identity (fantasy) and place in history even at the cost of loss of life.

How do these developmental issues differentiate adolescents from the 7- to 12-year-old child? How do adolescent issues evoke concerns regarding pedosexual contact? There is, perhaps most significantly, a normal increase in sexual behavior, both because of the issues of independence and identity and because of the onset of puberty. Although much of this sexual behavior is self-directed and controlled to some extent, it also is clearly affected by peer involvement. One must note that sexual behavior among adolescents is, in fact, statistically normal, with most having that experience before age 18 (Reinisch, 1990). "Normal" sexual expression is a perfect vehicle for the sexualized adolescent in that sex can be accepted and can be a useful tool for survival, coping, and controlling a scary situation. Having learned that sexual feelings can be exploited and used in a highly controlling fashion, the adolescent victim/survivor can obtain physical pleasure, attention, affection, peer acceptance, and even financial independence through the use of sex.

Conversely, a different set of victim/survivors goes into adolescence with an abhorrence and fear of sex, withdrawing from peers and typical adjustment needs with a pseudomature "I don't need them" attitude. These extremes of the highly controlling and the highly controlled are typical of sexualized adolescents and set them off from the sexual behavior of the nonabused adolescent. The victim/survivor may experience considerable difficulty in establishing any real intimacy patterns. Exaggerated control and intimacy dysfunctions of abuse survivors are, unfortunately, overrepresented among prostitutes and nude dancers and models and in sexually explicit media. (This does not necessarily represent a cause–effect relationship.)

Compared with younger victims, the adolescent victim/survivor is much more likely to attempt suicide and more likely to complete the attempt. (For helpful research and clinical data regarding adolescent suicide, see Capuzzi & Gross, 1996.) The desperation, powerlessness, and hopelessness of the abuse victim dramatically increase the risk of both attempting and completing suicide. Two studies make this connection effectively. Kosky (1983) reported that suicidal behavior was associated with losses, underachievement, divorce or other marital disputes among the parents, and abuse of the child. Several of these factors apply in many sexual abuse cases. McKenry, Fishler, and Kelly (1982) reported that factors such as family conflict, family cohesion, and parental behavior were critical. Again, both of these studies would point toward the abused (particularly the sexually abused child) as being at risk. Male victims may be at even higher risk because of intrapsychic conflict and homophobia.

The increased independence of the adolescent victim leads to two major concerns for counselors. One is that there is a significant resistance to treatment because there may not be a strong motivation to reunite with the family and, specifically, to have any contact with the offender, regardless of the level of trauma. The teenager may prefer to move out rather than have further contact as a result of the sexualization and pseudomaturation (this can also be a power play). The second, related, concern is that there is a clear risk of runaway behavior. This may take the form of a relatively typical overnight runaway, or it may be of significant duration. Again, this may be a power play, but the sexualized child is more likely to have a strong motivation for autonomy. (Conversely, one factor that may keep this client in the family is concern that younger siblings are being abused.)

Peer relationships are typically critical for adolescents. At the very least, adolescents want to be accepted; many want to be leaders. Ideally, adolescents have relationships with same sex and opposite sex adolescents. As noted in the discussion of sexual behavior, the extremes of peer relationships range from withdrawal and isolation to a strong need for acceptance. Both of these extremes tend to minimize the possibility of a strong, appropriate peer support system. The same behavior (e.g., sexual relations) that the victim uses to try to gain acceptance frequently backfires when the peer group attaches an unattractive label to the person (e.g., calling a female victim "easy" or a "boy-stealer").

The adolescent also runs a higher risk of developing severe reactions that may not typically surface until adulthood. These include dissociative reactions and various eating and other self-concept disorders, from anorexia to obesity. The counselor must be alert to these issues.

All of these typical adolescent developmental concerns regarding identity, autonomy, and acceptance by peers become magnified for the abuse victim/survivor. Even the brightest, most insightful adolescent will have significant difficulty with these tasks.

The Report

In either immediate or delayed intervention, the adolescent may be more concerned about confidentiality than the younger child.

Although this may cause some difficulty, it should not deter the counselor from making the report. The adolescent may be less vulnerable and better skilled at self-protection than the younger child, but he or she still needs the protection that is generally mandated.

Possibly more important than that sense of protection is the sense of validation that comes from making the report. This may be true at all age levels but is particularly important for the adolescent. Even if there are objections from the child or the parents, the report indicates that someone (i.e., the person making the report) thinks that the child is worth "the trouble" and worth caring about. Another reason the report is important is that other children may be at risk.

The adolescent may well see the system as nonsupportive during the investigation and may question the worth of the report, so an extra measure of support at this time is necessary. Even seasoned investigators sometimes express the sense that the adolescent could have said "No" or may have consented to and enjoyed the contact. Much more than the other age groups, the 13- to 18-year-old may even play out a heavily reinforced male fantasy. If the abuse is ongoing or was still occurring not too long before the report, there is also a good chance that it is a contact of long duration that began in preadolescence. Relatively few pedosexual relationships are initiated in adolescence (Finkelhor, 1984).

The delayed intervention presents unique problems with the report. The counselor feels a dilemma in reporting a pedosexual contact that last happened 3, 4, or even 10 years earlier. There generally is no "statute of limitations" involved in mandatory reporting laws, whereas there may be a limit (either statutory or practical) for prosecuting the offender. Theoretically, the counselor could be cited for failing to report a crime that could not be prosecuted. This would be extremely unlikely, however, and the counselor would be well advised to talk with the local Child Protective Services authorities to determine risk as well as the need for a formal report or investigation. If agency staff trust the counselor, they may take an "information only" or informal report, avoiding some of the legal considerations raised above provided that the child is safe.

Crisis Intervention

The crisis stage for the adolescent victim may be more difficult to deal with, because of the increased risk of suicide or runaway behavior. The counselor may have to do a considerable amount of general stabilizing before dealing with the abuse issues. Trust-building must be a major initial focus.

Any counselor who works with adolescents and preadolescents knows the importance of building trust. The skilled counselor masters the ability to gain both trust and respect while maintaining an appropriate adult role and an appropriate distance. Under ordinary circumstances, the adolescent has a difficult time trusting an adult who is either too close or too distant. This normal response is magnified by the pedosexual contact.

Sexual abuse strikes at the heart of the ability to trust. Whether or not the contact was initiated at a younger age, the adolescent victim is more likely to have kept the secret (despite physical and emotional pain) for a longer period of time than a younger child would have, with an almost constant feeling of betrayal along with the love-hate ambivalence discussed earlier. Even more so at this age, the victim is also likely to feel a lack of trust and significant rage toward the mother and consider her a coconspirator because she failed to protect. These feelings sometimes are stronger when directed at the mother than when directed at the offender.

Once these feelings are understood, it is easier to see the mistake that many counselors (of either sex) make—that of trying to act like a mother to the victim/survivor. This counselor reaction is much closer to pity than empathy and may include uninvited physical contact (hugs, hand-holding), loss of affective control (crying, anger), and verbal revictimization ("poor kid," "it must have been horrible," "how disgusting that must have felt"). In looking back on this time period, one insightful survivor commented that the worst thing was what she called "the big lie"—when adults say "I understand." The counselor must remain strong but not controlling, available but not intrusive, and honest in stating that he or she does *not* understand completely but would like to be a supportive and caring listener, with special experience to offer.

Counselors are also cautioned not to engage in "offender-bashing." As mentioned, it is easy for adults to identify with the rage the victim feels but less easy to identify with the ambivalence. Consider the following exchange:

Client: I just hate him! My skin crawls when I think of him touching me. I wish he would die!

Counselor: He sounds like a real son of a bitch. What a creep!

Client: Well, he didn't used to be. It was only when he was drinking.

The client quickly became defensive about the counselor's name-calling for two reasons: It pushed the ambivalence button and it took the focus away from the client's feelings. A more helpful reflection would have been, "You sound really angry." The victim's feelings should be the focus for support, even when they shift or seem unclear.

Regardless of whether intervention is brief or extended, the adolescent's trust is formed by the counselor's "being there." If at all possible, the same person should remain as the primary therapist for the duration of treatment. The adolescent may frequently test the counselor's limits and willingness to "be there" by calling the counselor between appointments, setting up phone calls between counselor and teacher or parents, or trying to "shock" the counselor with smoking, drinking, or sexual behavior or language.

The concept of "being there" is critical to a treatment contract that can be a useful option during this phase. Although part of this contract will act as an anti-suicide and/or runaway agreement, it will also serve as a more general, long-term agreement. It should be created anew in each case and remain flexible enough to be renegotiated as treatment progresses. It should emphasize counselor availability as well as the client's commitment to attend sessions and to call the counselor before taking impulsive action. It should also clarify the limits of confidentiality regarding what will be shared with parents, Child Protective Services staff, lawyers, and others. Adolescents will generally like the adult feeling of entering into a contract. Most important, the contract will act as an additional concrete bond in the trust process.

Related to the issue of trust is the adolescent's perception of the counselor's role as it relates to both "the system" and to parents. This goes beyond the confidentiality issue and raises a central question: For whom does the counselor work? The adolescent will have more difficulty with trust if the counselor seems to be an extension of "the system" or of parents—that is, if the counselor is another authority figure who is trying to get the child to "behave," force her or him home, and either push reunification or split the family. Conversely, the trust level will improve if the adolescent sees the counselor as an advocate within the system. Ideally, there is an added bonus if the adolescent perceives that the entire treatment team is working and advocating for him or her, but this may not be readily apparent, especially during the time of crisis.

As noted, the major issue to face during the crisis phase is the risk of suicide or other acting-out and self-destructive behavior. Trust-building is the initial step in accomplishing this, including use of the contract. It is important for the counselor to move quickly to clarify responsibility, which will be an ongoing task. In this phase, the adolescent not only has to recognize the offender's sole responsibility for the abuse but also clearly accept responsibility for his or her own recovery. The focus can be positive and centered around "here-and-now" issues as well as future planning. Even during discussion of the facts and feelings concerning the abuse, the focus can still be on how this history can be brought under control now. This is sometimes more difficult for the adolescent than for younger children because adolescents typically have a clearer memory of the painful details as well as the societal stigma. This positive focus on the present assists the adolescent to feel in control and avoid the sense of alienation that leads to high-risk behaviors. Alienation is significantly worsened if the mother does not believe the child, highlighting feelings of rejection.

The adolescent is less likely to experience the fears typical of the younger child. There is, however, a more subtle but pervasive sense of wondering "What's going to happen to me?" Although the adolescents' egocentrism helps to fuel a veneer of confidence, there is considerable anxiety over rejection before the self-identity is completely formed. It's the kind of doubt that even good bakers experience—the bread has risen, the crust looks brown, but how do we know for sure if it's done inside, especially when we have some concern about the reliability of the oven? The counselor has to address this concern of rejection by reassuring the adolescent that she or he will be involved in planning options and that even these options can be reviewed in terms of her or his comfort level. Note that this is not a promise that the teenager will be the one making all the decisions; to do so would only fuel the pseudomaturity and power issues.

The final general concern during the crisis phase (both in immediate and delayed intervention) is the issue of victim veracity. As noted in the earlier sections, the adolescent is more likely than a younger child to make a false allegation intentionally or, sometimes, to exaggerate symptoms. (This probably occurs only in a small percentage of reports.) Improved cognitive and verbal ability increases that possibility; however, the adolescent is also more likely to understand the consequences (separation from family, trial, incarceration, general family chaos). There are, certainly, some extremely dysfunctional situations where the child may accept these consequences as an alternative to an abusive or unstable situation. Unless the child is psychotic or severely antisocial, there is probably some severe problem if an untrue allegation is made. A plan for protection from further abuse may still be needed independently of decisions regarding prosecution of the offender. There also may be a need for a protection plan if the child recants the allegation, whether or not it was true.

Some unique issues pertain in the delayed crisis intervention. The first of these is the obvious one, to acknowledge the crisis. One might mistakenly believe that because time had elapsed since the last incident, there is no crisis. In fact, there are two major sources of crisis: divulging the abuse, and the precipitating problem (which may initially seem to be unrelated).

Like the adult survivor, the adolescent may divulge the abuse only after establishing a trusting relationship. Although this may occur with peers or family, the counseling relationship provides the atmosphere for most delayed reports. The presenting problem(s) may be relationship difficulties (boyfriends, sex, jealousy, pregnancy, rejection), school problems (academic, social, attention, homework, acting-out behavior), substance abuse, or issues of self-worth (depression, eating disorders, running away). These problems, in and of themselves, may be at the crisis level.

Divulging the abuse usually will precipitate a crisis because it represents such a departure from "the secret" and will be upsetting, at some level, to the status quo both intrapsychically as well as in the family system. This crisis may be met by minimization, rationalization, and denial coming from significant others (more so than in immediate intervention), and legal intervention is less likely to occur or to be effective.

The adolescent, then, may need considerable support in divulging the abuse. The counselor will have to create an atmosphere of trust and to ask the right questions. Many otherwise good counselors report hearing of only a few sexual abuse cases because they simply do not ask about it. This is particularly true in the adolescent delayed intervention. The "right questions" are actually permission statements rather than interrogatives; for example, "it's OK to talk about what happened in your family; sometimes feelings like yours are connected to stuff that happened in the past; it sounds like you've been keeping some sort of secret for a long time."

The counselor should first focus on the survivor's feelings rather than on the details of the pedosexual behavior. This should remain the primary focus, but the delayed intervention presents an exceptional situation in that the details may not be investigated or otherwise addressed. The counselor should give permission for the details to be discussed (rather than interrogating) and should also give permission for the details to be disclosed at intervals over time, allowing the picture to form as slowly as necessary.

The counselor will have to decide whether direct or indirect confrontation with the offender is appropriate. The "apology session" technique is discussed later in this section. The decision to adopt that as a goal must be made earlier in the crisis phase in the case of a delayed intervention.

The crisis intervention phase of treatment assumes added significance in delayed intervention. The adolescent is likely to panic once the abuse is divulged. The counselor may have to approach each session as though it may be the last intervention before the child leaves home, drops out of school, or moves with the family. The counselor may well have to "buy time" and offer as much support as possible.

Ongoing Treatment

Issues. Porter et al.'s list (1982) of 10 treatment issues apply to both immediate and delayed intervention; I relate them to treating adolescents.

1. *"Damaged goods" syndrome.* Adolescents are more concerned than younger children about the physical effects of sexual abuse, including pregnancy, sexually transmitted diseases, and hymen damage (even though the latter is also of concern to many nonsexualized children). These concerns can be related either directly or indirectly to the abuse. Adolescents also become aware that they may not be able to "save themselves" for a special first-time sexual experience. Clearly, sensitive medical intervention with counseling support is essential, even when there is no major physical trauma.

2. *Guilt.* The adolescent may feel responsible not only for the pedosexual contact, but also for any sexual or behavioral acting-out that has occurred. The counselor can assist the adolescent to assume responsibility and control over current behavior without feeling guilty for the sexualization. The adolescent may also feel guilty for not actively stopping the abuse at an earlier time, especially if the abuse was of long duration.

3. *Fear.* The fear issues, specifically the fear of alienation, have been noted previously. In ongoing treatment, the fear of alienation is closely related to trust of the counselor, peers, and, most of all, family. The adolescent may also fear retaliation, either in the form of physical threat or in the form of rejection and alienation from the family.

4. *Depression.* Ongoing depression and recurring suicidal ideation should be anticipated. The counselor should renew the suicide contract periodically. Antidepressant medication may be warranted for carefully selected clients.

5. *Low self-esteem and poor social skills.* Adolescents typically have concerns about self-esteem. These are greatly magnified in the victim/survivor, particularly as they relate to body image and a sense of general unworthiness. These image problems may manifest themselves specifically in various eating disorders. Although obesity may be observed and relatively easily monitored by the counselor, anorexia and bulimia may have less visible but disastrous effects. The counselor will have to monitor eating patterns directly with the adolescent and with the family. Although eating disorders are associated more often with female victims, male victims also have significant body image issues and may compulsively participate in athletic or bodybuilding activities or totally avoid them.

6. *Repressed anger and hostility.* Although more adolescents than younger children are able to express their anger and rage directly, many continue to repress or deny those feelings. Notice that we are talking about repressed feelings, not repressed memories. Defenses include withdrawal, minimization, passive-aggressive behavior, histrionics, and dissociation. The latter is a significant concern for counselors because the victim/survivor is in an extremely vulnerable position. Many adolescent victims show at least some dissociative behaviors that may be relatively subtle and easy to miss unless carefully monitored.

7. *Inability to trust.* As noted, trust and alienation issues are particularly important for adolescents in general and are magnified for the sexual abuse victim.

8. *Blurred role boundaries and role confusion.* Role boundary problems are usually set before adolescence. Because that system is difficult to modify, it may have caused major stress for the adolescent. If the role confusion has persisted, the victim will be understandably reluctant to give up the power of an inappropriate role, even if the power has been anxiety-provoking.

9. *Pseudomaturity and failure to complete developmental tasks.* Adolescent clients experience not only significant loss of power but also a sense of lost childhood. A frequently expressed part of the rage is the grief over lost or denied childhood experiences (e.g., "I should have been playing with dolls instead of his penis"). The loss of peer experiences may also be important because victims feel isolated from agemates and gravitate toward older friends or adults.

10. *Self-mastery and control.* These issues are discussed further in connection with empowerment. The adolescent needs to take responsibility for the recovery process and become accountable for current behavior in order to gain a sense of control of her or his own life in a positive way.

Treatment Strategies. In this section, I review treatment strategies sequentially with an emphasis on specific adolescent issues. Many of the strategies are used when treating younger clients.

Apology session(s). There are two unique issues for the adolescent in the apology process: resistance to the session and increased probability of rage reactions.

The older the child, the more likely he or she is to exhibit significant resistance to apology sessions. This resistance may take the form of "I never want to see that slime again," or "It's no big deal, it's over, why do we need the hassle?" This polarity of rage and passive-aggressive behavior is expressed not only by different victims but also by the same victim at different times. This resistance may be strong and of long duration, probably becoming even stronger as time passes without a confrontation. Although the victim's comfort level and readiness should certainly be considered, there may be a point at which the counselor may actively encourage or even push for the apology sessions, irrespective of the child's powerful resistance. Even a single apology session may be extremely valuable in exploring the resistance, ventilating feelings, and clarifying responsibility and may result in a significant therapeutic breakthrough. Allowing the adolescent to control totally the therapy process through resistance may reinforce power issues.

The other unique issue for adolescents in the apology process is the intensity of rage they may express during the confrontation session. Because of adolescents' verbal ability and the duration of the emotional repression, their rage can be strong and should be handled carefully by the counselor, balancing expression with control. In one apology session, I heard a 15-year-old girl string together 20-minutes worth of nonstop epithets, expletives, and anger in rather creative combinations. Fortunately, the offender was prepared and willing to listen, and the result was a clear therapeutic success. The girl was able to see the offender taking responsibility, acknowledging her feelings, and maintaining self-control.

The delayed intervention also creates a set of issues. The counselor, in consultation with the treatment team, when available, will have to determine whether the victim should confront the offender directly or indirectly. Factors in this decision include the victim's current relationship and contact with the offender, the extent and duration of the abuse, possible risk from the offender (rejection, retaliation), and whether or not a formal report has been made.

If a direct confrontation is planned, both offender and survivor should be prepared in advance, even if this means that the offender might refuse to cooperate (it's better to know that in advance). Ideally, both should also commit to several sessions (at least 3) to work through the various issues. The direct confrontation generally can have the same goals as other apology sessions discussed earlier, but with the added goal of dealing with "the secret."

Indirect confrontation can be handled in much the same way as it is with younger victims; the one difference is the possibility of greater resistance or rage.

Group strategies. After the immediate crisis intervention issues have been addressed and, perhaps, concurrently with the apology sessions, the adolescent can benefit from participating in a group. At least two types of groups should be considered: therapy and support.

The therapy group ideally should be led (or cofacilitated) by a counselor other than the primary therapist to provide a different perspective and further validation of the issues and the ability of the victim to deal with them. This group should have goals similar to those of individual therapy, with a special focus on validation. This validation includes reassurance about the report, support for the feelings of ambivalence as well as rage, and shared perceptions ("I'm not the only one in the world who felt like _____"). The group can help clarify roles and responsibilities, deal with empowerment, and greatly reduce the risk of alienation. Most successful groups are fairly homogeneous in age and, probably, sex; developmental issues as well as the desirability of same-sex or coed groups also need to be considered when forming groups.

After participating in a therapy group for 6 to 12 months, the adolescent can join a support group. The support group will continue the validation and empowerment process, including assertiveness and sex education. The support group can also deal with more "typical" adolescent concerns—relationships, school, career—and how these concerns may or may not be affected by the abuse. An additional therapy-oriented group subsequent to the support group may be useful for some adolescents.

Clarifying roles and responsibilities. This phase of treatment takes some of the results of the apology session and refines the roles and responsibilities within the family. As noted earlier, the adolescent may be well entrenched and enmeshed in a "parentified" role, a powerful position that has provided some of the few "positives" in life. It is more difficult at this age, of course, to give the adolescent permission to *be* a child. In effect, that process at this age would mean to *return to being* a child, a role that some victims have never learned.

There are some messages that can be helpful to the adolescent:

- It is not necessary to act like an adult in order to be accepted/appreciated/acknowledged.
- It's OK to have fun.
- Adolescents do have responsibilities, but they are not the same as those that adults have.
- Peers can understand and relate as friends.
- Time can be used as a part of the healing process and to avoid impulsive decisions.

During this phase, it is important to acknowledge not only the responsibility of the offender but also the role of the mother (or nonoffending spouse). The adolescent (more so than victims of younger ages) frequently shows what seems to be an inordinate amount of rage toward the mother for not protecting. The rebonding process begins in this phase with the clarification of what roles mother and child have been assuming. At this time, the mother may well acknowledge feelings of guilt, sadness, and jealousy. Depending on the maturity and emotional stability of the mother, she may see the adolescent as a "rival" at this point, which might further support her "choice" of the offender. These feelings may become so overwhelming that the mother may detach herself from the victim as a coping mechanism. The counselor should be aware of this possibility and provide additional support during this early part of the rebonding process.

One of the major concerns in this phase is familial resistance to treatment and blaming the victim. This is a special problem in adolescence because the family is more likely to see the victim as enjoying the contact ("otherwise she's old enough to have said no") and less in need of support ("if she/he doesn't like it around here, they can leave"). Normal and magnified adolescent limit-testing tends to aggravate this process. Combined with the "hassles" the family has experienced with Child Protective Services and the legal system, there is a high risk that the mother will, intentionally or not, choose the offender over the victim and either agree to an out-of-home placement or trigger a runaway situation.

Empowerment. As noted, both group and individual modalities should be used to empower the adolescent by reinforcing the report, rebonding, learning to be assertive, redefining paternal relationships, assuming age-appropriate roles, and practicing positive control and attitudes about sexuality. Two of these should be expanded as they pertain to the adolescent.

The process of rebonding with the mother is frequently more complicated and fragile with adolescent clients than it is with younger clients. There is a clear risk of rejection and alienation and difficulty in defining a relationship that is different from one that had existed for a long time. The counselor may find it helpful to explore common issues and concerns *outside* of the family and its history to balance the strong focus on the abuse. Examples of these include women's issues in society, career options, school planning and options, and peer relationships. This focus may actually encourage the opening of communication so that feelings about the abuse or the family dysfunction may be discussed more reasonably.

The second important focus in this age group is on the positive control and attitudes regarding sexuality. Because sexual behavior is likely to occur in this age group normally, the adolescent victim/survivor is likely to be (or to have been) involved with problematic sexual contact (e.g., involvement with a much older partner, engaging in high-frequency behavior, placing self at risk of contracting sexually transmitted diseases or becoming pregnant). The ultimate problem may be an increased risk of HIV, although this population has not yet shown the clear results of that risk.

The clear focus in both individual and group modalities should be on gaining control of the sexual behavior rather than on using sexual behavior to fulfill needs for acceptance and affection. This probably does not call for a "just say no" approach. Rather, the question becomes, "How can you feel more in control of the sexual situation and your sexuality?" There are several sexuality education approaches that effectively ask this question, including a relatively new concept called *puberty education* (McCann & Petrich-Kelly, 1999). This may include reducing the number of partners, intentional discussions with partners, use of contraceptives and safety barriers, masturbation (both as a "substitute" and a discovery technique for positive feelings), and, of course, accurate information about sex, which is almost always lacking.

A closely related issue is body image. The sexually abused adolescent may engage in sexual behavior to "prove" attractiveness and desirability and experience little real pleasure (anorgasmia may be typical). Victims/survivors may use excessive makeup or none at all and dress provocatively or plainly and use starvation or binging as ways to cope with a negative body image. Part of the empowerment process can consist of receiving information and support for nutrition, exercise, and self-care as well as information about the risks associated with smoking, alcohol, and other addictive or self-destructive substances.

Clients may engage in same-sex exploration. Although this may be normal for adolescents, the counselor should reinforce the issue of positive choice and control to ensure that this is not exclusively a reaction to the abuse. Certainly, an overreaction to same-sex contact could simply increase resistance. Gay, lesbian, and bisexual community support programs for adolescents may be helpful, either on a consultative or collaborative basis. Specific homosexual concerns for the male victim are addressed later.

Another effective strategy for empowerment is the use of stabilized adolescent survivors as peer facilitators for group therapy and support and as "sponsors" for other victims in earlier phases of treatment. This can be clearly helpful for both parties. This strategy can greatly improve the sense of control and accomplishment of the survivor, clarify issues, and provide role modeling.

Termination. Unfortunately, termination may not be clear or typical. The adolescent's independence is likely to lead to a client-initiated termination, perhaps before the counselor had planned. This typically takes the form of cancelling or missing appointments. Once the counselor sees this pattern, he or she should attempt to schedule a termination session in order to obtain closure.

The adolescent should be able to demonstrate self-protection, including the willingness to seek help from family, counselors, or the authorities.

Warning Signs. As noted in the crisis intervention phase, the risk of suicide remains real throughout the treatment process. The counselor needs to be aware of statements of depression, helplessness, hopelessness, and alienation from family or peers. Renegotiation of the suicide contract can validate the client's importance to the counselor and can be done from a positive perspective, emphasizing the areas where the client had gained control or made progress.

Runaway behavior also remains an ongoing risk. This could be either solitary or accompanied with a friend of either sex. Again, a contract is helpful; at the very least, the client should agree to contact the counselor for reassurance of safety.

The risk of dissociative behavior is more of a factor for the adolescent than for the younger client. Although this is usually caught early in the process, the counselor should still be alert to statements or behaviors that indicate a "tuning out" or a feeling of being a spectator to the abuse or other behavior, particularly in sexual relationships. This process may be part of the lack of pleasure that many survivors report.

Other Forms of Pedosexual Contact

Specific issues related to adolescent clients are briefly addressed here.

Pedophilia. Although pedophilia, by definition, applies only to prepubertal children, the taxonomy includes the two forms of adolescent preference, hebephilia and ephebophilia, under this category. Both of these forms may be closer in their dynamics to adult preference than is pedophilia (see chapter 3). Hebephilia may be a variant of heterosexual adult preference with an emphasis on the emerging development, "innocence," powerlessness, or fixation based on inadequacy. Likewise, in male offenders, ephebophilia may be a variant of homosexual adult preference with similar emphases, although this is certainly less clear. These adult arousal patterns do not alter the compulsivity involved.

The adolescent victim/survivor could, of course, have been victimized by a pedophile at a younger age and may feel uncomfortable or ambivalent about reporting the abuse. There may even be a lingering feeling of rejection if the pedophile has not kept various promises to the victim or if the pedophile has moved on to a younger child.

The victims of hebephile and ephebophile offenders may primarily feel exploited. They may have thought of the offender as a good friend, different from other adults. They may also have felt loved in an adult sense for the first time and, therefore, validated for their own attractiveness and maturity. When they discover that this validation was mostly, or only, for sexual purposes, they may totally reverse this validation and see themselves as "damaged goods," unattractive, and incompetent. For many victim/survivors this exploitation seems incongruous with the fun that they may have experienced, and it can set up a long-term dilemma. Loss of trust is a major issue in these situations.

Rape. Like adult rape victims, the adolescent victim feels both the trauma of the rape and the victim-blaming syndrome. Adolescents are susceptible to being castigated for short skirts or shorts, bare midriffs, makeup, or other "seductive" behaviors regardless of the relevance of these to the rape dynamics.

As discussed earlier, the rape victim has to deal with both physical and emotional trauma, including the probability of magnified reactions to the "damaged goods" syndrome and a strong possibility of male-bashing. Dissociation and gender dysphoria are both clear risks.

Addictive and symptomatic. Although younger children may gain some solace in realizing that these offenders are in some way "sick," the adolescent may feel increased ambivalence for the same reason (e.g., "I should have known that there was something wrong with him" or "How could I have let him?"). The counselor may need to attend to the responsibility issues at some length.

Ritualistic. It seems that adolescents are far less likely than younger children to be involved in ritual abuse, which is based on fantasy, fear, and submission to adults, all of which may be moot at this age. Again, it is certainly possible that ritual abuse started at an earlier age and continued into adolescence, but there is little indication of this. The key issue at this age level is in establishing self-identity, control, and responsibility.

The Male Victim

The adolescent male victim will have different reactions to the abuse depending on the sex of the offender. Although research is clear that most offenders are male (Finkelhor, 1984), it is not clear whether there may be different dynamics affecting adolescents that research has not identified because of the very effects of the problem. This is not to say that male offenders are in the minority but rather that there may be more "unreported" female offenders.

The female offender may see the male adolescent as a rejuvenating experience, particularly if she is under the influence of alcohol or other drugs. The male victim, having been programmed by movies and other media, may regard a sexual relationship with an older woman as a male fantasy come true. Although there may be some clear discomfort, particularly the closer the offender is to the victim (e.g., stepmother or aunt), the male adolescent is likely to see this as a positive experience at the time. Clinical experience verifies that adults looking back on such contacts may not see them as abusive or describe them as molestations (see also Finkelhor, 1990; Hindman, 1989; Hunter, 1990; Lew, 1988; Nyman & Svensson, 1997). We have to be careful about some counselor prejudice that predicts harm. How much of an impact such contacts generally have—positive, negative, or neutral—is simply not clear and should be explored thoroughly in each case.

The effects of the female offender on the adolescent boy need to be noted. The notion of female offenders goes against typical theories of offense based on power, control, and (primarily masculine) aggression, as noted in this book, and also goes against feminist perspectives (Elliott, 1993; Miletski, 1995). Women do appear to be different than men in that they are less coercive, violent, and threatening, and they may be less likely to deny the abuse (Matthews, 1993). There is a remarkable increase in emotional risk when the offender is a first-degree female relative (mother or sister) where it appears that shame and possible repression are more likely (Sgroi & Sargent, 1993). Sgroi and Sargent also noted increased problems for the victim/survivor in differentiation of self; establishing personal identity, committed relationships, and healthy marriages and sexual functioning; parenting; and establishing healthy relationships with children. Wyatt (1991) added that when there is no coercion involved or the behavior is defined as a "game," education, hygiene, or an act of love (as children may well experience a female offense), it may not be perceived as abusive. The rhetorical question for many adolescents that is crucial here is, "What child will risk losing his/her only loving family?"

The effect is much more clear and dramatic in the case of a male offender. Whether the contact happened during middle childhood and was not reported until adolescence, or whether it happened more recently, the male victim/survivor will probably have a strong homophobic reaction. He will have strong concerns that homosexuality was either the cause or effect of the abuse. This feeling is much stronger in adolescence and seems to occur even if heterosexual peer contact has already taken place. It is not clear whether, beyond this homophobia, there may be deeper sex-identity confusion because adolescence is a critical period for the establishment of identity. At any rate, the counselor will have to be extremely sensitive to these issues.

The Youthful Offender

The juvenile offender has become a topic of considerable interest, presumably as an offshoot of the general interest in pedosexual behavior (Perry & Orchard, 1992). Although most of these offenders are adolescents, some are prepubertal.

One of the tricky parts of this issue is the determination of the difference between sex play and an offense. Although some people would argue that all pedosexual contact is offensive, much of this contact is developmentally normal, especially between or among peers. The major variable that makes the contact abusive is a force/coercion/power factor that has not adequately been defined by research. The *DSM-IV* (American Psychiatric Association, 1994) cited a 5-year age difference based on Finkelhor (1984) as indication of a significant difference in power that would therefore define abuse. Although this is helpful, it defines only part of the abuse equation and does not deal with the coercion issue that Finkelhor also considered important. Clearly, children and adolescents can be coercive with another child or adolescent who is less than 5 years younger. This coercion can be physical or verbal, the latter being important for children who have been sexualized and have some "knowledge" advantage.

The issue of sexualization leads to the discussion of the offender-as-victim-as-offender. Although exact numbers are unclear, evidently a majority of youthful offenders have been victims themselves (perhaps untreated). Wieckowski, Hartsoe, Mayer, and Shortz (1998) noted that 12- to 15-year-old offenders seemed to come from multiproblem families, had a history of abuse in early childhood, and also had early exposure to sexually explicit media. Abuse may be the key issue in another study (Daleiden, Kaufman, Hilliker, & O'Neil, 1998) where young sex offenders seemed to have repressed normal fantasies. Although the effect of sexualization is the biggest factor here, the dynamics of the victim of abuse are similar to those of the offender in this age group: isolation, alienation, and a lack of intimacy. The sexualization acts as the magnifying glass, focusing these dynamics into a pedosexual contact.

How does a victim turn into an offender? Clinical observations may provide helpful information. The pedosexual behavior is likely to be limited to genital touching, although there may be other sexual behavior such as exhibitionism or voyeurism. The victim is likely to be prepubescent and known to the offender, whether intrafamilial or extrafamilial. The youthful offender is likely to have a history of physical or emotional abuse in addition to sexual victimization. This may reflect a generally chaotic family structure, sometimes held together by rigid rules and expectations. The offender may be rather compliant, withdrawn, and isolated from peers, with significant self-esteem problems (Monto, Zgourides, & Harris, 1998). Asocial behavior is as likely as antisocial behavior. There may well be gender-identity or sexual-orientation confusion and a generalized preference for nonsexual contact with younger children.

The youthful offender presents a picture of low self-esteem and inadequacy as well as immaturity, anxiety, and need for recognition, particularly in dealing with peers (Perry & Orchard, 1992). There is also a probability of school adjustment difficulties. Obviously, if there has been sexual victimization, most of these noted patterns could be exaggerated.

Risk factors or concerns that do not fit these patterns are as follows:

1. history of violence, particularly if violence or coercion seems to be increasing;
2. substance abuse or general antisocial behavior;
3. denial of responsibility or minimization;
4. multiple offenses or victims; and
5. compulsive or ritualized sexual behaviors.

Treatment of the youthful offender involves the use of elements of both victim and offender strategies. The major focus should be to promote a sense of clear responsibility and positive control.

The responsibility issue may be clouded because of the youthful offender's own victimization and age, so clarification of responsibility is vital. Although the offender's own victimization should be acknowledged and discussed in as much detail as possible, victimization cannot be used as an excuse or rationalization for an offense. The offender must clearly accept responsibility for the sexual behavior. This is also true regardless of age or maturity level despite possible difficulty in verbal ability. As clearly as possible, the youthful offender needs to take responsibility for the contact, antecedent behaviors, and impact on the victim.

These issues are best addressed in an atmosphere of supportive confrontation. This confrontation is accomplished in a combination of individual, family, and peer group modalities. Although this is similar to the supportive confrontation discussed in the offender section, there can usually be an added dose of optimism for the youthful offender.

Risk assessment is a critical part of the process, with exploration of concerns like denial, aggression, awareness of harm, and past treatment history. A system of subtyping juvenile offenders by their use of physical force emphasizes this variable (Butz & Spaccarelli, 1999).

The different modalities can reinforce each other, but some issues can best be handled in one or the other. Individual work can concentrate on affective awareness and expression, the offender's own victimization, control skills (thought stopping, fantasy control, antecedent control), and journal writing.

Family techniques deal with the cycle of abuse, appropriate modeling, and communication. The first two are particularly important in this age group and require cooperation from the whole family. There may be great resistance in exposing family secrets or changing behavioral patterns.

Group time can be used to develop interpersonal skills, affective expression (particularly anger), and self-concept and address peer concerns such as substance abuse. Group strategies may be the primary focus in residential treatment or correctional facilities where these offenders may be placed. In these settings, offenders are most likely to resist or discontinue treatment (McConaghy, Blaszczynski, Armstrong, & Kidson, 1989; Rasmussen, 1999).

Perry and Orchard (1992) referred to longer term prevention and treatment by a process that is called *generalization, maintenance, and transfer.* The focus is on returning to normal adolescent development through monitoring and educational and group approaches.

When treating youthful offenders, sexuality education should be emphasized. A special group should deal with sex information including psychophysiological response, psychosexual development, sexual orientation, sexual identity, and responsibility for behavior including contraception and sexually transmitted diseases. Gender role issues should be emphasized—identity, roles, stereotyping, expectations, and sexism. One study (Kaplan, Becker, & Tenke, 1991) noted the lack of sexual knowledge among offenders and provided four educational sessions of sexual information; the authors found that much more sexuality education was necessary.

The youthful offender clearly has unique concerns. Much more clinical experience and research with this population are needed in order to address these concerns.

Brief Interventions

Whereas treating younger victims with brief interventions may be tricky, this approach may work very well with adolescent victims. Even though trust is still a major issue, it is not something that is automatically gained with time, and many adolescents have a rather natural impatience to go on with life. When treatment is prolonged because of clinical or legal issues, it has been my experience that the teenager is probably the first member of the family to be ready to terminate and, as noted above, will self-initiate termination of treatment even when the counselor (who knows better!) thinks he or she should continue.

The brief interventions at this age are relatively easy adaptations of more extended treatment with emphasis on the crisis, apology, and empowerment stages. The interventions can also involve more than one counselor, allowing the adolescent a natural choice over the trust and identity issues. Brief intervention may not be useful when the abusive situation includes multiple victims, physical trauma, sexual offending, pregnancy, or the presence of a sexually transmitted disease.

The crisis stage can involve a team of counselors and support providers, including the primary therapist, family therapist, and appropriate school personnel (teacher, counselor, nurse, administrator). This results in a significant reduction in the number of sessions that are scheduled for the primary therapist. Of those team members involved, the teenager will probably gravitate toward the people she or he trusts most. This trusted person can then devote attention directly to the client regardless of the outcome of the legal and protective systems. The adolescent is also typically available for a group process very quickly. Referral to a crisis group, including peer facilitators, early in the process not only validates the report but allows peer support to set up other trusted relationships. The crisis group can be a time-limited closed group (perhaps 6–8 sessions), adding a sense of completion for this first phase.

While an ongoing group may follow the crisis group, with a stronger component of support than therapy, individual treatment may be put on hold until the time of the apology session(s). Here the adolescent should be seen individually to prepare for the session as noted above (reassurance of report, responsibility and progress of the offender, permission for feelings); this may be handled in 1–2 sessions. The apology sessions themselves may only be 2–3 sessions at this age, with, perhaps, one additional session in a nuclear or extended family session. It will be clear at that point if there are any major problems or obstacles and who has the responsibility to deal with them (e.g., the child, the offender, the mom, or the treatment team).

Empowerment includes preparing for the possibility of reunification or the family's options for long-term functioning or both. As noted, the group process is absolutely paramount in this arena. As these decisions come up, it would make sense to have a cluster of family sessions (3–5) to be clear about communication, protection, and appropriate power and control.

With interventions at these three crucial points, individual contact could be reduced to 15 total sessions over a period of about a year, much of which may be covered by managed care or other funding. Group treatment needs to be more extensive, with 20–30 sessions, perhaps at a lower cost and, again, with the possibility of outside support.

The educational component is crucial to the success of brief interventions with adolescent clients. As noted earlier, sexuality information is a major component and can be provided within a treatment program or cooperatively with Planned Parenthood or other church or community organization. Educational approaches to such matters as dress, make-up, health and nutrition, and tobacco and other substances are also important for self-esteem; attention should be paid to improving peer interactions. These approaches are an adjunct to the treatment process and may be provided in a very cost-effective way.

The key issue in brief interventions in particular is the stable availability of the primary therapist and the rest of the treatment and support team. The teenager will work on trust as long as he or she can call on the adults and obtain a quick and understanding response. Unforeseen crises need to be anticipated and can usually be handled very quickly.

CHAPTER 3

Intervention Strategies in the Treatment of Offenders

Remember the metaphor of sexual abuse as the snow-covered volcano? Treating the offender is a lot like scaling that mountain:

- At first, the task seems impossible and one wonders why anyone would undertake it.
- Early discouragement is predictable.
- Two steps forward are frequently accompanied by slipping backward.
- Obstacles are buried and may necessitate a quick change of plans.
- The task is best accomplished in teams with experienced personnel and safety measures.
- The climate may remain frigid, or there may be an early thaw.
- The whole mountain may blow up at any time, with or without warning.

There clearly is some reward at reaching the summit (or coming close to it). Most of the time, however, the counselor needs to gain satisfaction from simply making the journey. In this chapter, the focus is on the segments of that journey, from assessment and crisis intervention to empowerment and risk reduction. The major focus is on the regressed offender because that profile is encountered most frequently. Specific modifications are noted for other dynamic patterns.

The offender is probably the only family member mandated into treatment. Although juvenile court may order the child(ren) into counseling, failure to comply typically carries few if any consequences. On the other hand, the offender risks revocation of probation and incarceration for failure to attend counseling.

The concepts of voluntary treatment and counselor–client confidentiality have limited relevance when treating pedosexual offenders. The offender should be clearly informed of these limitations at the beginning of treatment. The counselor is usually required to report the following:

1. attendance
2. progress and problems
3. violations of probation conditions or court orders
4. financial status (payment of fees)
5. any new allegations of abuse

The protection of the child is *always* the primary consideration. In some cases, the client will have been advised by an attorney not to discuss details of an allegation until after sentencing or plea bargaining. This can be respected through the use of "hypothetical" or general discussions. Counselors will, of course, have to be aware of their own state laws regarding confidentiality or privileged communication. In some cases in local treatment programs, agreement may be reached with law enforcement or prosecutors for special confidentiality. The counselor may also have to ensure that the client is represented by an attorney.

How can the counselor establish trust and rapport with these kinds of limitations? The counselor is more likely than the client to perceive them as obstacles. The client is typically in crisis (pain, guilt, anxious about legal system) and in need of support, care, and information. Even the mandatory treatment becomes less of an issue as the clients become "hooked" into treatment. (It is my experience that this sense of getting "hooked" is applicable for many men in any therapy process, whether voluntary or mandatory; high resistance is often overcome by a positive experience in counseling.) Clients typically come to see the counselor as their advocate despite these limitations. The counselor is frequently, after all, the only support that the offender has at this point in the process.

The counselor also must determine whether treatment (or assessment) will be isolated or integrated. Isolated treatment involves only the offender. In this situation, there may be no plans for reunification of the family, or the offense may be extrafamilial. Integrated treatment includes other family members in the treatment plan, regardless of plans for reunification. Integrated treatment is almost always preferred because it builds a support system, increases the effectiveness of taking responsibility, and improves control. However, isolated as well as integrated therapy may occur at the same time. The offender undoubtedly has individual issues to resolve other than the abusive behavior and how if affects the victim. The independent issues may not be appropriate for discussion within the context of family treatment. The need or possibility of this will be partially determined by the time element.

The counselor should determine as quickly as possible whether treatment will be short term or long term. This will depend on the following considerations:

- *Incarceration.* The offender may be scheduled to be sent to prison within a few weeks. Some offenders may also be in jail while awaiting disposition, adding an obstacle.
- *Voluntary treatment.* If there are no legal consequences, the offender and family may terminate treatment early.
- *Divorce.* If there is an early decision to divorce (and relocation of children is involved), the isolated treatment plan might be somewhat shorter.
- *Limited mandated treatment.* It is possible that the courts or Child Protective Services may order a prescribed number of sessions or time duration for treatment. Most families do not voluntarily continue beyond that time.

If short-term treatment is likely, the focus needs to be on responsibility, impact on the victim, and risk reduction. There should be heavy emphasis on cognitive-behavioral approaches rather than insight or historical approaches. This is discussed further in the section on brief interventions.

Assessment and Evaluation

The counselor may be involved in three types of assessment processes:

- *Formal/consultation.* In this one-time or time-limited process, the counselor generally acts as a consultant and makes recommendations, and there is no expectation that the counselor will provide treatment. The types of recommendations are discussed below. It is important for ethical practice that evaluation be independent from treatment.
- *Formal/ongoing.* The counselor may be asked to do part or all of a formal assessment of a client who will continue in

ongoing treatment. Again, ethical issues should be kept in mind.

- *Informal/ongoing.* The counselor provides ongoing assessment of a client in treatment. This may include diagnosis, prognosis, and treatment plan modification.

Goals of Assessment

Any of the following types of assessment may be used with a variety of goals in mind:

- *Evidentiary.* The counselor may be asked to help determine whether the accused actually committed the alleged offense, what happened, and how often or whether the accused fits the profile of an offender.
- *Risk assessment.* The counselor may be asked to determine various kinds of general and specific risk factors. These may include the risk of a repeat offense, abuse of or threat to children, violence or danger to society, suicide, or probation violation. The risk assessment process can also be an ongoing part of a brief intervention.
- *Rehabilitation potential.* A somewhat different question is whether the offender has a good potential to change his behavioral patterns. This includes an assessment of the potential benefit from treatment or incarceration and may include an analysis of the offender's resources, both internal (intelligence, personality, health) and external (friends, family, career).

The counselor should know who the client is in these consultation assessments and communicate that clearly to the accused/offender. The client may be the defense or prosecuting attorney, the court/judge, probation department, Child Protective Services, juvenile court, or the offender himself. Although the assessment should be objective regardless of the client, the information may be used very differently.

Assessment for Treatment Planning

An assessment completed as part of a treatment planning process and an isolated evaluation have different goals. The primary advantage in the former is the stability and trust inherent in the counseling relationship. Counseling presents a much better atmosphere for supportive confrontation than does an evaluation, particularly regarding responsibility issues. The offender can discuss details of the abuse and the antecedents to it without the pressure implicit in a formal evaluation.

The goals for treatment planning must recognize the needs of both the offender and the victim. If treatment is isolated, without the direct involvement of the victim, consideration can still be given to the actual and potential victim(s). Goals should be broad enough to address concerns beyond the abuse issues to general self-control, responsibility, and self-esteem.

These latter general issues are extremely important for the treatment planning process. Treatment goals should not be defined too narrowly, focusing only on the sexual offense and assurances of no repeated offense. Although these narrow issues certainly must be thoroughly resolved, treatment of the more general issues may be an even better predictor of overall adjustment, stability, and control, thereby lowering risk factors. Early in the treatment process, many offenders will claim that they have "learned their lesson" and "will not do it again." Even though they may be sincere, they will feel much more confident and will be able to provide more specific assurances when the more general issues are resolved.

Assessment Techniques

1. *Clinical interview.* The clinical interview conducted by an experienced interviewer is central to any assessment. The interview should go beyond the typical mental status examination to include family, social, career, developmental, substance abuse, affective, and responsibility issues.

Information should be obtained regarding family of origin, current family, and past marriages and families. Significant relationships that did not involve marriage should also be noted. Patterns in relationships should be probed, especially dependency and control issues. The overall relationship of the offender to each of the children should be probed and should be supplemented by an understanding of each child's role in the family and family communication patterns.

The focus on social adjustment should include peer relationships (past and current), general relationships with women, isolative tendencies, and leisure activities. Social relationships with children should be probed, such as preference for child-oriented activities, leadership in child and youth groups and teams, or, at the other extreme, abusive hostility toward children.

Although specific careers may not be predictive of a sex offense, there may be a tendency for offenders to choose isolative or dependent job settings. Employment stability and relationships with employers and other employees should be noted.

A developmental history should include physical, cognitive, and intellectual development. A brief medical and educational history should focus on perceived areas of strengths, weaknesses, and, specifically, disability or potential rejection.

Patterns of substance use and abuse are a concern not only because of addictive behavior but also as evidence of chronic or episodic crisis-oriented dependency. Denial and minimization should be expected and confronted; those who restrict their drinking to beer may not consider their drinking a problem. (When substance abuse is present, beer is most likely to be the substance misused because of the typical "macho" dynamics.)

Affective awareness is a critical area. Many offenders are particularly unaware of (or unable to express) feelings. This extends not only to relationship feelings—love, anger, resentment—but to more general feelings like sadness, frustration, and anxiety. The counselor should gather information about the offender's "affective history"—feelings throughout childhood, adolescence, and adulthood, particularly regarding patterns of affection, nurturance, and dependence.

Finally, responsibility issues should be clarified as much as possible. Ideally, the offender should be able to fully accept the responsibility for his actions. At the time of assessment, however, even those with positive prognoses may not be clearly aware of responsibility early in treatment or may be under legal obligation not to admit liability. In other words, whereas clear acceptance of responsibility is a positive predictor, the absence of it may not be a negative one. The clinical interview can be part of an active assessment, concurrent with a brief intervention.

2. *Sex history.* A structured sex history should be done separately from the clinical interview. The separation between the two helps in maintaining a systematic approach to the sex history. The history should clearly include all sexual behavior and arousal patterns, with a special focus on early sexual experiences with peers and adults. These childhood experiences should not be labeled as *molestations* or *abuse* by the interviewer in order to circumvent typical denial patterns. Fantasy patterns should be questioned in a similar way because initial responses will probably be superficial and minimal.

3. *Psychometric evaluation.* As noted earlier, there is considerable disagreement about the efficacy of psychometrics. Again, part

of the problem is in the classification of offenders. MMPI profiles that may apply to rapists, for example, generally are not valid for most pedosexual offenders. The MMPI may, however, be helpful in developing a general diagnostic picture and as a cross-check for credibility and openness versus guardedness. The Multiphasic Sex Inventory (MSI; Nichols & Molinder, 1984) or the Derogatis Sexual Functioning Inventory (Derogatis, 1978) may be helpful in a similar manner, as a validation of the sex history. The Millon Clinical Multiaxial Inventory (2nd ed.; MCMI-II; Millon, 1984) may be useful as an alternate or supplement to the MMPI. Projective measures may be helpful, depending on the evaluator's experience, but may be more difficult to defend within the judicial system. An intellectual/cognitive measure (e.g., the revised Wechsler Adult Intelligence Scale; WAIS-R; Wechsler, 1981) or Kaufman Adolescent and Adult Intelligence Test (KAIT; Kaufman & Kaufman, 1993) may be needed if there is some question regarding ability to effectively gain from verbal therapy modalities or, perhaps, to document a significant learning disability. The Abel Assessment for Interest in Paraphilias (Abel, Huffman, Warberg, & Holland, 1998), a relatively new addition to the psychometric field, combines a self-report with a time measure of attention to various visual stimuli, including the possibility of adjunctive plethysmography. The use of this instrument is still somewhat exploratory with adults; specific cautions have been raised about its reliability and validity with adolescent offenders (Fischer & Smith, 1999; Smith & Fischer, 1999).

4. *Psychophysiological measures.* Perhaps the most innovative work in the area of assessment has come in the form of psychophysiological measures—the penile plethysmograph and the polygraph. Although neither of these have yet been ruled as admissible evidence in court, they can provide helpful techniques in penetrating the barriers of denial and minimization (Abel & Becker, 1984; Blasingame, 1998; Freund & Blanchard, 1989; Howes, 1998; Lalumiere & Harris, 1998; McGovern & Peters, 1988). Although questions of reliability remain, these measures have been useful, particularly in identifying and confronting pedophilic patterns and comparing rapists to nonoffenders. In 1998, Blasingame called for more research into the use of polygraphy, an indication that this technology has yet to be put to its best use.

The plethysmograph (also referred to as *phallometric measurement*) provides a visual readout (graph or digital) of penile arousal through a transducer attached to the penis. Arousal is then measured while the man is exposed to various stimuli—audio and visual tapes, slides, or films with various themes, both normal and "deviant," including children, nudity, rape, or seduction. Patterns of arousal are noted and explored with the man, either while on or off the plethysmograph.

The polygraph (lie detector) can be used as a supplement to the plethysmograph to detect arousal patterns in the general physiology as well as to detect "lies" and denial mechanisms.

Psychophysiological techniques provide useful information in the assessment process but may be even more useful in the treatment process. When used as an intrasubject appraisal, the data can be used as a monitor, particularly for behavioral treatment modalities. There may be more validity to this approach. These data may also be critical in further research on normal and pathological response patterns.

Although these techniques are promising, they are associated with important caveats. Perhaps the most obvious is that a trained technician must administer the procedures. Using these techniques adds complexity to the process, and there is also the additional expense on top of a significant capital expense for the equipment (several thousand dollars, depending on computerization options). Validity questions must be addressed. Do we know enough about normal arousal? What patterns do "normal" men show? Does arousal predict behavior? If so, at what levels? What specific stimuli predict specific behavior?

Cautions Regarding Assessment

Assessment of accused or admitted offenders presents several unique problems. Primary among these is the dichotomy between those who talk "too much" and those who talk "too little." The latter is, perhaps, obvious. The offender may be facing a long prison sentence; loss of family, job, or financial security; and societal condemnation. Denial and minimization are frustrating but understandable and particularly painful when a child has to testify against a father. As prison sentences increase, the tendency will be toward more denial and less acceptance of responsibility. This affects all components of the system: the family, treatment, the criminal justice system, and child protection agencies.

The other half of the dichotomy, talking "too much," is not anticipated by many counselors. Many offenders, particularly within families, eagerly confess to the pedosexual contact immediately on confrontation with the authorities, whereas others confess within a month of the report. Both types of groups may abrogate their own rights because of feelings of guilt and shame. In some cases, this guilt release seems appropriate and could be therapeutic; however, it is also essentially irreversible and can result in later bitterness, resentment, and minimization. The irony is that some of the best candidates for treatment, those who accept responsibility, are sent to prison because of their confession, whereas deniers are likely to avoid prosecution.

Another caution is that despite the presence or absence of a confession, there may be significant discrepancies in the reports from one person to another and also from one time to another. These discrepancies may be normal and tolerated if they do not affect the overall responsibility issues. For example, the discrepancy in specific dates, times, places, and frequency may be acceptable if the nature of the behavior, extent, and approximate duration are clear.

A typical confounding variable in the responsibility area is the claim of an alcohol- or other drug-induced blackout. Accused offenders frequently claim vague or no memory of a pedosexual contact as a result of a blackout. Some offenders try to sidestep the responsibility issue by agreeing that they "might have" or "could have" done "something" (e.g., "if she said I did it, then I must have"). Others totally deny memory and even use alcohol as a defense, claiming that they could not have offended because of lack of consciousness, absence from the home, or erectile incapability. Although the possibility of substance-induced amnesia should be acknowledged, many if not most of these cases do result in partial or total appropriate recall during the treatment process. While waiting for this recall, the offender's responsibility for the substance use or abuse should be a clear focus. If the denial process continues, the offender may not be a candidate for treatment.

The final assessment caution lies in the potential for manipulation by the offender. This caution is also applicable to treatment. The offender may well act charming, pathetic, or passive-aggressive in an attempt to ally with the examiner and convince him or her of the need for leniency. The manipulative behavior may also serve as the offender's way of assuring himself that his behavior was not harmful or serious.

The possibility of brief(er) assessment procedures should be addressed here. As noted earlier, an ongoing assessment can occur during crisis treatment, creating an "active assessment" process, mixing treatment with the gathering of information. In some cases, this is essential because of outside constraints. Although ethical issues are raised when a counselor both evaluates and treats the same client, the necessity for immediate crisis intervention along with assessment may outweigh other considerations.

Diagnosis, Categorization, and Treatment Planning

Assessment of the offender goes beyond the typical issues of diagnosis and prognosis. Risk assessment and treatment planning are both essential components and add to the complexity and difficulty of the task. Treatment planning should be considered even if incarceration is anticipated. Integration of diagnosis and pedosexual taxonomy categories essentially adds four axes to the diagnostic system.

Most pedosexual behavior is not specifically classified in the *DSM-IV* (American Psychiatric Association, 1994). The exception, as noted earlier, is pedophilia, classified as 302.20 on Axis I as one of the paraphilias. The criteria for the diagnosis of pedophilia are quite specific although less so than in the third edition of the *Diagnostic and Statistical Manual of Mental Disorders* (*DSM-III*; American Psychiatric Association, 1980). The criteria are essentially the same as the third revised edition (*DSM-III-R*; American Psychiatric Association, 1987), with some broadening of the nature of impairment. There are three components:

> A. Over a period of at least 6 months, recurrent, intense sexually arousing fantasies, sexual urges, or behaviors involving sexual activity with a prepubescent child or children (generally age 13 years or younger).
>
> B. The fantasies, sexual urges, or behaviors cause clinically significant distress or impairment in social, occupational, or other important areas of functioning.
>
> C. The person is at least age 16 years and at least 5 years older than the child or children in Criterion A. (p. 528)

There are also notations to specify if the attraction is to male individuals, female individuals, or both; whether the behavior is limited to incest; and if the arousal is exclusive to children or nonexclusive.

Offenders may have any of the other Axis I diagnoses, but the most likely would be in the affective disorders, sexual disorders, or substance abuse. The diagnosis of an affective disorder is difficult because of reality influences and stresses and the frequent overlay of personality disorders. For many offenders, however, there is considerable depression, perhaps chronic, that could be diagnosed as dysthymia (300.4) or major depression (296.xx). My clinical experience suggests that depression may be far more typical than originally thought and that it can exist concurrently with a personality disorder.

Although sexual disorders seem to be a reasonable corollary of pedosexual contact, they may not be more prevalent in the offender than in the nonoffending population. Possible disorders include other paraphilias, sexual dysfunctions (ejaculatory and erectile), and compulsive sexual disorder. The latter may fit for the addictive-compulsive sexual offender. Compulsive behaviors could include masturbation, use of sexually explicit media or prostitutes, voyeurism, exhibitionism, or a combination. These behaviors may not meet the criteria for paraphilias but still contribute to a compulsive sexual disorder.

Substance abuse may be a diagnosable condition. Careful assessment is essential in this area because of the impact on both risk assessment and treatment planning. Specialized treatment may be needed.

Offenders are more likely to have Axis II diagnoses (in addition to Axis I), such as dependent, narcissistic, passive-aggressive, and borderline personality disorders, or mixtures of these. These long-term patterns of behavior set the stage for the triggering dynamics and disinhibition. Essentially, this pattern emphasizes the learning of harmful behavior over a long period of time, a model that fits what is known about offenders. Specifically, an individual with a dependent personality and a dysthymic disorder has a particularly strong tendency toward poor self-esteem, lack of appropriate feelings of power and control, lack of affection and affective awareness, and use of alcohol or sexual behavior to fill other needs. Interestingly, antisocial personality disorder is not a typical diagnosis; most offenders have little or no history of overt antisocial behavior. Instead, they exhibit rather rigid, conservative, and traditional tendencies.

Pedosexual Taxonomy

The pedosexual taxonomy described in chapter 1 can be a helpful framework because it focuses the dynamics of the pedosexual offender in a much narrower way than the *DSM* system can. Although, as noted, the six categories—regressed, pedophile, addicted/compulsive, rapist, symptomatic, and ritual—are not completely discrete, I believe that they do separate out some factors that assist in risk assessment.

Regressed. If the assessment does not indicate pedophilic patterns or other serious psychopathology, the offender probably fits the regressed category. The offender probably had a reasonable psychosexual development, with adult partners preceding the pedosexual contact. Dynamics include general stress, lack of control, poor self-esteem; history of physical or sexual abuse; marital or family dysfunction; and disinhibition factors, including alcohol use.

There may well be a a powerful machismo veneer covering a sense of dependency and helplessness. Although this exists even before the pedosexual contact, it is worse after it, with the addition of significant guilt. That guilt, in turn, may trigger defense mechanisms, primarily projection and denial. Although the regressed offender presents a complex picture, prognosis for treatment is good if the offender accepts responsibility for his behavior. Treatment will be long-term (unless a brief intervention approach is adopted), and rather confrontive in order to deal completely with issues of responsibility, control, and power. If these issues are successfully addressed, the regressed offender presents a minimal risk of recidivism.

Pedophile. The criteria for *DSM-IV* diagnosis of the pedophile also should be followed for the pedosexual taxonomy. Although the term *preferred arousal* was eliminated in the shift from to *DSM-III* to *DSM-III-R* and then *DSM-IV*, it may still be a good operative word in exploring pedophile dynamics. Not only do pedophiles prefer children as sexual objects, they globally prefer to be with children and feel more comfortable with them than with adults. As one pedophile client (Case Study D) succinctly summarized, "I love children. I *really* love children." Although criteria call for a pattern of at least a 6-month duration, most pedophiles will acknowledge almost a lifelong preference (at least a global or generalized preference) for children. This is particularly true in the male-male combination, whereas the dynamics involved in pedophiles with arousal to females may be closer to intrafamilial or regressed offender dynamics for this "emotional congruence" (Wilson, 1999). They frequently present as kind, gentle, and generous individuals who may be seen as the best baby sitter or caregiver in the neighborhood, giving gifts and taking children to the circus, zoo, and so forth. It is important to note that this behavior is not simply seduction or set-up with the prospects of sexual gratification—there is truly a preference for being with children at all of these activities. Although they may have had some adult sexual relationships, including marriage, they remain essentially asexual in regard to adults.

Pedophiles may also have a heightened chance of having been abused as children (Freund & Kuban, 1994; Freund, Watson, & Dickey, 1990). This emphasizes the importance of the awareness of survivor issues.

Pedophiles may be more likely than regressed offenders to choose male children. However, such individuals should not be referred to as *homosexual pedophiles,* as noted earlier, because the preference is very different than the orientation of the adult homosexual.

The pedophile may find great difficulty in focusing on responsibility and frequently sees nothing wrong with his behavior and sees no harm done to the children; he often considers his gentle concern and affection toward children as superior to the parents' hostility or apathy. He may also have been involved with or aware of some pro-pedophile groups, which now have increased visibility on the Internet (Li et al., 1993). Because of this difficulty with responsibility as well as the long-term preference and arousal issues, exclusivity, and urge intensity, the pedophile is generally seen as being at high risk for recidivism. Even when the pedophile is cooperative with treatment, mandated or voluntary, treatment efficacy generally has been poor.

Recent research provides some insight into pedophilia. R. Blanchard and Dickey (1998) reported that same-sex arousal to adolescents has more etiological factors in common with adult arousal (androphilia) than does same-sex pedophilia. In a second study, R. Blanchard et al. (1999) included intellectual functioning as a variable and noted that high maternal age "(or some factor it represents)" (p. 111) increases the likelihood of exclusive sexual interest in boys. Intellectual deficiency seems to decrease the likelihood of exclusive sexual interest in girls. These two factors combine so that a pedophile with both factors is more likely to be sexually interested in boys than a pedophile with only one factor. These results point to developmental factors, an etiology that fits the typical clinical picture.

Addicted/compulsive. The sex addict or sexually compulsive individual is marked by the sense of a loss of control over sexual behavior. Any sexual behavior or combination of behaviors may be the compulsive focus. Masturbation and use of sexually explicit media may be the most common behavior, with voyeurism, exhibitionism, and use of prostitution as other possibilities. Other nonsexual addictions are likely, including alcoholism and eating disorders. Pedosexual contact in this group may not be one of the most frequent behaviors among these offenders but may become more of a focus as more is learned about the addictive/compulsive patterns. As mentioned earlier, the sex history should bring out this information, although the emphasis should not be on either specific behavior or frequency, but rather on the sense of lack of control over the behaviors. With clear acknowledgment of responsibility (not only guilt or remorse), prognosis for treatment may be good, particularly if specialized treatment is available. Even with this prognosis, however, there may be significant risk concerns. These risks may not be related primarily to the pedosexual contact but rather to

exual risk behaviors (e.g., peeping, drunk dri-
bstance-related theft).

ey behavior pattern of the rapist is power
ace. The typical risk dynamics of adult rape are
hildren are the victims. Given current lack of treat-
ment th rapists in general, the pedosexual rapist is an extremely hig risk offender for both sexual and physical assault. This offender would not be an appropriate candidate for treatment of pedosexual issues, particularly in a community program.

Symptomatic. Prognosis and risk assessment for the symptomatic offender depend on the primary disorder. The frequency and type of pedosexual contact may be strong factors, however, in risk assessment. As in other areas, the ability and willingness to take responsibility are of primary importance.

Ritual. Little is known about the ritualistic offender, clearly fitting the overall sense of mystery, incredulity, and skepticism in this area. Risk assessment should focus on the level or intensity of compulsivity involved. There may or may not be a diagnosable Obsessive-Compulsive Disorder; determining the presence of this disorder obviously is important in the treatment planning, including the possibility of medical intervention. As with other compulsive disorders, prognosis is cautious at best.

Treatment Planning

If the consensus of the evaluation, risk assessment, and the criminal justice system indicates treatment rather than long-term incarceration, the counselor may become a critical part of the treatment planning process. This process probably will be ongoing and integrated, with the probation department and Child Protective Services both likely to have input. Although the process will be dynamic over time, it will consistently identify modalities, intervention approaches, and goals. Timelines, frequently used in treatment planning for other types of interventions, should be flexible and individualized. Regular treatment planning meetings, preferably formal and scheduled (with room for emergencies and crises), should be held to revise the treatment plan.

Treatment of the pedosexual offender is best when it is multimodal and involves more than one therapist. The presence of a therapy team discourages controlling and manipulative behaviors by the offender and the family and may improve both flexibility and accountability in treatment. The following modalities should be included:

1. *Individual therapy.* The individual therapist may be designated as the primary therapist and should be the most stable, long-term influence, both during and after treatment. If possible, this person should be willing to commit to long-term (at least 2-year) direct and indirect involvement with the family. Even in brief interventions, the primary therapist may have to provide some elements of case management, treatment coordination, and ongoing risk assessment over a significant period of time. The individual therapist is also at the core of accountability.

2. *Family therapy.* Whenever possible, marital and family therapy should be used even if reunification is not a goal. Specifics about family therapy approaches are noted in chapter 4. Family therapy can be supportive, confrontive, preventive, and curative. Cotherapy should be used when possible. Marital therapy should also include sexuality education, enrichment, and therapy as appropriate.

3. *Group therapy.* Groups are absolutely essential in the treatment process for both support and confrontation (i.e., getting the offender to assume responsibility for his behavior). Groups can be segregated to offenders or, at a later point, include spouses or partners. They should be homogeneous for pedosexual offenders and probably for regressed offenders as well.

4. *Self-help.* Many offenders and families benefit from socialization skills, practical and emotional support, and information from self-help organizations like Parents United. This group, founded in San Jose, California, as part of Giaretto's (1982) integrated treatment program, now has chapters across the country, empowering families to help themselves, elect their own officers, and regain a sense of control over their lives.

5. *Educational groups.* Particularly in the later stages of treatment, educational groups can focus on issues like communication, parenting, and sexuality.

Specific intervention approaches include the following:

1. *Behavioral, cognitive, cognitive-behavioral, rational-emotive.* These strategies may include a variety of techniques of desensitization approaches and may include monitoring with the plethysmograph or other psychophysiological measures. Restructuring the thought–action pattern is crucial.

2. *Psychopharmacological.* This approach may include standard antidepressant and antianxiety medication if appropriate, although few offenders seem to have received this, perhaps because they are not seen as suffering from depression by many evaluators despite a

persistant pattern in that regard. There are also reports of the selective serotonin reuptake inhibitors (SSRI) family of medications being useful in dealing with the obsessive components of some pedosexual contact. In fact, "self-medication," particularly with alcohol, may be more likely than prescribed. One controversial treatment has been the use of an anti-androgen, medroxaprogesterone acetate (MPA or Depo Provera) or another anti-androgen, sometimes called "chemical castration." Despite reports of success with some offenders, chemical castration is still generally considered a treatment of last resort. For an updated and comprehensive review of medical interventions, see Bradford and Greenberg (1996).

3. *Probation.* Supervised probation is an intervention for many offenders. Although some clinicians may not see probation as an intervention in the typical sense, it clearly has a major impact on the offender and his family, particularly as it applies to issues of power and control. Probation may be supervised at various levels of control, from monitoring by monthly report to surveillance and continued telephone contact. Technological advances have included electronic "banding" and monitoring. The court issues conditions of probation specifying restrictions on travel, visitation, use of substances, and other behavior.

4. *Jail.* The offender may be ordered to spend some time in incarceration as a condition of or precursor to probation. Sentences may vary from 30 days to 2 years and may include special programs such as work furlough or weekday release to allow continued employment and family support. The imposition of "jail time" generally is intended to have a punitive, rather than therapeutic, effect, but it can be a significant intervention (positive or negative) regarding power and control issues.

Treatment goals will vary, but certain goals seem consistent despite modalities and specific interventions. I have grouped these into six areas: responsibility, power, control, affective awareness, communication, and interpersonal relationships. Notice that these goals are far broader and more inclusive than just focusing on the behavioral patterns.

Responsibility. The offender will

- clearly accept the responsibility of the pedosexual contact without reservation or rationalization;
- clearly acknowledge the actual and potential harm to the victim, himself, and the family;
- accept the ongoing responsibility for support and protection of the family regardless of reunification decisions;

- demonstrate responsibility in employment, finances, and similar areas;
- demonstrate responsibility in attendance and utilization of therapy opportunities;
- accept and adhere to conditions of probation and other directives of the criminal justice and child protective systems; and
- differentiate between responsibility and guilt.

Power. The offender will

- acknowledge the inappropriate power relationship inherent in the pedosexual contact;
- identify and correct inappropriate power relationships in the family;
- identify areas of individual powerlessness and plans for change;
- assist in empowering the victim (e.g., by validating the report); and
- demonstrate ability to share power in the marital, familial, or work situation.

Control. The offender will

- demonstrate control over sexual arousal, behavior, and fantasy;
- acknowledge disinhibitors and plans for controlling them;
- describe the "set-up" for the contact and plans for controlling these (relapse prevention);
- demonstrate general impulse control, including control over "temper" and substance abuse;
- demonstrate control over day-to-day decision making for himself; and
- understand and resolve issues regarding need for control over others and relinquish this need.

Affective awareness. The offender will

- identify the full range of his feelings consistently and with understanding;
- express the range of feelings and clarify same to the counselor and the family;
- demonstrate ability to understand, clarify, and take appropriate action on others' feelings; and
- demonstrate specifically the ability to appropriately express anger.

Communication. The offender will

- demonstrate ability to use "I" messages and active listening;
- demonstrate ability to express and receive thoughts, feelings, opinions, and beliefs;
- develop effective extrafamilial communication (work, social, etc.); and
- demonstrate improved parenting skills.

Interpersonal relationships. The offender will

- demonstrate improved relationship with spouse or significant other;
- demonstrate awareness of intimacy needs within relationships;
- show appropriate sexual relationship(s) with adult partner(s); and
- demonstrate improved socialization skills and reduced isolation.

Treatment

In this discussion of treatment interventions, I assume that treatment for most offenders is mandatory and long-term. If either assumption is inaccurate, the treatment goals must be modified, with an emphasis on crisis intervention, responsibility, and control, as elaborated in the section on brief interventions. As in the treatment of victims, the stages of treatment for offenders overlap and are flexible. Crises will occur throughout the process up to and beyond formal termination. The stages are roughly parallel in either an individual or group modality.

Crisis Intervention

All of the major family members (victim, offender, spouse) should be considered suicide risks. Even while denying allegations in the initial stages, the offender may attempt to resolve conflicting feelings by suicide. Clearly, any attempt could be devastating for the victim and family.

When the report and arrest are made, more so than at later times, the offender is likely to perceive issues as "black and white." The counselor can make use of this black-and-white perspective with a clear treatment contract, including a suicide contract. Because many offenders have dependent features, the most effective suicide prevention strategy may be to tell the offender, "Don't do it!"

For the most part, however, the counselor needs to emphasize and validate the gray area—that there will be few easy and clear answers. The initial crisis phase is marked by extreme confusion and fear. Information received by the family is usually ambiguous and elicits many questions: Will the child be removed, the father arrested or prosecuted, siblings removed, the father incarcerated? The counselor cannot answer these questions and obviously should not make any promises about outcomes. In fact, the counselor should acknowledge and even emphasize that the family does not have control over these decisions; rather, they have to focus their efforts on the small amount of control that they do have. This reframing is critical. Too many times, I have seen inexperienced but well-meaning counselors reassure offenders, victims, or families that "everything will be OK," when in fact the counselor has no control over the outcome.

As noted earlier, the offender is likely to enter this phase in a denial mode (either by outright denial of the pedosexual contact or by minimization of the extent, frequency, duration, or effect of the contact; Schlank & Shaw, 1996). Even those who readily admit to the contact will have accounts that differ from the child's report, for many reasons. The offender can be supported in his need to protect himself and yet be confronted about his need to accept responsibility for the good of his family and himself.

This concept of supportive confrontation, nicely described by G. Blanchard (1995) as "respectful firmness," is critical not only in this crisis phase but throughout treatment. The counselor must be able to support the client while still confronting the client on issues of responsibility, control, and accountability. The counselor consistently must walk the thin line of concern for the client and responsibility to the victim. One technique for accomplishing this is to ally with the offender in his concern for the victim. Most offenders are cooperative in this regard, making it somewhat easier to deal with responsibility issues.

As part of the support, the offender can be assured that he is not the only one in this circumstance. Despite the heavy, negative societal condemnation and, more than likely, tremendous self-condemnation, the offender can be shown that his and his family's problems are not unique and that many families have recovered. Without diluting any responsibility for the offense, the counselor can show unconditional positive regard and reinforce the basic "OK-ness" of the offender. In most cases, the offender's lack of previous criminal record can be helpful, as can an emphasis on the previously mentioned alliance to protect the victim.

Once that support is given, responsibility becomes the biggest issue of the crisis phase. The offender must clearly accept responsibility for the offense. This is probably the most important treatment goal in the whole process. The responsibility must be unequivocal; that is, without excuses or rationalizations. The offender must go beyond simply acknowledging the behavior to accepting responsibility for the set-up; statements of threat, coercion, and confusion made to the victim; damage to himself and others; and consequences (jail, probation, separation of the offender's family). There can be, and probably will be, specific differences in details between the accounts of the offender and the victim. These differences can be explored during treatment if the basic responsibility is clearly accepted. The offender may need several sessions and considerable supportive confrontation in order to accomplish this.

The responsibility issue should be addressed in a positive manner, the emphasis being that responsibility allows the treatment process to begin. Responsibility, in a positive way, becomes the best route for the offender to take control of the treatment process and establish the first step in a more general positive control. The emphasis on positive responsibility is in contrast to the disabling guilt that many, if not most, offenders feel. Although a certain amount of guilt is to be expected, it becomes self-destructive and counterproductive unless the counselor can turn it around into positive responsibility.

Apology Sessions

The apology sessions become the bridge from crisis intervention to ongoing treatment. The number of sessions and session timing are flexible. The goals are responsibility clarification, apology, validation of the report, and commitment to treatment.

As noted earlier, the apology sessions are not held until both victim and offender are prepared, with emphasis on the victim's safety and support. The offender should be prepared to focus on the responsibility issues and should have enough affective awareness to clearly respond to the victim's feelings. Role-playing is one method to prepare the offender for a variety of victim responses, which may range from coldness to rage.

The offender is expected to initiate the first apology session by acknowledging complete responsibility for the offense and apologizing for the contact. The victim is then encouraged to respond with feelings or questions. The offender should accept any feelings expressed by the victim. These feelings may be expressed over the course of several sessions. The other goals should be accomplished in the first session (although they may be repeated). The report should be validated as appropriate and the first step in "making things better," and the offender should make a firm commitment to treatment and to making whatever changes are necessary for the victimized family to recover and for the victim to be safe.

Continuing apology sessions should include the rest of the offender's family, especially the spouse or partner. Apologies should be directed to other family members, with clear acknowledgment of the harm inflicted. The details of the contact should be discussed in order to have an improved sense of protection and in order to disrupt the "family secret" pattern.

If the offender's family is not available for apology sessions, the process should still be completed using role-play (perhaps with another counselor) or letter-writing. If the children are not available, the apology sessions should be held with the spouse with, again, the details of the contact discussed, even if the spouse if not initially eager to hear them.

Pattern Analysis

Once responsibility issues have been clarified and communicated, the major treatment task involves pattern analysis. This includes an understanding of individual and systems dynamics, history, disinhibition, arousal patterns, and affective awareness.

The offender should bear as much responsibility as possible for work on pattern analysis. The counselor should facilitate the process and be accountable for progress toward the treatment goals, as well as for integration of the patterns.

The pattern analysis may be the biggest part of the jigsaw puzzle analogy mentioned earlier. The offender must painstakingly put together the puzzle, sometimes piece by piece, sometimes several pieces in a cluster. The counselor can understand how puzzles fit together but does not know in advance how this particular one will look. Moreover, the puzzle may never have all the pieces in place.

The first step in putting together the puzzle is to clearly identify the pieces. The offender must be able to discuss the details of the pedosexual contact and identify the direct antecedents to the contact. This is sometimes called the *set-up* or *seduction*, although the latter is not an accurate description when viewed in the typical adult way. The details should include frequency and duration as well as progressive patterns (stroking to digital penetration to oral-genital contact). Victim and offender responses should be queried. Offender techniques for convincing the child not to tell should be elicited. Offender arousal patterns during the contact should be as specific as possible (e.g., how much of an erection, at what point, for how long?). Information regarding time and place will help to determine how protection mechanisms (e.g., rest of family) were circumvented. Finally, the offender should clearly understand how the report came about.

After the details of the contact have been determined, disinhibiting factors should be considered. These factors include any that clearly serve to disinhibit the offender from sexual contact with children. Disinhibiting factors may be relatively overt, like alcohol use or misuse, or more subtle, like elaborate rationalizations. The latter may include the child's "need for sex education," "need for affection," or "medical necessity." They also may include a child's initiating, enjoying, or demanding contact, spousal rejection, or the child's being asleep. One of the great ironies is that the offender could have used the contact as punishment for sexual behavior such as normal childhood masturbation or peer exploration. Multiple disinhibition factors are likely to be present.

The disclosure of details and disinhibiting factors may take a considerable amount of time. Just like the process of sorting out and turning over pieces of a puzzle, the effort may seem nonproductive and time consuming, but it does unravel patterns and helps to "hook" the puzzle solver into the task.

One strategy of completing a puzzle is to identify the straight-edged pieces and complete the outer perimeter. This accomplishes three goals: It establishes the outer limits and dimensions, sets a structure for at least some of the patterns, and provides positive reinforcement and encouragement by narrowing the number of possible combinations and by making connections. In the pattern analysis, this phase examines the individual's family and sexual history.

The offender is encouraged to look at his family (or families) of origin with an emphasis on patterns of power, dependence, control, communication, discipline, and affection. The parental marital dyad is discussed with an emphasis on models of affection, intimacy, and sexuality. Many offenders describe a rather rigid, nonaffectionate family with either an absent or authoritarian father, physical abuse, or a strong punishment orientation. In my informal clinical research, fewer than 10% of offenders have reported any physical affection from their fathers (hugs, strokes, shoulder pats, lap sitting). Encouraging the offender to write his autobiography may be a helpful technique in gathering this information.

The sex history should be structured so that the counselor can feel assured that it is as complete as possible. More information is likely to surface in treatment rather than in assessment because of improved trust. It seems obvious that the possibility of a history of sexual abuse should be thoroughly pursued. Many interviewers, however, end their pursuit by asking the question, "Were you ever molested or sexually abused?" Most offenders answer this question negatively because they do not think of their early experiences as abusive. The more helpful prompt might be, "Tell me about early sexual experiences you had with an adult or a much older child." This can be followed by a discussion of details and reactions, both past and current. The offender can be encouraged to reframe such experiences as abuse if the counselor considers that it might be helpful. The sex history should also look at behavioral and fantasy arousal patterns, including masturbation and use of sexually explicit media.

The sex history and arousal patterns in most regressed offenders tend to seem quite normal but limited. Homophobia is typical, as is a small number of close heterosexual relationships. Sexually explicit media may be a disinhibiting factor, but not to the extent that they are a factor for the pedophile or rapist and generally not with children as objects. Explorations should include fantasy patterns involving children, adolescents, or particularly young or small women and fantasy patterns of control over partners, including instruction and experimentation. Force, if present, magnifies all these noted concerns.

If arousal patterns, either during childhood or during the pedosexual contact, are of concern, the counselor might consider two options: psychophysiological assessment and treatment and fantasy control. In the former, the plethysmograph can be used to assess and monitor treatment as a feedback measure. With or without the plethysmograph, arousal and fantasy patterns can be controlled through aversive conditioning (use of noxious stimuli such as smelling salts or use of visualizations), masturbatory satiation, or thought stopping. These techniques typically are used by specially trained therapists.

Once the background issues have defined the perimeter of the puzzle, the next strategy may be to group the puzzle pieces by color and shades of color to see if designs can be perceived. It should be noted that the puzzle process is not rigidly sequenced, so that some pattern and color grouping may occur while the perimeter is being assembled.

The colors are supplied by the awareness and clarification of individual and systems dynamics. Individual dynamics include personality and affective awareness and exploration of functional and dysfunctional behaviors. Typical dynamics include dependent and passive-aggressive personality patterns. These need to be continually challenged by the counselor, not in terms of right versus wrong or black versus white but in terms of productivity and effectiveness. Although not all these dynamics may require change, the offender must become aware of their role in helping to set up or disinhibit the sexual behavior. Most offenders do change their behavior significantly, although they still may meet criteria for personality disorders. The awareness of these dynamics may be more important than major behavioral changes.

In addition to recognizing behavioral patterns, the offender must be able to demonstrate affective awareness. It would not be unusual for an offender, when asked to describe a feeling, to respond, "I feel like you're wrong." Integration of sensory and affective awareness and separation of thoughts and feelings may be totally novel concepts. Many offenders report crying for the first time since childhood or for the first time ever. Permission to cry can be an effective lead-in to permission for feeling appropriately angry, sad, hurt, and so forth.

It is important to explore system dynamics that affect and are affected by the offender. The family system is obviously central, but employment, social, and extended family systems also may be important. The offender should become aware of roles, interactions, expectations, and other typical systems dynamics. Family systems issues are discussed in chapter 4. One critical relationship issue should be stressed, however. The typical offender seems to have particular difficulty in handling intimacy, both within the marital or sexual relationship as well as in friendship and extended family systems. Concepts of vulnerability, trust, and openness may be difficult to explore and require considerable counselor patience.

One last pattern to explore is substance use and abuse. This pattern should be investigated not only in terms of disinhibition but also in terms of personality, relationship, and lifestyle issues. Although most offenders may not have addictive patterns—at least not yet—substance use, particularly beer consumption, has a significant impact on isolative and insulative behaviors, passivity, rationalizations, and finances. The general consumption pattern is typically out of control and needs to be challenged as such. Again, the presence of probation as a "hammer" may be very positive.

Throughout all this pattern analysis, as in the previous phases, there has to be a recurring emphasis on responsibility, power, and control. These three underlying factors may be the most important in initially being used inappropriately, and thus creating the problem, but later acting as agents of change and ensuring the prevention of relapse.

Empowerment

The abuse of power may be one of the key factors in facilitating the pedosexual contact.

The inequity of power within the family is exemplified by the great irony of intrafamilial sexual abuse. The offender feels powerless for a combination of reasons at the same time as he perceives the child as powerful and tries to "fight fire with fire" by using sexual contact as a power tool. The powerless offender becomes powerful and then, after the report, again powerless. One of the major treatment tasks is to empower the offender in order to produce an equitable power balance within the family and improve related issues such as self-esteem, independence, and self-confidence.

Empowerment is linked with control. Independence and assertiveness can be encouraged through decision-making skills, option exploration, and negotiation skills. Within the family, particular attention can be paid to parenting and financial issues, both of which are closely identified with power. Outside the family, empowerment can take the form of outreach to others, either generally or specifically within the pedosexual self-help programs.

Career issues also can be the focus of empowerment. Many offenders have had a history of unemployment, underemployment, and serial employment resulting in both economic and psychological problems. Many also lose their jobs as a result of arrest, conviction, or incarceration. Career exploration, decision making, and stability therefore become empowerment possibilities.

Termination

Even a seemingly clear-cut issue like termination is complex. There may be several different points that seem like terminations: family reunification, Child Protective Services case closure, "graduation" from self-help programs, release from mandated treatment, or release from probation. For the purposes of this discussion, I focus on termination from treatment, although the other milestones also deserve attention.

Because most offender treatment is mandated, termination decisions involve more than the completion of treatment goals. The treatment team has to agree, sometimes unanimously, on the demonstration of those treatment goals and to be convinced that the risk of repeated offense is minimal. The termination process may include an independent clinical or psychophysiological reevaluation.

In assessing the risk of repeated offense, the risk can never be considered nonexistent. Even in the best situations, the risk is considered minimal but still present. Essentially, the treatment team must determine not only an offender's consistent compliance with the treatment goals but also his ongoing commitment to change and self-monitoring. The offender should also be able to show access to an ongoing support system.

The offender's commitment should include a clear agreement to return to treatment after termination if necessary. In my experience, the most successfully treated offenders have returned at least once after termination to deal with a new problem. In contrast, about half of the incidents of repeated offense occur after termination, and all have been related to a resumption of substance abuse behaviors. If the offender remains on probation after termination, the probation department should conduct regular urinalyses and possible psychophysiological measures.

Treatment of Other Types of Pedosexual Offenders

In describing treatment strategies, I have intentionally focused on the regressed offender because that is the type of offender counselors and therapists encounter most frequently. Many of the same interventions are appropriate for other pedosexual offenders, but some specific issues should be emphasized.

Pedophile

Responsibility and control issue are critical with the pedophile and must be emphasized in every session. If at all possible, arousal patterns should be consistently monitored. If treatment is to be successful with the pedophile, those patterns will have to be shifted completely. The pedophile will also have to alter his pattern of nonsexual contact with children, in most cases an extremely difficult task. Research in the treatment of pedophiles will have to be conducted in correctional facilities, with all of the attendant difficulties that it entails.

Rapist

Clinicians in the corrections field have found that treating the rapist and the dynamics of the rape situation and its issues of violence generally call for specialized training (Groth, 1979). Although the dynamics of rape are becoming better understood, most offenders have difficulty acknowledging responsibility. Child rapists may be even more difficult to treat, although research does not indicate that clearly.

Addictive/Compulsive

Treatment of the addictive offender is still in the early stages, but it seems that a "12-step" recovery program may be helpful and effective. Inpatient programs, similar to other addiction programs, also have been established. For the pedosexual offender, coordinated treatment between an addictions specialist and the primary counselor seems necessary. As with the regressed offender, group treatment is helpful and perhaps essential. The two approaches can be complementary and should be coordinated.

Symptomatic

The key element in treating the symptomatic offender is coordination between treatment team members dealing with the primary disorder and those dealing with the sexual contact. Clearly, the relationship between the primary disorder and the symptomatic pedosexual contact should be thoroughly understood.

Ritual

As noted in the risk assessment discussion, treating the ritual offender requires treating the presumed obsessive disorder. Treatment has to focus on nonobsessive behavior as a positive alternative. Some nonoffending obsessive behavior may also need to be accepted.

Female Offender

Much remains to be learned about the phenomenon of the female offender. Although the overwhelming percentage of offenders are male (with both male and female victims), clinical experience with adult offenders and survivors leads to the conclusion that many unreported contacts involve female offenders. Allen (1991) estimated that offenses by female individuals may have involved well over a million victims. Female abuse may be more of a taboo because it is more threatening and does not fit the male aggression and power issues or the victim/survivor orientation of feminist theory and advocacy (Elliott, 1993; Miletski, 1995). There is also a generalized sense of societal disbelief, getting down to even the basic notion that women cannot "molest" because they don't have penises, a basic misunderstanding of the sexual abuse process (Rosencrans, 1997).

The major statistical problem is that male victims do not report as often as female victims because they are less likely to perceive pedosexual contact as abusive, and female children report abuse by adult women even less frequently (Wyatt, 1991). Many offenders report sexual contact as children from baby sitters or aunts, but relatively few situations directly involve the natural mother. When the mother is the offender, substance abuse generally is a major factor, leading to the conclusion that the offender was in a symptomatic pattern or that unusually strong disinhibition was necessary. Although this symptomatic pattern may also be linked to psychosis, more recent information indicates that this is not likely (Mathews et al., 1989).

An interesting aside: I have observed that female offenders are less frequently charged, convicted, or incarcerated. These observations seem to be supported, at least in part, by Allen (1990) and Finkelhor, Williams, and Burns (1988). It is unclear whether this is a pattern of reverse bias in the criminal justice system or a convergence of factors including the strong denial of female offenders, investigative inadequacies, young age of victims, or general difficulty in substantiation (Dunbar, 1999).

Despite the similarities between male and female offenders in such areas as powerlessness, dependency, and need for control, the differences between them are worth noting. Female offenders appear to use less force and coercion, yet they may be physically abusive outside of the sexual arena. Although one study found that female offenders accept responsibility for offending more easily than male offenders (Matthews, 1993), another found that female offenders have a much stronger denial mechanism and ability to keep the secret than have male offenders (Allen, 1991). Women tend to start abusing younger children than male offenders do; in one study, the average age of victims was 3.2 years, and the abuse may last for 8–10 years (Rosencrans, 1997). There seems to be a stronger likelihood of a history of abuse as a child, to be discussed shortly under dynamics. Women tend to have lower incomes and occupational statuses and may have a more active sexual desire and experience, and they may be relatively pessimistic about the possibility of change (Allen, 1991). Female offenders have a stronger need for emotional or relational connections, although this may simply be an underidentified issue in male offenders.

Categorizing female offenders may shed light on dynamics issues. Mathews et al. (1989) described three categories: teacher/lover, predisposed (intergenerational), and male-coerced. There are other systems that look at the independent offenders and active or passive co-offenders (Davin, 1999). The focus of research has mostly been on the independent offender, who is seen as being more psychologically disturbed and having suffered more severe sexual abuse as a child; chemical dependency was not a significant factor in either group (Davin, 1999). Female offenders showed more dependency than controls, but they were not significantly different from controls in family-of-origin history, although the intensity of their own sexual abuse did not correlate with the intensity of the abuse perpetrated. This study contradicted other research (Hislop, 1999) in its finding that female and male offenders do not differ in salary, occupation, or number of sexual partners. The importance of primary mother-daughter attachment, female identity formation, and related sense of abandonment is seen as crucial in treatment planning (Dunbar, 1999). The one true commonality in all this research is the history of physical and sexual abuse, with victimization of female children leading to offending by these victims when they become adults on an even more predictable basis than for male victims (Turner & Turner, 1994).

Treatment of the female offender can be similar to that of the male offender, perhaps more so with the approach that we have taken with male offenders as compared with that of other models. Typical issues of nurturance, intimacy, and dependency should be explored fully as should the almost consistent victimization history. It would not be an exaggeration to say that all female offenders should be seen as victims (although this is not a rationalization for their behavior). Because of this history and the resultant ambivalence and emotional isolation, a period of attachment with their own childhoods and that of their own child's is essential. Women may hang on to guilt feelings and shame longer than do men and they may be more self-destructive, with even stronger suicide potential. Group approaches to discuss these issues may be particularly helpful.

Disinhibiting factors require extra attention. The basic goals of encouraging appropriate responsibility, power, and control are essentially identical to those for the male offender, although the female perspective in our society should obviously be taken into consideration.

Cultural Diversity in Offender Treatment

Within the counseling profession, perhaps even more so than in allied professions, we have struggled with issues of cultural diversity. We have produced media that deal with the cultural issues in general and with the role of the counselor in making appropriate interventions (Lee, 1997; McFadden, 1999). Specific issues related to cultural diversity in sexual abuse treatment are addressed in a new volume, edited by Alvin Lewis (1999a). This book reviews some general issues for treatment of culturally diverse clients and then specifically addresses issues in six cultural groups: Native Americans, African Americans, Hispanics, Alaskan Natives, Asian Americans, and Maori. The book does not mention the concerns of sexual minorities; they should also be considered in the context of differences described below, despite the apparently low incidence of abuse.

Although no data indicate any identifiable ethnic, racial, or sexual minority group as having an unusual incidence of sexual abuse, it is clear to anyone involved with the criminal justice system that ethnic minorities and the socioeconomically disadvantaged are overrepresented in the system (R. Jones et al., 1999). My experience is that it is far more likely for the upper middle-class offender to hire a specialized attorney and receive a plea bargain, acquittal, or early termination from treatment. It is not clear whether this is related to cultural dominance or economics or both. Again, this is a reflection of the whole system, not just the agencies dealing with sexual abuse cases. Informal research in a community treatment program indicates that the ethnicity of the participants is very congruent with the general population. See Case Study B.

The dominant culture, called either *Anglo, Anglo-American,* or *Anglo-European* in the Lewis book (somewhat confusingly, *Anglo* refers to English), is seen as setting values and standards for a variety of expectations including criminal offenses and therapy (in the broad context), with poorer outcomes in traditional therapy for disempowered groups (R. Jones et al., 1999). Clearly, there are potential barriers to treatment with these groups that have been identified as early as Sue and Sue's (1990) pioneering work. These barriers are identified in R. Jones et al. and include the following:

- institutional racism (perpetuating the differences among groups),
- ethnocentrism (using dominant standards to judge other groups with attendant self-deprecation of the groups themselves; Comas-Diaz & Griffith, 1988),
- systemic and professional ethnocentrism (either not acknowledging or addressing cultural factors as part of the search for more "universal" determinants; Brislin, 1990), and
- individual ethnocentrism (assuming that methods and techniques from the dominant culture will work for others and not recognizing cultural perspectives, including spirituality).

Turning specifically to sexual abuse issues, there initially had been an assumption that the taboos against sexual contact with a child are universal. In fact, some historical and contemporaneous cultures have looked on sexual contact with children as soothing, educational, or as a rite of passage. When cultural contexts have been suggested, both the judicial and mental health systems have emphatically rejected them, typically because of the perception that the children needed protection above all else. Arguments regarding cultural relativity went unheeded.

It has been postulated that historical and sociopolitical experience has produced acculturation stress and that related factors like "historical hostility" (Vontress & Epp, 1997) have played a role in the creation of aggression. Specifically, the disempowered male may use sexual aggression as a means of gaining power and control. This fits with the discussion of powerlessness as being one of the huge contributing factors for offender behavior. It is not clear whether any particular groups may be even more vulnerable to this influence.

These power and control issues also carry over into the counseling relationship where cultural factors may be important in building trust and rapport. Some individuals may have a much more difficult time in trusting the counseling/therapy process (perhaps regardless of the counselor), especially when the treatment is mandated, as it is in most sexual abuse situations. Culturally competent therapists will recognize this and utilize options to assist the process, such as allowing more time for trust development, emphasizing active rather than passive cognitive foci, and serving as an unconditional client advocate. As noted elsewhere in this book, this advocacy is essential and independent of issues of offender responsibility or victim advocacy, which are complementary.

Lewis (1999b) discussed cultural issues and barriers that might be involved in the evaluation and treatment of sexual abuse. Assessment concerns include gender of the evaluator, extent of acculturation by the client, and level of family involvement. In some cultures, the family unit might be reluctant to participate openly in treatment because of a perceived violation of the norms of respect, which would call for silence. Although not specifically discussed, one might expect that such family norms may also affect the number of reports that are made; some cultures show an underrepresentation in reporting and, therefore, treatment.

Vargas and Koss-Chioino (1992) emphasized the dilemma that some client families may experience between traditional values or practices and that of the dominant culture. However we may recognize the normality of some of this diverse behavior, we are functioning within the sociolegal context that demands accountability.

The following factors should be noted and addressed by counselors (Lewis, 1999b):

- *Biculturality.* This is the ability for an individual to function in two cultures; for example, exhibiting different behaviors in different cultural context (traditional or mainstream).
- *Family tradition and structure.* This is a key factor because sexual abuse treatment as described in this volume is strongly dependent on family dynamics as etiology and treatment modality. The relevant power of mother versus father as well as the status of children (individually or collectively) is a crucial issue and must be addressed in the treatment planning process.
- *Degree of acculturation.* The assessor must explore this variable, getting some clues from dress, language of preference within the family, and issues of respect, dominance, and submissiveness.
- *Language.* The understanding of English is crucial for clients working with monolingual English counselors. That seems obvious, and we are probably more aware of the issue than other more subtle cultural influences. We should note whether a client's ability to use and understand conversational or standard English is adequate in comprehending the terms that are used in individual or family treatment (e.g., *bonding, pseudoadult, dynamics, sexualization,* and *fellatio and cunnilingus*); if an interpreter is needed, there may be concerns about the gender, participation, and possible biases of that person. Children, who may know English better than their parents, should not be used as translators; to do so would dramatically affect the power balance.
- *Help-seeking behavior.* Many disempowered clients have not had the experience of seeking help outside of the family or

community. This concern is exaggerated by the probability of mandated treatment.

- *Eye contact.* Some cultures will avoid eye contact or direct the eyes downward as a sign of respect and lack of understanding. Even within the family, children may avoid eye contact with the parents.
- *Spirituality and religion.* The counselor must be aware of the impact of these two different variables that can have an impact on the family's view of norms, acceptance, healing, and reconciliation. The use of, or consultation with, native healers may be particularly helpful.
- *Privacy.* Many cultural groups would consider discussion of either family or sexual issues to be an extreme violation of privacy. In fact, privacy is a very typical concern for most families in treatment, and sexual discussions make them very uncomfortable. We are essentially a sex-negative society with clear proscriptions against open sexual communication. This may be exacerbated with some other normative systems.
- *Social tolerance for deviant and dysfunctional behavior.* Many aspects of sexuality, including pedosexual contact, may trigger differing levels of acceptance or aversion. Although most societies do not endorse this behavior, condemnation and punishment may be remarkably variable, with a higher priority of castigation for substance abuse, adultery, theft, or other criminal offense.
- *Psychometrics.* Some of the instruments used in offender diagnosis and classification clearly are affected both by contextual language and normative assumptions, from gender roles to the perception of pathology. Instruments like the MMPI, MCMI, and other "personality" assessments are particularly susceptible to this kind of influence. It is certainly clear that psychophysiological assessment would also be vulnerable to differing arousal patterns and stress reactions, particularly in this relatively invasive setting.
- *Choice of therapist.* The gender of the therapist is a typical concern, so too are the therapist's cultural background, social class, experience with diversity, general acceptance level, and comfort with sexual issues. If the individual or family is, in fact, able to be involved in the choice of therapist, their commitment level may be significantly enhanced.
- *Treatment modalities.* Family treatment modalities, as noted, may be difficult for many cultural groups. Other typical treatment techniques, from behavioral to cognitive to family systems, can all be difficult to implement.

- *Storytelling.* The use of stories, past experiences, metaphors, and self-disclosure may all be viewed as positives by some individuals. The healer in many cultures is seen as reflective, wise, and observant rather than verbal, directive, and prescriptive.
- *Pharmacology.* Groups may have differing beliefs regarding the use of typical psychoactive medications that may be primary or adjunctive treatment. Again, it is likely that a large proportion of all clients, particularly men, would be concerned about negative effects (antidepressant-induced anorgasmia, loss of desire with anti-androgens) but also generally concerned about the vulnerability involved in taking any medication. This fear or concern may, again, be exacerbated in some cultures.

The recognition of cultural diversity can be the key factor in dealing with a wide range of individuals. This perspective, which includes sex positivism, development of positive power, and unconditional acceptance, is adopted throughout this volume. Specific positive strategies include learning as well as teaching; modeling help-seeking behavior through consultation; increasing awareness of specific, even idiopathic, differences; and, perhaps most important, conveying a sense of genuine respect. These strategies and the positive perspective of awareness should be emphasized in counselor education, supervision, research, and program development, with continued encouragement by professional organizations (Johnson & Cuestas-Thompson, 1999). The American Counseling Association has certainly devoted increased attention to diversity issues in their programs and media.

Doing therapeutic sexual abuse work with diverse groups adds yet another challenge to an already complex process. Fortunately, the same qualities generally required for effective treatment noted in the previous philosophical assumptions stand the counselor in very good stead for any "curve balls" that may occur when treating the minority client.

Warning Signs

As noted in the assessment phase, the offender has many good reasons to deny and minimize the offense as he faces sentencing. This continues to be a risk during treatment although less so after sentencing. What does continue is a tendency to generally minimize problems and emphasize progress in counseling. Vague comments such as "I'm feeling better" or "Our communication has improved" or "I won't do it again" should be challenged and confronted with a statement like "Tell me exactly how." Most offenders and their families (including the victim) believe they are ready to terminate counseling after a few months, but when looking back with hindsight at the actual termination time, they see how much additional progress they have made since that time they thought they were ready.

A related issue is that an offender with a dependent personality will eagerly cooperate and say exactly what the counselor wants to hear. The offender's question, in fact, is specific: "What do you want me to tell you?" This, of course, fits right into the black-and-white, rigid pattern of the offender's pathology.

The length of treatment itself frequently becomes a therapeutic issue. The counselor often is under significant pressure to reduce the length of therapy. The pressure may come from the victim, offender, or nonoffending spouse. There also may be financial pressures on either the private practice or agency counselor to limit treatment duration. The best metaphor I've used to deal with this issue is that whereas 90% is wonderful as a "grade," this situation requires 99%, and that takes time, even beyond what seems like compliance with the treatment goals.

Brief Interventions

Time, various experiences, and repetitive opportunities for new behaviors help to cement the lessons learned in therapy and increase the effectiveness of treatment and lower the risk of recidivism. Although specific statistics are not available, clinical observations indicate that for many regressed, intrafamilial offenders, a great deal of risk reduction may take place when the report is made. Assuming even basic responsibility and admission of harm, that percentage may continue to improve in the initial stages of treatment. It is the continuing honing of experience that brings on the last few percentage points, primarily in the empowerment phase.

Are we as a society ready to reduce treatment duration and, perhaps, increase the risk even a small amount? The answer seems to be "Yes." In our general mental health treatment approaches, psychosocial support levels, managed health care, and funding for a variety of clearly helpful and effective programs, we have consistently made the decision to limit access to resources and do the minimum whenever possible.

The flip side of that argument is that with many clients, we can provide excellent care with episodic treatment, similar to that noted in other brief interventions. In fact, treatment of isolated offenders (those without goals of reunification or opportunity to deal with the victim/survivor) indicates that duration can be much shorter. Some research in treatment efficacy (Marshall & Anderson, 1996) shows that protracted relapse protection programs may not be necessary or more effective.

One source of timesaving can be in the area of assessment. Although the criminal justice and child protection systems have their own needs for assessment, the level of assessment for treatment planning may be reduced. The most effective assessment may well be part of the treatment process, rather than a separate, identified process. Again, this is the "active assessment" approach. Risk assessment becomes a longer term issue.

The treatment goals, particularly the emphasis on power, control, and responsibility, remain the same when treatment is of short duration. The cooperation of the offender is clearly essential. A minimum of 5–8 sessions should be devoted to the crisis stage in order to shift guilt to responsibility, reduce suicide risk, and "hook" the offender into treatment concepts. While the "hook" is more likely in longer therapeutic relationships, it can still be used as a way of expediting the whole process and helping the victim.

The apology session(s), if needed or available, call for another 3–4 sessions in preparation, meeting, and resolution. If that is successful, treatment may move as quickly as possible to family interventions. Family work, to be described in the next chapter, including Solution-Focused Brief Therapy, can be shortened with little loss of overall effectiveness (Fleming & Rickord, 1997). Although abused families certainly present extra risks that are not typical in Solution-Focused Brief Therapy, the principles remain similar. Five to 10 sessions in family therapy, including dyads, triads, and whole family combinations, may be required. Thus, a total of 15–20 sessions over a period of a year may substitute for over 50 sessions in more traditional approaches.

As in the other brief interventions, the group process is crucial, both for treatment and self-help and support. The group can provide the most information, validation, and encouragement. The duration of group work can be reduced by emphasizing the crisis stage, acceptance of responsibility, and creation of positive options. The self-help group may be more helpful than traditional therapy groups if there are restrictions or limitations.

The offender, more than the other family members, may also benefit from changes in counselors/therapists. Although the counseling relationship is crucial in the early stages of treatment, the treatment goals can also be addressed by a new therapist, releasing one therapist from the burden of having to provide the full range of services. Sometimes, managed care and other funding sources may be willing to provide new limitations with each new therapist.

CHAPTER 4

Intervention Strategies in the Treatment of Family and Adult Survivors

Intervention Strategies With the Family

Most pedosexual contact occurs within the family (referred to as *intrafamilial child sexual abuse*). In this chapter, I discuss ways in which the whole family can recover from the devastation of sexual abuse and provide the most effective strategy for breaking the cycle of abuse.

The focus on the family does not necessarily imply that dysfunctional families cause abuse, nor does it ignore a child's victimization outside the family or the possibility that the offender also may seek a pedosexual contact outside the family. It also in no way removes responsibility from the offender for his behavior or excuses it. A family systems approach can be an effective treatment intervention because it functions as a preventive approach, preventing contact within and outside the family, in turn preventing the intergenerational cycle from repeating, and further preventing at least some other problems aside from sexual ones through improved family functioning.

Friedman (1988) reviewed the family systems strategy and other models of family intervention. Some of those concepts are integrated in this discussion. First, however, it will be helpful to highlight two specific roles that have not been discussed: the mother/spouse role and the sibling role.

The Other Victims

Although *victim* in this context is used to refer to the one who has been involved in the pedosexual behavior with an adult, it would not be incorrect to view the other family members similarly, if not equally, as victims. This may include extended family members, friends, and associates; here, the focus is on the mother/spouse and sibling roles.

The offender and victim both have major issues to resolve and heal, but the mother probably has more numerous and more significant issues than either; these issues are emotional and logistical (and the impact of the latter should not be discounted).

The major dilemma for the mother, of course, is the schism of loyalty to her husband and protection of her child. The woman in this situation is like someone who is glued to both sides of a vise—the force threatens both to pull her apart and crush her. The dilemma will last at some level, through and beyond the treatment process, and gets expressed in questions such as "Whom do I believe?" and "Can I ever leave them alone?"

The mother's initial dilemma arises in dealing with the report. Disbelief is probably her most common reaction. Even if she had previous suspicions, it is still difficult for her to believe that the sexual behavior happened. The mother will undoubtedly question the child about details in order to test credibility. Typically the details given by the offender and the victim differ. Most mothers believe the victim but it may take them anywhere from a few hours to several months. The question of belief, however, is not as important as the sense of protection. The mother may have doubts and confusion about what happened but can still act to protect the child by having the father move out, cooperating with Child Protective Services, supporting the child, and so forth.

Even after enough details are known to "convince" the mother, she may continue to be torn. The mother can be encouraged to provide support for both husband and child and express the appropriate feelings such as anger, rage, and hurt. Whenever possible, the mother can give priority protection to the child and not be forced into choosing between the two loved ones. In some situations, of course, the mother may choose between victim and offender, and the treatment plan can be modified to adapt to that.

It is easy to lose track of one important consideration amid this chaos of feeling torn. The mother frequently feels guilty or responsible for the pedosexual contact. She feels that she must not have been a "good enough" sexual partner or a good wife and mother generally. She reasons that had she done better, her husband would have been satisfied or the child would have come to her for help. This feeling may be reinforced if the details refer to sexual behavior in which the wife refuses to engage (e.g., oral sex) or if contact with the child occurred right after she declined sex or when she was ill or disabled. Offender responsibility must be strongly emphasized.

The mother may well go through cycles of intense anger and depression. She will be angry not only at her husband but also at the child and, most of all, at herself for not protecting her child and not recognizing the problem. Her depression primarily results from her sense of hopelessness, helplessness, and lack of control over herself and her family. Individual and group therapy should focus not only on these issues but also on the opportunity for her to explore issues in relation to her family of origin, including the possibility of having been a victim herself of either sexual or physical abuse.

Finally, the issues of logistical pressures on the mother should not be overlooked. In most situations, she becomes for all practical purposes an instant single mother. With a good chance of husband or children being out of the home, reduced income, increased expenses, and transportation to several therapy sessions a week, the logistical and economic strains alone are formidable. Mothers need as much support as possible with these issues.

Siblings who actually have no knowledge of the abuse start out in a position that seems to be in contrast to the mother's. Rather than feeling central to all the emotional and logistical struggles, siblings frequently feel "out of it." They may feel that they are the last to know and that they are clear about only part of the information being discussed. Neither the victim nor the parents are eager to reveal the details to them. Siblings are typically ignored in treatment strategies and by Child Protective Services and the judicial system during the crisis phase, except for being questioned about whether they were abused or whether they were witnesses. Even after this questioning, they frequently still do not know what happened.

When the details are brought out, the siblings invariably do not believe the victim. Like the mother, they feel a loyalty to the father, but even more than in her case, there is clear dependence on him and fear of abandonment if or when he is removed from the home or incarcerated. Even after believing that the abuse occurred, they go through a stage of "blaming the victim," reasoning that things would still be "normal" if the report had not been made. The apology sessions, which should include the siblings, must clearly address these issues.

At times, siblings know or strongly suspect that abuse is occurring but may protect themselves or others by denial. They then may feel disloyal to the identified victim and may experience guilt, which is exhibited by withdrawal, anger, or confusion. Supportive therapy is necessary to help these siblings to reveal their knowledge or suspicions and rebuild the sibling relationship. They should also be helped to realize that they too have been victimized by the situation.

It is only after these stages that the siblings may show the fear or concern that they are, or could have been, victims themselves. Their protection system (mother, counselor, Child Protective Services, probation, teacher) should specifically be identified to them, and the counselor should obtain an age-appropriate agreement to go to these people if it should ever be necessary.

Family Treatment Goals

Family treatment goals can be established to parallel those of the offender and victim. These can be established somewhat independently of reunification decisions and be flexible enough to change if the reunification option changes. If the decision is made to stay apart, the family still will need considerable counseling and support. Ideally, the father can still be a part of the family sessions. In too many cases, however, the mother quickly opts for a divorce and, perhaps, relocation, and therapeutic follow-up is not possible.

Family treatment should include the following minimal goals:

1. clear understanding of the details of the pedosexual contact;
2. clear acknowledgment of offender responsibility and cessation of blaming the victim;
3. improved communication, including affective communication, and clear role boundaries.
4. appropriate power relationships with a focus on mutual cooperation and firm, but not dictatorial, parental control;
5. appropriate sharing of responsibility for day-to-day functioning;
6. ability to have fun together; and
7. reduction of family isolation by socialization with other families or organizations.

Family Characteristics

The sexually abusive family may have the following tendencies:

1. An overly dependent yet unclear marital relationship may prevail. Each partner may be unable to meet his or her own

needs and unsuccessfully tries to please the other, at least early in the relationship. The sexual relationship may suffer because of intimacy problems but, in and of itself, may be no worse than that of most couples. (Clearly, offenders do not seek out children because of isolated sexual problems in their relationship.)
2. The child takes on a pseudoadult role in an effort to make peace in the family. Intentionally or not, the child gains significant inappropriate power that leads to anxiety and, in turn, an increased drive for power.
3. Lack of appropriate role boundaries can be created because of one or more of the dynamics noted earlier—dictatorial father, irresponsible/dependent father, or pseudoadult child.
4. The family becomes enmeshed and therefore isolated from other social contacts. This is related to perceived risks of rejection, failure, or abandonment.

Interventions

Although some therapists emphasize the need for family treatment as the first and primary modality, it has been my experience that initiating family treatment too quickly may add to the confusion and dilute responsibility, making it less effective than at a later point. With the exception of the apology sessions, the focus for the first year or more of treatment should be on the individuals involved—offender, victim, mother, siblings—with a progression toward family therapy through the use of dyad and triad or subsystem therapy. Returning to the jigsaw puzzle metaphor: The goal is to form the big picture, but that has to happen by putting two pieces together over and over.

Dyads. There are three critical dyads in the family system: mother–child, husband–wife, and father–child. Dyad sessions with these three combinations, in that order, should begin as soon as the crisis phase is under control and after the child has been sufficiently prepared to confront the abuser. Sessions may take place with one or two therapists. The dyad process begins the emphasis on the family as a support mechanism, one of the most crucial parts of the recovery process (Stroud, 1999).

Mother–child. The mother–child dyad is addressed first because of the need for clear lines of protection. The child should feel that the mother believes enough to provide that kind of safety. There is a deeper, longer term goal of bonding or rebonding this relationship. Frequently, there has been a sense of competition and even jealousy rather than bonding. Issues related to trust, vulnerability, and fear of abandonment or rejection need to be addressed. A clear understanding must be established that the child will report sexual or other problems to the mother and that the mother will listen and take appropriate action regardless of the consequences.

Marital dyad. The marital dyad clearly is a major focus of treatment; this is the case even if there is a decision against reunification. Although I use the terms *marital, wife,* and *husband,* the discussion applies equally to couples who are not legally married. Initially, the focus should be on both information and feelings regarding the report. The wife should be encouraged to express her rage, hurt, and fears, and the husband should be encouraged to accept and validate those feelings without excuses as part of his acceptance of responsibility. Each can be encouraged to "take care of self" in expressing feelings, needs, and concerns and asking for help and support without dependence. Treatment emphasizes communication techniques, particularly active listening and "I" messages. Mutual analysis of each other's history and dynamics will be revealing and helpful (what did I learn in my individual sessions?). Parenting issues, especially information on normal development and new options for child rearing and discipline, are essential. Discussions should also focus on more gender-equitable sharing of responsibility, power, and control within the dyad and within the family.

Sex therapy is an absolutely essential component of the dyad work, even if the couple does not initially have any complaints about sexual functioning. If possible, participation in a sexuality class or group should be part of the treatment program. Like other couples, the couple in an abusive family probably has little or no information about their sexuality. Counseling and educational components should include information on anatomy and physiology, human sexual response, psychosexual development, alternative lifestyles, values and beliefs, sexual dysfunction, and communication. Typically, these couples demonstrate a narrow range of behaviors, lack of sexual communication, reluctance to experiment or explore in a healthy way, and lack of sensuality and intimacy. If sexual dysfunction is present, it is most likely in the form of ejaculatory timing, absence of orgasm or, perhaps, lack of desire. In proposing the discussion of sexual topics, I assure the couple that we will, together, make their sexual relationship better, no matter how it has been in the past or present. Sensate awareness and nonsexual touching is typically emphasized.

Father–child. The most delicate dyad to deal with may also be the most rewarding. As noted in chapter 2, the father–child relationship must be totally redefined. The father must regain a clear parental role, with appropriate power, in making decisions and setting limits for all the children, particularly for the victim. It should be specified that the victim cannot use the threat of a report to avoid reasonable paternal discipline or expectations. Appropriate affection should not only be discussed but specifically demonstrated, with feedback from the child as to comfort level of certain behaviors (e.g., hugs, kisses, sitting close, shoulder hugs). Father should specifically encourage and validate the child's creation of protection and support systems and clarify changes he has made.

Triads. The child, mother, and father triad should meet with some regularity during the second half of the treatment process to act as a check and monitor unit. The triad may be similar to an executive committee in an organization. The individuals can accomplish a great deal as a small group but they also function as monitors to make sure progress is being made, identify problem areas and possible solutions, and confront each other in a supportive atmosphere. The triad is the ideal unit for clarifying communication and goals both among the triad and between the family and the therapists/treatment team.

The family unit. Working with the whole family unit is a significant challenge for the counselor(s); therefore the dyad and triad sessions should be a helpful preparation. The whole family should be present, although children younger than 3 or 4 could be present for only one or two sessions. Two counselors should be at each session, one of whom should clearly be the victim's advocate. Most, if not all, of the sessions should be planned for 1½ hours.

It will be helpful to initiate sessions with the children to ensure their participation. Emphasis should be placed on the rights of each person to speak and, particularly, to express feelings. This creates a model and permission for mutual respect, equity, and communication. The counselors' role is to model and guide the family in its process with a minimum of intervention; intervention should consist more of reinforcement and encouragement than analysis. This can be accomplished while still providing accountability for the treatment goals.

Topics for family sessions should include responsibility issues, role boundaries, self-control, support systems, household functioning (jobs, chores, projects, finances), sexual/dating concerns, work and career issues, and plans for (or results of) reunification and visits.

Visitation

One of the most effective ways of monitoring family functioning and adjustment is through the use of controlled family visitation. In this approach, the father is gradually reintroduced into the family through a long series of planned visitation sessions that are carefully monitored, either directly or by verbal report. The goal of this controlled approach is to empower the family, particularly the mother, toward independence and self-protection.

The exact structure of the visitation process may take different forms (Wolf, Conte, & Engel-Meinig, 1988) but essentially consists of four stages: preparation, public visits, home visits, and overnight visits. Because court or probation orders may prohibit the offender from having contact with the children, the probation department has to be involved in the visitation decisions. The probation officer's presence may be a helpful controlling force.

Preparation for visits should include a set of predetermined rules for contact. The children should have a clear voice in making these rules based on their comfort level. Rules may include limitations on physical contact, agreement to not discuss the pedosexual contact, avoidance of arguments, and limit setting and time control by the mother. One critical rule for the whole visitation process is that the mother must be present and act as supervisor at all times. (We actually have had therapeutic success with the father having limited unsupervised time with the nonvictimized children late in the process.) The mother must be clearly committed to this component of the treatment.

The first visits will be public (park, mall, restaurant) and last about 2 hours. Emphasis is on a positive experience; expressions of discomfort are aired in the therapy sessions after the visits. The duration of visits is then increased to accommodate the most uncomfortable member of the family. The mother's ability to control the visit is carefully monitored.

Initial home visits last about 4 hours once a week. Activities should be planned in advance with an emphasis on doing at least one fun thing. This time period can be increased and dinner visits added—2 hours each, once or twice a week. Home visits will gradually be increased to 8 hours on Saturdays and Sundays and 4 hours each on two or three weekdays.

Overnight visits frequently create concern among the children because mother's protection will not seem to be available. Added preparation will be helpful with discussion on "how to feel safe." Options might include closed (or locked) doors, night lights, or rules against the father going into the children's rooms. One overnight visit, typically on the weekend, will then be discussed thoroughly before continued visits are allowed. Overnights are then gradually increased to four or five a week before reunification is considered.

Reunification

For most families in the treatment program, the word reunification attains a new, almost mystical level of importance. It is a more important goal than terminating therapy or completing probation.

The treatment team makes the decision for reunification when the family has completed most or all of its goals and clear safety and protection have been demonstrated in the visitation process. An independent reevaluation of the offender may be required. Areas for continued family improvement are identified. All the children are carefully questioned individually about their readiness. The family agrees to a continued treatment plan of at least 3 to 6 months.

Like the other treatment interventions, family treatment is a careful, time-consuming process. Time is an important ally, allowing some problems to emerge and be resolved. Patience is an important therapeutic tool.

Brief Interventions

The overall treatment, supervision, and monitoring of the family and possible reunification are a long-term commitment. The time is necessary for the safety and protection of the child, as well as in emphasizing the complexities of family functioning.

Work with the family counseling itself can certainly be shortened compared to earlier approaches. Solution-Focused Brief Therapy (Fleming & Rickord, 1997) and cognitive-behavioral models (Bera, 1990; McCarthy, 1990) both facilitate shortened work with families. These approaches and the goals noted earlier are very clearly aimed at the current and future functioning of the family. The counselor's role and expertise is in using the dysfunctional patterns of the past—roles, esteem, identity, and the violation of intergenerational boundaries—to help create goals that are appropriate for the family, reducing the overall number of sessions needed. Each session, of course, can cover multiple topics.

The use of homework for all family members can be highly effective with time and cost. The family can accomplish a great deal during visitation time by practicing problem solving, improved communication, and communication of feelings and recording these efforts in a journal.

Interventions With Adult Survivors

Discussion of family sexual abuse involves confusing dichotomies—the love and hate of the victim for the father—offender, the offender's machismo and powerlessness, and the mother's conflicting loyalties. The dichotomies of the adult survivor are even more dramatic: courage and vulnerability, strength and weakness, the pain of reality and the escape of dissociation.

How do we know what we know about sexual abuse? How did we really start to understand about its extent and "the numbers"? How do we know about the damage it causes? We know because of the stories of countless courageous survivors of abuse, mostly women, who have told us not only about the behaviors but also about their fears, nightmares, compulsions, rage, and self-destructiveness.

Treatment of the adult survivor has appropriately received increasing attention in recent years. This attention has come from four somewhat disparate types of groups with similar goals: sexual abuse treatment programs, substance abuse treatment programs, rape/sexual assault recovery groups, and feminist advocacy and support groups. Although approaches may differ, the similar goals include confrontation of the issues, clarification of responsibility, stabilization, and positive control.

A special note should be made regarding the feminist perspective. Both female and male counselors should not only be aware of this perspective but also use the many positive powerful factors involved. Although most counselors of adult survivors have typically and understandably been women, the sensitive male counselor can provide a helpful model and balance to treatment. Treatment teams might be an effective tool as well. There is also, I believe, a great benefit to be gained if the counselor of adult survivors also has experience with child victims and offenders.

As noted earlier, I have intentionally separated the terms *victim* and *survivor* (with some use of both together, e.g., *victim/survivor*). I believe the term *victim* emphasizes the child's powerlessness, whereas *survivor* puts a positive focus on the person who has been living with this issue, whether the person has or has not received treatment. The term *adults molested as children* (AMAC) is used in some of the literature but is not used here because of the vagueness of the term *molestation. Adult survivors* is used to describe both in-home and out-of-home childhood experiences.

The attention and focus on survivors has produced information and research about or with adult survivors. Some studies focus on research and analysis (Bass & Davis, 1988; Finkelhor, 1984; Finkelhor & Dziuba-Leaterman, 1994; Herman, 1981; Indart, 1999; Knopp & Benson, 1996; Rush, 1980; Russell, 1986). Others have focused on the survival process (Bear, 1988; Hunter, 1990; Lew, 1988). Advocacy and victims speaking out are noted in others (Bass & Davis, 1988; Bass & Thornton, 1983; Brady, 1979; Davis, 1991; Fraser, 1988; McNaron & Morgan, 1982; Morris, 1982). These studies provide a valuable addition to our knowledge and also emphasize that research in this area is relatively recent.

Presenting Problems

Although the four types of groups noted above may be doing most of the work with adult survivors, the female survivor is likely to seek help initially from a counselor or other helping system. It is essential that the mental health counselor, college student counselor, or sex therapist ask questions having to do with sexual abuse. Those questions may be the turning point in the life of a survivor. It should also be emphasized that these questions do not lead to jumping to the conclusion of abuse; confused memories and other variables affect the conclusion drawn.

More often than not, the survivor who seeks help has the following types of presenting problems:

- depression: feelings of vulnerability, hopelessness, poor self-esteem, unclear identity;
- eating disorders: obesity, anorexia, bulimia, body image problems;
- sexual problems: dysfunction, lack of desire, addictive/compulsive patterns, anorgasmia, dystonic homosexuality;
- dissociative patterns: "spacing-out," fear of loss of reality contact, delusions, isolation; there may also be a vague feeling

that something has happened but the specific memories cannot be accessed;
- somatic concerns: loss of feeling, chronic pain, gastrointestinal distress, recurrent gynecological concerns, chronic fatigue; and
- interpersonal problems: relationships, intimacy and closeness, social isolation, work or career instability.

Although this list is neither exhaustive nor unique to the survivor, it helps to build an awareness of the kinds of issues that can take the form of presenting problems. It takes only a few minutes during an evaluation or initial session to ask about any sexual contact as a child.

Confronting the Issue

Once the right questions have been asked, the survivor can be encouraged to explore and confront the issue of the abuse. This is a difficult decision for survivors to make. Counselors value self-exploration and insight, but survivors may feel that they are exposing themselves to great pain with only a hope that the effort will eventually produce positive results. Precautions related to suicide should be taken.

The counselor not only has to provide major doses of encouragement but suggest multiple options. For example, details of the abuse could be discussed all at once or over a period of time, relaxation techniques or hypnotherapy could be used, names could be omitted or changed, a female therapist or cotherapist could be introduced, or a support person could accompany the survivor to the session(s). Once these options are discussed, the survivor should make a firm commitment to go through with this phase. If such an agreement is not made, there is a good chance that the client will not return because of the fears involved.

The disclosure itself should be made at the client's pace and in her or his own words. Some survivors may have repressed or simply forgotten certain facts, which they may be able to recall as therapeutic work continues, with accompanying intense psychological pain. The counselor can certainly clarify information as well as acknowledge feelings and should be prepared to offer support that might include more frequent therapy sessions for a limited time. Encouragement can entail recognizing the uniqueness of a client's experience as well as the commonalities with other survivors. Caution should be used against judgmental statements (e.g., "that's disgusting," "how horrible," "they should hang the bastard"). Finally, the survivor should receive reinforcement for having told her story.

Counselor support does not mean an unquestioning belief of the specific details that may be evoked. Previously discussed issues of difficulties in memory suggest that one should exercise care, but this does not change the supportive approach of hearing and encouraging the feelings, regardless of any objective validity. These do not have to be challenged.

The survivor should be referred to a support group early in treatment. The group can provide an important sense of validation and support for continuing the process. Group therapy has been shown to be consistently effective (Marotta & Asner, 1999).

Clarifying Responsibility

It is critical to clarify that the offender bears complete responsibility for the abuse. It seems almost obvious that the survivor would blame the offender, but this is frequently not so, and the survivor may have significant guilt issues. The survivor must realize that the offender is responsible for the sexual contact, no matter what she did, said, or felt, and no matter what promises or threats were made. She is entitled to rights over her own body, and the offender bears responsibility for violating those rights.

At this point, the counselor should decide whether it would be helpful to discuss some of the abuse dynamics, not so much to analyze the past but to reinforce the offender's responsibility and validate the survivor's position. The survivor, like everyone else, wants to know the "why" but benefits more from learning the "how." In my experience, many counselors increase the pain of survivors and functionally revictimize them by spending too much time in the analysis of the past.

As part of the clarification process, the survivor can begin to confront the offender psychologically. This may become a recurring issue throughout and beyond the treatment process. The survivor can confront the offender through role-playing or Gestalt work or by writing letters or a journal. She can be encouraged to vent her feelings, although they may not surface initially. Feelings can encompass rage, fear, hurt, sadness, confusion, and ambivalence. All of these should be supported.

There is frequently a question of whether the survivor should confront the offender directly if that is physically possible. There may be some significant benefit to this in terms of closure and validation, but there are also risks that the offender will deny the contact with such force and conviction (perhaps aided by "false allegation" support groups) that the survivor can suffer major damage. Clearly, this step should be taken only after careful preparation for the possible consequences and only after the psychological confrontation has been settled. It may even be necessary to obtain assurance that the offender will, in fact, cooperate and assume the responsibility (less of a possibility now that litigation may be forthcoming). This confrontation should not be viewed as necessary for recovery.

Stabilizing

The longest phase of recovery could also be labeled as *processing*, *empowering*, or *healing* because it is all of these. It is partly putting the jigsaw puzzle together and partly "moving on." It is a process of grief and anger, finding the lost childhood, and self-empowerment (Bass & Davis, 1988).

Recognizing the need for grief acknowledges that a significant part of the survivor's life was lost, a part of childhood that cannot be replaced. Regardless of how "mild" or "severe" the abuse was, that loss is equally real. The survivor can grieve for the joy that was lost to pain, for the innocence that was lost to guilt, for the intimacy that was lost to exploitation, and for the love that was lost to violation. Anger and sadness are part of the grief and needs to be repeatedly acknowledged. Group work and writing exercises can be especially helpful in this process. Visualization techniques can also help the healing dramatically by emphasizing self-control.

"Finding the child" is a process that does not encourage living in the past or replacing the lost childhood; rather, it attempts to recreate the child within us without using this "inner child" as an excuse, rationalization, or cop-out. The concept of taking care of oneself is vital here. The survivor can look at ways to nurture herself or himself in the areas of health, career, finances, and play. While still feeling in control, she can give herself permission to relax, have fun, and use support systems, all of which may be more difficult than what one might think.

Two relatively new techniques for survivors should be noted here. One is the increased use of Eye Movement Desensitization procedure to treat trauma-related memories (Wernik, 1993) and the other is the use of bodywork; specifically integrating bodywork with psychotherapy (Timms & Connors, 1992). Both of these are psychophysiological and intended to uncover memories in the body. These techniques seem to be promising; both require specialized training. Unfortunately, they also may become a target of those who are critical of the validity of repressed/recovered memories.

Empowerment processes include techniques that build self-esteem, self-confidence, and a sense of positive control over one's life. These might include additional education, improved decision making, outreach to other survivors, creation of support systems, expansion of the social arena, and a positive approach to spirituality. Parenting issues should also be addressed, as noted earlier (Armsworth & Stronck, 1999).

One specific area that needs emphasis is sexuality. Survivors need information about healthy sexual functioning and enjoyment. Wendy Maltz (1991; Maltz & Holman, 1987) was the first to identify sexual symptoms of sexual abuse, including false ideas about sex, sex negativity, lack of desire, and automatic reactions; she reframed these into healing through a touch continuum that emphasizes intimacy, communication, and sensuality. Positive information can be gathered from written (Barbach, 1975, 1982; Heiman & LoPiccolo, 1988; Zilbergeld, 1978), group, and video sources, including appropriate fantasy, like some of the newer feminist-produced explicit and nonexplicit media (e.g., the Candida Royale series of videos). Emphasis should be on engaging in sexual contact from a positive perspective rather than as a way to please someone else. Intimacy and communication should be encouraged, particularly with the use of relaxation, nonsexual touching including massage, and respect for limits placed by the survivor.

The Male Survivor

The male survivor is like the "Stealth" bomber—invisible to radar, revealing itself only when totally safe, and potentially explosive. As noted previously, the male victim and the male survivor are not likely to report pedosexual contacts because they tend not to see them as abusive and are not likely to recognize their harmful effects. We are aware, however, of a clear increase in the number of individuals who are surfacing as a result of offender retrospection and referrals to treatment programs.

Three beliefs (Johanek, 1988) distort views of male victimization:

1. "Real men" would fight or resist abuse.
2. Sexual response "shouldn't" happen.
3. Offenders are homosexual and "taint" the victim.

The male survivor has problems and concerns similar to those of the female survivor with two additional concerns: homophobia and the magnification of weakness. Because male victims are typically abused by male offenders, issues of possible or potential homosexuality are typical but not always in the survivor's conscious awareness. Homophobia must be clearly and directly addressed in therapy.

Hunter (1990) also pointed out that male survivors of female offenders may have even more difficulty in coming forward to address their concerns. The grief aspects of abuse—denial, sadness, anger, bargaining—as well as very typical feelings of fear, guilt, shame, and rage are emphasized for men who are frequently inexperienced at dealing with feelings.

There is also a clear societal concern that the survivor feels vulnerable and violated in a society that requires men to be powerful, strong, and in control. It is the same problem that female survivors face but with added obstacles and vilification. This is particularly true in the sexual area where there are strong expectations that men are initiators or aggressors and have a much stronger desire and sexual stamina, all of which may be severely affected by the abuse experience. This "failure" may be more visible because erectile reactions are so much more obvious and there is less societal permission to "fake it" or pretend to enjoy the responses.

The male survivor discovers that support groups may be difficult to find and may choose to focus on individual counseling or more general men's groups. Issues of trust and vulnerability are obvious. Again, because of societal pressures and role expectations, the male survivor might be more likely to direct his rage toward others and engage in sexual or other acting-out behavior. Although not all men who were sexually abused as children necessarily become sexual abusers as adults, the majority of adult offenders were themselves abused. Sexual addiction/compulsion and isolation both may be possible effects. Suicidal risk is high at various points in the process.

Because of the difficulty in finding groups, the male survivor may have to turn to bibliotherapy to gain that sense of validation. Hunter's (1990) book is invaluable because it lists several real stories that effectively cover a wide gamut of experiences.

Supporters of Survivors

Increased attention is now paid to individuals who serve as supporters for both male and female survivors (Davis, 1991). These partners should be involved in the counseling process and be provided with information, written and verbal, about pedosexual contact, abuse, and the recovery process. The extent to which specific information is disclosed is, of course, up to the survivor. The partner's involvement certainly becomes crucial in the sexual healing process. Most partners, with appropriate education, are very happy to move in the direction of nonsexual touching and reduced demands. Much of this happiness is rewarded when couples frequently and dramatically improve their sexual enjoyment.

Brief Interventions

There are two unique reasons for addressing brief interventions with survivors: the lack of funding from community and government resources (Child Protective Services, probation, and victim programs) and the reticence of survivors to endure the perceived pain of therapy.

Adult survivors are not seen as crime victims in the typical sense because of the time lapse involved. Thus, there are few financial support mechanisms to support treatment (unless, ironically, they become offenders!). Fortunately, many victim and offender treatment programs piggyback a survivors' group program on to their agenda. This gives the advantage of a continuum of service in dealing with abuse concerns and also provides the possibility of normalization of contacts among the three affected populations—victims, survivors, and offenders. Some well-reconstructed offenders have served as sounding boards for survivors in an incredibly powerful way, with benefit for both.

The reticence for treatment is experienced both before initiating the request for help and after. Survivors show extraordinary difficulties with trust and may "shop" for several therapists before settling on one who meets their expectations. Unfortunately, the switching may just reinforce their paranoia and fears and simply avoid vulnerable discussions. There is also a sense that the counseling/therapy will be painful, somewhat akin to going to the dentist after not having seen one in many years—one hopes for the best but is really expecting the worst. Although many survivors, particularly those with dissociative and borderline personality concerns, spend years of their life in various therapies, the majority look for dramatic breakthroughs and insights but have difficulty in accepting "one step at a time" recovery and focus on self-control that is crucial in profiting from brief treatment.

As noted for male survivors, bibliotherapy and general self-help can be a good adjunctive resource, although some of the earlier lay-oriented books probably resulted in overidentification of abuse, some false allegations, and a pervasive feeling of societal male-bashing and pessimism. Many of the readers of these books, of course, did not seek out treatment, assuming the worst.

For many clinicians, dealing with the abusive family or the adult survivor is the biggest challenge. The unique combination of adults and children requires great skill, perseverance, and flexibility. The temptation to fall into societal sex negativity is strong and pervasive, and courage is necessary to maintain the necessary optimism.

CHAPTER 5

Case Studies

One of the most productive ways to gain insight into pedosexual problems is to study actual cases with both typical and unique components. The cases selected are all actual cases although identities, descriptive statements (age, work, etc.), and some details of the offense have been changed to protect confidentiality without changing patterns of dynamics. Cases represent "successes" and "failures" in terms of treatment across a spectrum of pedosexual situations. Two case studies illustrate the use of brief interventions.

Each case study is preceded by the pedosexual taxonomy shorthand noted in chapter 1: (a) age of participants: child (C), adolescent (Ado), or adult (Adu); (b) family setting: intrafamilial (I) or extrafamilial (E); (c) level of coercion: high (H), medium (M), or low (L); and (d) offender dynamics: regressed (R), pedophile (P), rapist (Ra), symptomatic (S), addictive/compulsive (A), or ritual (Ri).

Case Study A
C/Adu, I, M, R—Dictatorial/Possessive Father

Presenting Problem

Joan, age 16, in a discussion with a friend about sexual issues, revealed that she "had sex" with her father on many occasions. Her friend, in turn, discussed this with her mother, who reported it to

Child Protective Services. A male investigator from the agency and a female detective from the sex crimes unit of the police department interviewed Joan at school the next day. She initially denied any sexual contact and angrily refused to talk with the investigators, demanding to know where they had received their information. The investigators requested assistance from the school counselor, who was reported to have a good relationship with Joan.

The counselor focused on the positive aspects of reporting, particularly on Joan's right to her own privacy and body. Joan tearfully acknowledged that her real concern was that the father may have "had sex" with her younger sister, Beth, age 13, and she did not feel she could talk to Beth about that.

Joan reported that she had sexual contact with her father from the time she was 11 until the age of 14. Behavior included mutual genital stroking, fellatio, and approximately five incidents of penile-vaginal coitus. The sexual contact stopped when she refused. She also refused two subsequent suggestions. She reported that she felt disgusted but that she had never been hurt. She had not reported earlier because it hadn't felt like a "big deal" and because her father had told her that her mother would be very hurt and might "divorce them both." She guessed that her father was "having sex" with Beth because they had been alone together more often in recent months.

The Child Protective Service and police investigation team questioned Beth at her school. She angrily reported that her father had stroked her genital area through her underwear on three occasions in the last 2 months, and a week before had coerced her into fellatio. Beth said that this made her sick (literally) but that she was afraid of reporting because her father might hurt her. She also reported that she had seen her sister and father "making love" (coitus).

Investigators interviewed the mother, Carol, who said that she believed the stories and said that she had suspected some problem but "not this." She agreed to protect the girls and to cooperate with their father's removal from the home. The girls were brought home.

The father, Dave, was questioned at work at a construction site. He denied the allegations and angrily told the investigators to mind their own business. He became agitated, was placed under arrest, and was transported to the county jail. The next morning he agreed to make a statement and admitted that the allegations were correct. He was released, escorted home to pick up personal belongings, and transported to a friend's home. He was ordered to have no contact with his children.

Descriptive Information

Dave, age 37, was a construction worker (carpenter) and Carol, age 34, was a waitress. They had been married for 17 years and had three children: Joan (age 16), Beth (age 13), and Roger (age 9). They had lived in this community for 2 years, after having moved four times in order to obtain employment. Dave was in the army for a year and received a general discharge after two AWOL incidents. He had no criminal record but had two convictions for driving while intoxicated. Carol had worked outside the home for most of their marriage. The children generally performed satisfactorily at school. There had been no previous reports to Child Protective Services.

Crisis Intervention

Beth, Joan, and Carol were referred to one counselor and Dave was referred to another. Dave was arraigned and released on his own recognizance.

Beth and Joan were seen individually, and each was also seen together with Carol. Beth was angry with her father, saying that she was glad to have him out of the home. She expressed fear that he would retaliate for the report and wanted to know what would happen to him. Her mother and the counselor assured her that she was safe. Her mother was able to accept Beth's anger.

Joan indicated that she did not want to talk about the abuse and that she was sorry that she had made the report. She said that she did not feel at risk and that Beth could have stopped the contacts by refusing to participate. She also refused to talk with her mother about the report, telling her to "listen to the tape" of the investigation interview. She reluctantly agreed to continue counseling.

Dave was seen individually by his counselor. He admitted the sexual contacts although he did not think they were as frequent as Joan had reported. He said that he loved his children and that they enjoyed the sexual contact. He said that Joan had initiated several of the fellatio incidents by saying that she wanted to "make you feel good." He didn't understand why Joan wanted to stop. He also discounted Beth's reluctance, saying that she would have "liked it better when she did it more." Generally, he consistently emphasized that the children were "*his* children" and that nobody had the right to interfere with his family. He agreed to continue the counseling process and signed a suicide and treatment contract.

During subsequent crisis sessions, Joan was increasingly able to discuss her anger with her father and acknowledge that he was responsible for the behavior even though she had sometimes enjoyed "feeling like a woman." She remained reluctant to discuss specific details of the abuse but was able to discuss general issues with the counselor and with her mother.

Beth continued to be angry but shifted from never wanting to see her father to never wanting to "have him touch" her. She did not want him to go to prison because then the family "would be poor." She reported liking counseling because it was the first time that she felt she could talk about herself and her own problems.

Dave increasingly accepted responsibility for the sexual contacts even though he maintained that Joan consented to the behavior. He was able to develop some trust in the counselor. He denied memories of victimization by sexual abuse, but he reported a history of physical abuse from both his parents. He was able to recognize that his father had a similar possessiveness over his family members. At this point, Dave still had some difficulty seeing the general problem with his behavior, although he began to acknowledge the harm created by the pedosexual contact. He also acknowledged drinking about six beers a day although he denied being "an alcoholic." Throughout the crisis stage, he adhered to the restrictions imposed regarding no contact with the children. He was formally charged with two counts of attempted sexual conduct with a minor under 15. Partly because neither Beth nor Joan was willing to testify in a trial, a plea bargain was arranged and Dave was sentenced to 7 years probation.

Carol was seen individually during the crisis phase, with frequent sessions with the children and with Dave. She expressed a great deal of anger toward Dave and discussed the possibility of divorce. When she directed this anger at him in person, he accepted it with some minimization. Carol expressed guilt over not being a satisfactory lover, but Dave told her that their sexual relationship was not a causative factor.

The first apology sessions ended the crisis phase, approximately 3 months after the report. After preparing the children and securing their agreement, separate sessions were scheduled for Joan and Beth with Carol and Dave. Joan remained passive and generally silent throughout the session, accepting Dave's apology and acknowledgment of responsibility with minimal expression of feelings. At the end of the session, she asked, "Is that it?" Beth, on the other hand, was agitated throughout her session, pressing for reasons as to why Dave "did it." She expressed anger that he "screwed up" the whole family. She wanted to know details of Dave's contacts with Joan, which were supplied.

Ongoing Treatment

During the next 7 months of treatment, Joan was seen in individual treatment, group therapy, and dyad work with her mother and with Beth and in triad and family apology sessions. In the individual sessions, Joan became more at ease and openly discussed the details of the abuse. She reported being initially afraid and confused over the genital touching but agreed that after a few months, she enjoyed the "special" attention, affection, and sexual arousal. Her father had told her that she was going to experience "being a full woman," and she welcomed the coitus when he first attempted it. She reported enjoying both the sexual arousal and the feeling of "pleasing him," although she became more concerned about the possibility of pregnancy and more interested in "other" boyfriends. With time, she became more disgusted with the sexual contact and felt that Dave was taking advantage of her.

During treatment, Joan gradually acknowledged Dave's full responsibility for the sexual contact. She remained somewhat defensive in the dyad sessions with Beth, however, because she felt that she had set up the pattern. Beth assisted this process by clearly identifying that she was angry with Dave and not Joan. Joan's dyad sessions with Carol were initially very tense until Carol expressed her feelings of resentment and even jealously toward Joan, after which Joan laughingly acknowledged the same feelings toward Carol. From that point on, Joan and Carol felt closer and began a rebonding process.

Triad apology sessions (Joan, Carol, and Dave) continued to focus on Dave's responsibility for the sexual contact but also dealt with his general possessiveness and control over the family. Both women confronted Dave about his exploitive behavior. This theme also surfaced during the family apology sessions, with the counselor suggesting options for alternative family communication and decision making. The family sessions also addressed Roger's confusion and clarified the nature of the sexual incidents for him. Roger seemed torn between a loyalty to Dave and Carol, feeling that Dave was "mean" but that "the girls picked on him" during sessions.

Joan began to attend an adolescent survivors' group. Initially, she was rather passive and was clearly reticent to discuss any facts or feelings about the abuse. It was not until several months had gone by, when she heard a story similar to hers, that she was able to identify and discuss her experiences openly. She then began to identify common experiences with other group members' trust issues, power struggles, and ambivalence. She gradually became one of the most productive and supportive members of the group.

In a parallel time frame, Beth was seen in individual sessions, group therapy, dyad sessions with Joan and her mother, and triad and family apology sessions. In the individual sessions, Beth was able to express her anger toward both parents—toward her father for the abuse and generally being "mean" and toward her mother for "allowing" her father to "be like that" and not divorcing him. She worked on somewhat typical birth-order issues like feeling "left out" or different and not receiving attention like either Joan or Roger. The counselor was able to focus effectively on the positive aspects of "being different": independence, peer relations, and assertiveness. Beth was also able to use the female counselor as a role model and develop skills in dealing with adults, resulting in improved school performance.

Beth participated in a young adolescent group. In contrast to Joan, she was quickly able to open up with the group and discuss both her and Joan's experiences. At times she was disruptive to the group process because of sexually explicit language and profanity and general limit-testing behavior. She became adept at confronting other group members in a productive way.

Carol was seen in individual treatment as well as the previously mentioned dyad, triad, and family sessions. She was also seen in marital dyad sessions. Carol initially presented as an articulate, powerful woman who, however, remained in a dependent position in relationships. She perceived that she had "no choice" but to stay in her marriage to Dave because he was the sole financial support, and she did not want to "destroy the family."

Carol's family of origin was discussed. Carol was the oldest of three children. She denied a history of sexual or physical abuse. Her parents divorced when she was 9 years old and her mother worked full-time, placing Carol in the role of "assistant mother," a role she retained until she married Dave at age 17. She described the marriage as having met her expectations, which, in retrospect, she saw as low. She thought that initially the alcohol "mellowed" Dave and made him less demanding, but then it seemed to exacerbate his irresponsibility and verbal abuse.

By the end of the treatment phase, Carol had decided not to divorce Dave but felt comfortable that this was a clear choice. She was clearly placing herself in the "protector" role, with marital progress contingent on the safety of the children. Marital sessions focused on a more equitable distribution of power in the relationship and, as a part of that, improved communication. Slow progress was made on these issues; Dave gradually acknowledged Carol's strengths and the possibility that she did not have to be dependent on him. He was less willing to see himself as demanding, noting that he saw himself as inferior to Carol in many ways. It was not until late in treatment that he was able to see both of these working together (demands and inferiority feelings). Dave had a much more difficult time listening to Carol than she to him, and he showed much defensiveness. However, Carol reported that she felt that Dave heard her more consistently and thoroughly than at any time in their relationship. She reported a sense of ease in expressing her needs, even when Dave did not fulfill them.

Carol also participated in a women's group. After an initial period of reluctance, which she attributed to lack of confidence, she contributed consistently to the group by describing her own experiences and by supporting other group members. She particularly befriended one member of the group. The group experience was a major vehicle in helping Carol resolve the pull between Dave and the children and also in improving her self-confidence and related assertiveness skills.

Dave's response to treatment was slow but consistent. A working diagnosis of passive-aggressive personality disorder was established. Dave adhered to the conditions of probation, although he consistently spoke with hostility about his restrictions and "the system." With the cooperation of the probation department, he was not mandated to be free of alcohol, giving him the opportunity to stop drinking voluntarily, which he successfully accomplished. Whenever possible, Dave was given choices such as this in order to improve his sense of appropriate control and to reinforce active rather than passive behaviors. He remained consistently aware of his responsibility for the sexual contact.

In reviewing Dave's family of origin, he described his family as being "large and close." He was the fourth of seven children raised in a rural setting. He remembered clear expectations and rules in the family, with his father in a strong authoritarian role. He described significant corporal punishment that could well be described as abusive. He also described his father as a "heavy drinker." He noted that he had always said that he respected his father but that he realized that he really "hated him." Dave became significantly remorseful when he identified his behavior with his father's abuse, with concern that his children hated him.

It was not until over a year of treatment that Dave acknowledged his own victimization. During discussion of his sex history, specifically focusing on control and consensus issues, Dave became silent and tearful. He reported that an uncle had anally raped him at age 9 while on a camping trip. He had not reported the abuse earlier because he felt "ashamed" and felt that it "wouldn't do any good —it's not an excuse." He was upset at himself for crying, saying that he had not cried since that abuse incident. The next several sessions dealt with his vulnerability, "macho" defenses, homophobia, and the keeping of "the secret," including the corresponding issue of acceptance of authority. He also role-played confrontation with the uncle (who was deceased). He cried several times during these follow-up sessions. He also cried during one family apology session and received support from the rest of the family.

Dave concurrently attended a men's group. For the first several months in the group, Dave presented either of two behavior patterns—passive, silent, and marginally responsive, or hostile toward "the system." He verbally pursued any situation in which Child Protective Services, law enforcement, the county attorney, or probation department was "out to screw" the average family, whether it involved his family or another. Several weeks after he accepted responsibility in individual therapy, he still refused to acknowledge fully the same responsibility in the group because it was "none of their business." With some encouragement from the probation officer regarding his need to cooperate, Dave acknowledged in group his responsibility and reluctantly discussed the details of his offense. He retained some verbal hostility regarding "the system" for about 6 months although he actually continued to cooperate. By the time he acknowledged his own victimization in individual therapy he was trusting enough to also discuss it in the group at the next opportunity. He noted that the support of the group was an important "permission statement" for him. He did not cry in the group despite receiving specific permission to do so.

Empowerment

The empowerment process for this family focused on the following: (a) increased focus on marriage and family sessions and more frequent visitation, (b) improved socialization, and (c) leadership in self-help and group activities. More frequent marriage and family sessions began even while Dave was continuing his individual sessions. The major focus was on communication, problem solving, parenting skills, and appropriate individuation. Of these tasks, communication remained difficult if more than a triad (of any combination) was present. There seemed to be increased competition for attention and increased defensiveness. This continued as a moderate problem area through reunification. The other tasks were accomplished by using subsystems of the family. Each member of the family became stronger individually.

Marital therapy also included sexuality issues, specifically enrichment and consensus. With the assistance of a sexuality class, Dave and Carl were able to get more information regarding options for their sexual behavior. In particular, they reported pleasure from increased nongenital touching, including stroking and massage. Carol also became comfortable in initiating sexual contact, which both she and Dave saw as positive.

Once the apology sessions were under way, the visitation process began. The family began with supervised public visitation, then home visits of increasing duration. After some initial discomfort expressed by both Dave and Beth, the visits seemed to be an important bonding opportunity. The family reported that it was the first time they consistently had fun together. After gradual increases in time together, overnight visits were introduced, were carefully monitored, and were seen as successful.

The amount of socialization clearly increased for family members individually, for Dave and Carol as a couple, and for the family as a whole. The parents became good friends with a couple from their therapy group and, for the first time in their married life, engaged in social activities with this couple (movies, football games, etc.). The children, particularly Joan and Roger, enlarged their circle of friends both through the treatment program and at school. Both Beth's and Roger's school performance improved.

Within the self-help component of treatment, Carol, Dave, and Joan all assumed leadership positions. Carol was elected vice-president of the self-help group and acted as a sponsor for three women new to the program. Dave coordinated the group's support committee, assisting other families with home repairs, vehicle repairs, and a food and clothing bank. Joan was elected president of the children's component and organized several new activities.

Termination

After approximately 2 years in the treatment program, the family was reviewed for reunification. Dave underwent an independent reevaluation by court personnel, who saw him as significantly improved but still retaining some passive-aggressive features. Recommendations were made for continued treatment after reunification. The family met with the treatment team to clarify and review comfort levels, protection strategies, and relapse prevention.

The family committed to continued treatment. The treatment team approved their reunification, and the judge lifted restrictions on contact and visitation.

The family continued in treatment for 6 months after reunification. The children and Carol terminated their individual therapy after monitoring the effects of reunification. This monitoring was also the focus of Dave's individual sessions and conjoint family sessions. After commitments were made for ongoing contacts, Dave and the family were successfully terminated from treatment approximately 2½ years after the report of abuse.

Case Study B
C/Adu, I, L, R—Dependent Father

Presenting Problem

Kevin's 4th grade teacher referred him to the school counselor and nurse because of a dramatic change in behavior, including aggressive incidents toward peers almost daily and three incidents of enuresis during class. Kevin angrily denied any problems, saying that he was simply defending himself against other children and that the fighting and arguing was worse since his "accidents." A follow-up session with the counselor was approached in a more indirect, supportive manner. Kevin admitted that he was worried about his stepfather "losing his job again." Even though he liked having more time to spend with his stepfather, Kevin didn't like the fact that, in the past, it also meant that his stepfather would be "drinking beer and smoking pot." When asked what would be the worst thing about that, Kevin said that they would play "weird sex games." He said this included "touching and licking each other's weenie" and that he didn't like to do that because it felt funny. The counselor assured Kevin that he did not have to do that and that it was understandable that he didn't like it.

The school counselor reported the conversation to the school nurse, principal, and Child Protective Services. An investigative team of Child Protective Services and police personnel arrived later that day. After an introduction from the counselor, Kevin discussed the sexual contacts with the investigators. He reported three incidents of mutual penile stroking and fellatio during the previous 6 months. In each case, the stepfather initiated contact "when he was pretty drunk." All three incidents happened while his mother was at work. There was apparently no ejaculation or attempt at anal penetration. Kevin had been told that it would be "our secret," but his stepfather exerted no overt threats or force.

The investigators interviewed Kevin's mother, Karen, and stepfather, Danny, at home. Danny admitted to two incidents as alleged by Kevin but didn't remember a third. He stated that he felt ashamed and worthless and that he had been depressed and drinking excessively, having lost 3 jobs in the last year. Karen was extremely angry, initially wanting him arrested but then wanting him "locked up in the hospital." She indicated that he had talked about suicide on several occasions and that she didn't want him to do that. He acknowledged past and current suicidal ideation. He was taken into custody and placed in the mental health unit of the county jail on a suicide watch. Kevin was returned home.

Descriptive Information

Danny, age 28, was unemployed at the time of the arrest, having worked as a dishwasher, short-order cook, and delivery driver; Karen, age 30, was employed as a receptionist. Karen had one child, Kevin, age 9, from a previous relationship. This was the first marriage for both. They had been married for 2 years after having lived together for 3 years. They both had lived in this community since they were children. Both had completed high school. Karen had been employed at three different clerk and receptionist jobs since graduation, leaving one because of her pregnancy. Danny had not held any job for more than a year and estimated that he had had 15–20 jobs. He described himself as a "slow learner" and that he typically got fired for "making stupid mistakes," although recently he was fired from two jobs for smoking marijuana on the job. He had no criminal history. Kevin was a 4th-grade student who had been receiving excellent grades until the last 6 months prior to the report. There have been no previous reports to Child Protective Services.

Danny and Karen were both of Hispanic background. This may have had a bearing on the employment difficulties and on the general sense of powerlessness. They did not report any outright discrimination but noted that it seemed to have been more difficult for them to be upwardly mobile. Danny also felt that the neighborhood environment, whether culturally or economically, played a role in the creation and maintenance of his substance use history.

Crisis Intervention

Danny was arraigned and released from jail in 5 days after two evaluations by the jail consulting psychiatrist. He moved into a trailer home. He was immediately assigned to a counselor and a sponsor from the self-help organization. He acknowledged his continuing depression, guilt, and shame but denied further suicidal ideation, saying, "getting caught was the best thing that ever happened to me." He agreed to a suicide contract and an abstinence agreement, saying that drinking and marijuana use were the cause of all his problems. (As a condition of release, he was also required to submit to urinalysis twice a week.) Although the counselor supported Danny' s decision to abstain, he also confronted Danny with his simplistic answer. Because Danny reported that he felt more dependent on daily marijuana use than on alcohol, he was also referred to Narcotics Anonymous and began attending daily groups. He was formally arrested and agreed to a plea bargain of a guilty plea to one count of attempted sexual conduct with a minor. He was sentenced to 7 years probation, 1 year in the county jail work release program, and mandatory abstinence from alcohol and other drugs. He began work as a short-order cook and began serving his jail sentence, with release time for work and therapy.

Karen was assigned to an individual counselor and crisis group. She remained angry with Danny but hoped that the report and arrest would "straighten him up." She expressed guilt that she frequently joined him in his marijuana use, although she denied any knowledge or suspicion of the pedosexual contact. She described the marital relationship as good except for Danny's "irresponsibility." She generally described their sexual relationship as "very exciting and active," but lately she had been concerned that their sexual activity depended on their use of marijuana as a relaxant. She expressed considerable concern about her choice of "losers" in relationships but did not express any intention of divorcing Danny. Although prior to this incident Karen had not seen her marijuana use as harmful, she agreed to voluntary abstinence. She seemed clearly supportive and protective of Kevin.

An individual counselor saw Kevin, with a focus on play therapy and expression of feelings. He verbally and nonverbally expressed anger toward Danny but hoped he would "get help." He was kept informed of the criminal justice process. He expressed hope that the family could get back together after Danny was "fixed" and was given support that he would be safe. Kevin had told his friends that Danny was "in trouble for drugs," therefore avoiding dealing with the sexual issue. Generally, he seemed to be able to take care of himself in a reasonable manner. He continued to see the sexual behavior as "weird" and was worried that Danny might have done something that hurt, although he denied any physical pain (or pleasure) from the contacts. After preparation, apology sessions were held with Kevin, Karen, and Danny, and the counselors involved. Danny tearfully apologized and accepted responsibility for the three incidents. He cried throughout the first apology session. He positively reinforced the report, saying that he was proud of Kevin. Kevin remained passive during the first two apology sessions, accepting and understanding Danny's verbalizations but not showing any affective response. He quickly agreed with the counselors' suggestions that he was still afraid. Both parents spontaneously supported his fear as being understandable. By the third apology session, he initiated hugging Danny but still remained affectively passive.

Just as the decision to allow family visitation at the jail was being considered, Danny tested positive for marijuana use in a routine screen. A subsequent search revealed two marijuana joints in his locker. His work release and visitation privileges were cancelled for 90 days, and counseling sessions were held at the jail. At the end of the 90 days, another apology session was held so that the family could deal with this setback. Both Kevin and Karen expressed their anger at Danny.

Ongoing Treatment

Danny was seen in individual, group, marital, and family sessions as well as Narcotics Anonymous. Individual sessions focused on responsibility issues (general, drug-related, and sexual), positive control, and self-esteem. Working diagnoses were dysthymia and dependent personality disorder.

A review of Danny's history showed that he was the youngest of three children from an intact family. He remembered his childhood as being "very normal" with no major problems. He denied abuse. He reported moderate alcohol use by his father. He described consistent problems in school, having been retained in one elementary grade and then dropping out of high school in the 9th grade. He reported starting to use marijuana at that time, quickly becoming a regular user. He started drinking beer at age 18 but continued to prefer marijuana. He denied other drug use.

Danny described his sexual history as "frustrating" prior to his marriage. He reported consistent masturbation and two or three heterosexual contacts. Further exploration of the masturbation patterns yielded a sense of addiction, at least during his early adulthood. Danny reported that he would sometimes masturbate five times a day and that he frequently experienced penile irritation. He denied homosexual contacts. He remembered severe self-esteem problems related to his inability to attract or maintain sexual partners. He connected this with a significant fear of loss of his relationship with Karen, with whom he has had a "wonderful" sexual relationship.

Treatment strategies of supportive confrontation focused on issues of self-control, responsibility, and personal power. Control was improved with consistent monitoring for further drug use and through the 12-step Narcotics Anonymous program. General control was improved, with assumption of control over progressively more complex decisions. Power and responsibility were likewise increased, with positive emphasis on his job. Assertiveness skills were addressed. The incarceration in the county jail seemed to add a sense of structure to Danny's life that he had previously lacked. Although he reported "hating" his time there, he had functioned on a more consistent basis and seemed to have improved motivation.

Marital dyad sessions focused on power sharing. This became particularly important as Karen became stronger and more assertive regarding her needs. Communication was initially very basic, with considerable emphasis on affective awareness. Dynamics of dependency and codependency on each other and marijuana received special emphasis. The sexual relationship was viewed both for its strengths as well as its contribution to the dependency problems.

Parenting issues and skills were addressed in both marital and family sessions. Kevin seemed to engage in frequent power struggles with both parents, testing limits particularly regarding bedtime and responsibilities (chores). By eventually handling these struggles, both parents were able to improve their self-esteem and Kevin seemed more secure.

Danny's group provided important supportive confrontation. Group members, who identified with each other, consistently addressed responsibility issues. Danny's drug issues seemed to be unique to the group, but other members seemed to translate the issues to their own dependency problems. Danny participated more in group but remained somewhat passive.

Karen was seen in individual, marital, family, and group sessions. Individual sessions focused on her dependency issues and ways for her to feel more powerful and in control of her own life. Decision-making skills were emphasized. Karen's history showed several areas of strength—positive school history and apparently normal family background and skills in dealing with people. As she had indicated earlier, however, she did not feel confident in her relationships with men. She had engaged in several relationships beginning in high school with similar results—dating would lead to a sexual relationship and then the relationship would end. This series of relationships also resulted in conflict with the values of her extended family, reducing the sense of support from them and increasing her sense of guilt. She had felt used and dissatisfied until she began dating Danny. Because Danny seemed less demanding, she felt more comfortable, feeling that they could "take care of each other." She initially saw their mutual use of marijuana as a bond, preferring it to the possibility of Danny going off on his own to drink or smoke (which he had, in fact, also been doing).

After several months in treatment, Karen admitted that she had not felt as satisfied with the sexual relationship as she had originally stated. Although she appreciated Danny's affection and his finding her attractive, she saw the contacts as increasingly repetitious and dependent on the marijuana for arousal. Danny consistently seemed to demand fellatio as his means of satisfaction, with decreasing concern for her needs. As noted, this became a major focus in the marital sessions.

Group sessions seemed to be particularly helpful for Karen. She gained support from identifying with the other group members and improved her self-esteem through comments from the group about her strengths, attractiveness, and competence. She became a quiet leader of a small subgroup of Hispanic women in the group, seeing this as a way of reducing her inner conflict about alienating her extended family. The group also became a resource for parenting issues.

Kevin was seen in individual and family sessions. He participated briefly in a play therapy group but was seen as too mature for the young children's group. At that time, there were not enough male victims to form a separate group. Later in treatment, he became a helper in the young children's playgroup.

Individual sessions for Kevin focused on his feeling of being "left out" of the family and his attempts to gain power in order to become more like the adults in the family. He was encouraged to take appropriate responsibility in the family and was praised for his school performance. He also began an after-school sports program for the first time.

Empowerment

The empowerment process focused on family communication and activities, particularly those with other families. After Danny's release from jail, family visits were scheduled with increasing duration. The visits decreased Kevin's feelings of isolation within the family because he was given an active voice in planning the activity of a particular visit. The activity focus also countered Danny's passivity and supported each of the family members' decision-making skills. Karen in particular was able to establish a network of friends within the treatment program, and the family as a group became more involved with church-related activities. They had been marginally involved with church early in their marriage but had not been involved at all with the related social activities. They felt comfortable with large group activities (dinners, volleyball) and maintained contact with two of the other families between activities.

Partially because of the setback in treatment after Danny's marijuana use and partially because of the treatment team's concern about possible relapse, the family remained in the treatment process longer than most families. Although this engendered some frustration, the family also became better able to advocate for itself and, yet, accept the limits imposed by society. Danny was able to speak assertively, but with control, with members of the treatment team.

Termination

Almost 3 years after the report, the treatment team approved reunification for the family. The family continued in treatment as a unit for 4 months after that. Danny was mandated to continue attendance at Narcotics Anonymous and required to submit to random urinalyses for the duration of his probation.

Approximately 1 year after termination, Karen and Danny returned for four sessions of marital therapy to deal with his termination from employment. These sessions focused on his self-esteem and her concerns about Danny's repeating old patterns. These issues seemed to have been resolved, Danny obtained new employment, and there did not seem to be any new concerns.

Case Study C
Ado/Adu, I, L, R—Pseudoadult Child

Presenting Problem

Marianne, age 17, requested a pregnancy test from her family physician, fearing that she was pregnant as a result of sexual intercourse with her father. She disclosed one incident of penile-vaginal penetration with ejaculation and multiple incidents of genital stroking, fellatio, and cunnilingus. The pregnancy test was negative. After discussion with Marianne, the physician reported the information to Child Protective Services.

Marianne disclosed the same information to the investigators, saying that she and her father had been "having an affair" for the last 6 to 7 months that included progressively more overt sexual behavior, almost on a daily basis. She guessed that there were at least 20 incidents of cunnilingus. She confirmed only one coital contact, occurring 3 weeks before the report. She denied any violence or threats; saying that she was willing to do "the other things" even though she didn't like it, but that she was afraid of getting pregnant or contracting AIDS if he continued to "make love to me." She reported that she had refused a subsequent advance by the father and he had not approached her for the 2 weeks prior to the report. She said that she didn't want to get him in trouble if he would stop.

Because there was no mother in the home, Marianne and her younger brother, James (age 12), were placed in the home of their paternal grandparents after it was determined that this would be a safe environment. The investigators interviewed the father, Tom, who admitted the contacts and said that he was "waiting for something to happen after I went too far." Tom was arrested and released to his own custody after agreeing to have no contact with the children or with his parents and not to visit their home.

Descriptive Information

Tom, age 36, was a landscape foreman, having worked with this company for approximately 7 years. He had been a single parent since his wife, Mary, left the family 10 years before. None of the family had had contact with Mary since that time, and they presumed that she was living in another state. Both Tom and Marianne described Mary as "nice but flaky" and stressed-out by the demands of parenting. Tom reported no significant relationships since Mary left because he "didn't have time" and "didn't feel comfortable" around women.

Marianne, age 17, was a junior in high school. She reported average grades but limited extracurricular activity because she has always "taken care of" her brother and father. This included cooking, housecleaning, and most of the laundry. She remembered "watching" her brother essentially since her mother left. She took over most of the cooking at age 11. She denied any particular relationship with a boyfriend but indicated that she had lots of friends at school.

James, age 12, was a 5th-grade student who had been retained in first grade. He received fair to poor grades but was described by his teachers as a "hard worker." He denied any knowledge of the sexual contact between his father and sister. He also denied any contact between himself and his father.

The family all described themselves as "close" and used to working "as a team." They reported frequent contact with the father's parents and with the father's sister and her family, who also live in the community.

Crisis Intervention

Child Protective Services filed a dependency petition and was granted legal custody of Marianne and James, physical custody remaining with the grandparents. All parties agreed to a plan for foster placement with the aunt and uncle after their home was reviewed and licensed as a foster home.

After learning of the possible prison sentence that her father faced, Marianne recanted her story, saying that she had been angry at her father and that she had really "had sex" with a boyfriend, whom she refused to identify. Because of this recantation, the lack of physical evidence, and inadmissibility of the father's "confession" because of civil rights procedural errors, the county attorney dismissed the criminal charges against Tom. The dependency, however, continued in force, including the "no-contact" provisions.

Tom voluntarily agreed to treatment, regardless of the dismissal, with the hopes of reuniting the family. He was assigned an individual counselor but declined group treatment because he feared he might incriminate himself. He was fully cooperative with the individual counselor and quickly developed a trusting relationship. Crisis issues included suicide prevention and focus on regaining control over his life. Initially extremely guilty and depressed over the loss of his children, he came to see the advantages of having opportunity to "regroup" and build a new relationship once the charges were dismissed. Because he did not have a spouse or significant other, a crisis support team was established by scheduling counseling twice a week and involving two of his work colleagues. During the "no-contact" period, his counselor maintained contact with the children's counselor in order to reassure Tom of their progress.

Marianne was assigned to an individual counselor and support group. She refused to talk directly about her report on the allegations against her father but agreed to "listen." In both settings, she received support for both the report and the recantation, with messages that each was a reasonable way of taking care of herself. She was given permission to discuss more general issues, including her feelings about being placed in the pseudoadult role and related issues of her loss of childhood. She responded positively to this permission and actively participated in both modalities.

James was assigned to the same counselor as Marianne. He indicated that he believed Marianne's initial report but that he still wanted the family to "get help" and get back together. He seemed to make a good adjustment to living with the grandparents, who he felt were also supportive of reuniting the original family. He reluctantly expressed anger toward his father. He did "not exactly" see Marianne as being in a maternal role but did agree that he was dependent on her.

Ongoing Treatment

Tom continued in individual treatment. Goals included a more balanced, controlled approach to parenting and caring for himself, including increased socialization and active, positive planning and decision making. Redirection of sexual outlets was also clearly a major goal.

Tom's history indicated that he was the younger of two children and that he was in close contact with his family of origin. He reported a lifelong history of obesity to a greater or lesser degree and related peer problems (name-calling and rejection). He also reported a negative body image and very poor self-esteem, leading to suicidal ideation during adolescence. He had not made any suicidal gestures and denied further ideation. He saw his wife, Mary, as somebody who "felt sorry for me" and "liked me because I was loyal and dependable, like a puppy dog." He described the marriage as good for a few years with a sexual relationship that felt good for Tom but never seemed to satisfy Mary completely. He felt that the birth of James was a last effort to save the marriage and expressed surprise that Mary left him to care for the children. He described the children as the "only thing I've got" and saw the relationship with Marianne as "always affectionate." He acknowledged his responsibility for the sexual contact as well as the more general responsibility for placing her in the pseudoadult role. His sex history had been limited to masturbation and occasional (once or twice a year) visits to prostitutes since his divorce. He denied sexual arousal to children and reported fantasies of women finding him attractive. At the time of treatment, he was moderately overweight but had good muscle tone. Working diagnoses were dependent personality disorder and major recurrent depression.

Treatment strategies included reinforcing positive decision making and creation of options rather than adhering to his previously rigid style. Tom was encouraged to pursue socialization with women, which resulted in several "dates" and dramatically improved his self-image. He was invited to create controlled fantasies regarding some of these women.

Apology sessions were held initially with Marianne and later with both Marianne and James. Tom tearfully apologized to both children and accepted responsibility for both general and sex-specific issues. Marianne confronted him with feelings of anger, focusing on the sense of the loss of her childhood.

Marianne's individual and group sessions were accelerated because of the limited time frame of the dependency petition. She was able to identify feelings of anger and ambivalence and, most clearly, loss of both her mother and her own childhood. She became able to define appropriate roles and tasks for herself and redefine her relationship with James as a result of the placement with the grandparents and, later, with the aunt and uncle. She developed a close relationship with a boy at school and began dating.

Family visits began early in the treatment process, shortly after the apology sessions. Initially, visits were supervised by the aunt but shifted to unsupervised 2 months before Marianne's 18th birthday. Marianne reported positive feelings of comfort during the visits, noting that both she and her father had changed. These visits and family counseling sessions focused on planning appropriate roles in the family and setting up support systems (friends and extended family) and protection mechanisms (e.g., locks on bedroom and bathroom doors, family discussions).

Termination

The dependency status of both children was dropped on Marianne's 18th birthday. With the lifting of restrictions, the family reunited after an accelerated treatment program of 7 months. The family voluntarily continued family treatment sessions for 3 months and then terminated.

A 1-year follow-up indicated that Marianne was preparing to be married in the near future and would be leaving the state with her new husband. Tom acknowledged mixed feelings about the marriage but thought, overall, that it would be good. He reported continued dating but "nothing serious" and an occasional sexual contact with one of these dates. James was continuing to struggle in school. An invitation to return to counseling was refused.

Case Study D
C/Adu, E, L, P—Pedophile

Presenting Problem

Norman, age 26, was referred by a clergyman after an allegation of sexual conduct with a 4-year-old child had been investigated and deemed unsubstantiated. Norman had expressed concerns regarding his sexuality to the clergyman, who referred him for specialized treatment.

At his initial appointment, Norman seemed to be extremely anxious and tearfully described his problem by saying, "I love children. I *really* love children." He reported that he was extremely frightened about the investigation and the possibility of going to prison. Without specifically acknowledging his responsibility for the pedosexual contact, he described himself as a "sick man" who desperately needed help.

Descriptive Information

Norman was a clerk-typist employed in a large real estate business. At the time of the referral, he lived with his mother because of financial difficulties but had lived on his own during two periods of his life for as long as 2 years. He was a high school graduate with 1 year of community college credit. He had been employed by three different firms since high school graduation; he left the two previous firms because he felt like he "wasn't getting anywhere" and reported similar dissatisfaction with his current job. He described himself as a "hermit" who only wanted to be involved in activities that include children.

Crisis Intervention

The major focus of the crisis phase was suicide prevention. In the initial session, Norman described himself as worthless and "the lowest of the low" and said that he had considered taking "an overdose of something" but hadn't acted on it. He refused a recommendation for voluntary hospitalization but agreed to a suicide contract and telephone contact between sessions. After discussions with Norman, the counselor also confirmed with his mother that she was available to him for support and that she would report any concerns or problems. Norman was willing to acknowledge to his mother only that he was depressed; he would not acknowledge any of the sexual issues.

Ongoing Treatment

Norman remained in treatment for 2 years, with goals of redirecting his sexual preference and generally reducing his dependence on children. It became apparent that Norman had actually engaged in sexual contact on one occasion, that being an incident of active genital touch of the aforementioned 4-year-old boy. He had had a long-term obsession with children with sexual arousal to young (prepubertal) boys. He described, in a rather childlike manner, his desire to play with children, teach them, and hug and kiss them, most of the time without sexual arousal. He described himself as a "Pied Piper" in that children seemed spontaneously at ease and playful with him. He would frequently take friends' children to the park, zoo, or other activities and was regarded as "the best baby sitter of all time."

Norman was an only child, having been reared by his mother after an early divorce. He did not remember any contact with his father. He described himself as a "sissy" in that he was frequently picked on at school for his somewhat meek behavior and his eyeglasses. He had seen himself as an awkward and clumsy child. Although he denied any pedosexual contact with an adult, he remembered several incidents of sex play with other boys, including mutual genital stroking and fellatio. Between this and a lack of interest in girls in high school, he had assumed he was gay but did not act on that belief. After high school graduation, he began to date girls and was surprised to find himself enjoying the experience and becoming aroused, although there was no overt sexual behavior. He also had one same-sex experience, mutual fellatio, which he found moderately arousing. Based on information that he had read, he concluded that he was bisexual but really did not find sexual contact with either men or women consistently arousing.

While in high school, Norman began babysitting. He enjoyed this and received a lot of positive comments. He remembered being curious and then, later, aroused by catching glimpses of young (3- to 5-year-old) children's genitals and set up situations where he assisted them in changing or going to the bathroom. Children younger than 5 did not seem aware of his behavior. He would indirectly contact the genitals by tickling, hugging, or wrestling. Within the last year before this referral, he began taking pictures of children in bathing suits, underwear, or nude. He denied exposing himself or having direct genital contact except for the one reported incident.

During the first 6 months of treatment, Norman refrained from any contact with children. He redirected his attention toward career concerns and toward exploring relationships with adult women. He dated two women who had young children and quickly shifted his attention to the children, which initially made him even more attractive to the women but eventually turned them off. He did not engage in sexual contact with the women. Norman interpreted these relationships as rejecting. For the duration of treatment, he made some initiatives toward women but generally felt inept, unable to converse, and uncomfortable. He had no social friendship relationships with adult men.

Norman had some success with fantasy redirection. He was able to masturbate to fantasy themes involving women and denied similar behavior involving children. He reported being more aware about his sexual orientation as being heterosexual.

Norman reported continued contact with children in supervised or controlled situations and expressed pleasure over his nonsexual contact with children. He felt most positive about his ability to relate to children and keep it nonsexual, giving him a feeling of "the best of both worlds." At one point he became rather depressed when he had not had contact with children for a week. The counselor confronted the obsessive nature of the behavior more frequently, which sometimes increased his guilt. When his contacts with children became less supervised and he reinitiated babysitting activities, he was confronted even more strongly and encouraged to alter his behavior.

Approximately 2 years after the initial referral, a 9-year-old neighbor boy reported that Norman had licked his penis while he was sleeping at Norman's house. Norman was arrested while holding a knife to his throat and was placed in custody at the mental health unit of the county jail. A police search revealed several photographs of children. He was convicted of sexual conduct with a minor and multiple counts of sexual exploitation (due to the photographs) and is currently serving a 38-year sentence.

Case Study E
C/Adu, E, L, P—Pedophile

Presenting Problem

Frank, age 52, was referred for evaluation by his defense attorney. Frank had been charged with molestation (specifically, genital touching) of a 5-year-old friend of his granddaughter. The evaluation was requested to substantiate this contact as an isolated incident and rule out pedophilia, which would affect the sentencing decision.

Evaluation Summary

Frank presented as an unusually well-dressed and well-groomed individual. He was retired from the military and at the time of the referral had a senior management position in a computer company. He described the allegations against him and accepted the responsibility for his behavior, tearfully stating that it was a "stupid, stupid mistake" and that he had no idea why it happened. He reported that he has been asking himself "Why?" and could only think of the great stress he had been under since his recent divorce and business problems. He specifically denied any other pedosexual contacts or extraordinary interest in children.

Frank's psychosocial history did not yield any significant indicators of concern except for possible alcohol misuse. His sex history, likewise, seemed to indicate typical psychosexual development and arousal patterns. He reported peer contacts during adulthood with no preferred arousal to younger women. There did not seem to be any interest in sexual power and control issues. Sexual orientation had always been heterosexual; he was mildly homophobic.

Psychological testing showed above average intelligence, strong memory and attention, and a valid, normal Minnesota Multiphasic Personality Inventory profile. Thematic Apperception Test and Incomplete Sentences responses were descriptive and somewhat concrete but seen to be within normal limits.

Psychophysiological assessment using the plethysmograph detected consistent penile arousal to pictures of young children. When confronted with the graphic evidence, Frank admitted that he had been aroused by child pornography for "many years," particularly by photographs of nude prepubertal children. He denied other direct pedosexual contacts because of fear of incrimination.

He acknowledged that he did have a "small collection" of pictures and videotapes that he had destroyed after this recent report. He refused to answer whether he had taken any of these pictures.

On the basis of the persistence of the arousal pattern and the strong probability of other pedosexual contacts in his history, Frank was classified as a pedophile in the report submitted to the court. Because of his lack of previous convictions and exemplary military and employment record, a plea bargain was accepted that resulted in "no contest" pleas to attempted molestation and sexual exploitation. At last contact, he was serving two concurrent 5-year sentences in the state prison.

Case Study F
C/Adu, I, H, R and Ado/Adu, I, H Ra—Adolescent Survivor

Presenting Problem

Cindy, age 16, was referred for counseling by the juvenile court after a second arrest for prostitution and possession of marijuana and cocaine. Previous treatment for substance abuse had apparently been only marginally effective. She has been a runaway for 2 years and her family had not been located. Sexual abuse has been suspected but Cindy has consistently denied it.

Crisis Intervention

Cindy was initially seen while still in the juvenile detention center. She was extremely hostile and resistant to counseling. She was granted her request for a female counselor. She minimized the referral problems by saying that she was not using drugs as much as she used to and that the prostitution should not be against the law because "nobody gets hurt" and "it's good money." She asserted that she had been supporting herself "real good" for the last 2 years by "having sex, which everybody agrees is fun."

To diffuse Cindy's resistance, the counselor allowed her to choose topics for the counseling. She chose to vent anger and hostility at "the system" for unfairly punishing her and, by the third session, began to talk about her anger and concern that a boyfriend had "dumped" her. This led to a more general discussion of problems with boys and men. In the 10th session, she was angrily stating that "all men fuck you over" when she started to cry for the first time. She sobbed that, "I really got fucked over!" She reported that her stepfather (mother's second husband) had physically abused her throughout her childhood, beating her with a belt on her bare buttocks on a weekly basis for anything she had done wrong. After he had "disciplined" her, she would have to remain nude from the waist down and bent over a chair so he could "make sure I wasn't really hurt." During one of these sessions at age 11, she peeked and noticed that he was masturbating. He invited her "for a closer look," and from that time until she was 13, replaced the weekly beating ritual by giving Cindy the "choice" of fellatio instead. Cindy finally reported this to her mother when he began forcing her to swallow his ejaculate. Mother "kicked him out of the house" but told Cindy not to tell anyone because she (mother) might get into trouble.

Continuing the history over a lengthy crisis session, Cindy reported that her mother began living with a "boyfriend" when she was 14. One evening when her mother was working the night shift, the boyfriend became drunk and woke Cindy. He threatened to beat her if she made a sound and proceeded to perform cunnilingus and then forcibly penetrate her (penile-vaginal and penile-anal). He slapped her once when she cried in pain. After he passed out, she gathered some possessions and ran away from home, spending the night in a riverbed. When she called home the next day, her mother was very angry and didn't believe her story, saying that Cindy wasn't "going to cost me another man." Her mother told her to return home immediately or "forget it." Cindy did not return home.

The crisis intervention shifted at that point to focus on Cindy's rage and lack of trust in men, with role-playing, visualization, and writing (the latter limited by Cindy's expressive language problems).

Treatment

Cindy was placed in a group foster home and was monitored for alcohol and other drug use. Individual sessions continued to focus on her rage as well as her guilt over her behavior. She felt that she had, in fact, chosen the fellatio over the physical punishment and should have instead "taken her punishment." It took several sessions before she was able to clearly see the stepfather's manipulation and sexual motivation. Likewise, for some time, she was convinced that she had done something to cause the rape because "why would two men want to do the same thing?" She dealt with similar issues in an adult survivors' group that she attended.

Six weeks after the placement in the group home, she was caught smoking marijuana. She was detained for 48 hours and placed in another group home. She again minimized the marijuana use but agreed to abstain. Treatment emphasis was shifted to focus on her own recovery regardless of the traumatic history. She seemed to stabilize and abide by the rules of the group home. School attendance became consistent. After 6 months, treatment issues were expanded to include relationships, self-esteem, rejection, and power issues. She continued to deny or minimize problems that did arise.

One year after the initial referral, Cindy ran away from the group home after being accused of sexual conduct with another girl in the home. Two years after that, there remains no evidence of her whereabouts.

Case Study G
C/Adu, E, L, P—Adult Survivor

Presenting Problem

Debra, age 28, self-referred with concerns about "confused feelings regarding sex." Sometimes she felt "turned on" with her boyfriend but at other times she felt repulsed, particularly when he engaged in cunnilingus in a similar manner as she had experienced during a pedosexual contact. She indicated that she had sexual contact between the ages of 5 to 7 with a neighbor who "was like another father." She had recently been reminded of this contact when she saw this man and saw her father cheerfully wave to him. This infuriated her. She denied other problems or concerns unrelated to these.

Descriptive Information

Debra was an assistant manager in a retail business. She was a graduate of a community college and has been employed for 6 years. She lived with her family in her childhood home although she spent as much time as possible in her boyfriend's home. She was the younger of two children; she had a brother 3 years older. Her parents were in their first marriage. She had been in her current relationship with her lover for 2 years. During the time, she described having had a very good sexual relationship and good intimate communication. She noted that her lover was supportive of her regarding the current issues.

Crisis Intervention

Debra described the history as she could remember it, although she reported that much of the details remained "fuzzy" because of the time lapse and because she had "tried to block it out." She remembers that her father never seemed to have time for her, so she spent a lot of time with a neighbor, John, and his daughter. During that time, roughly between the ages of 5 and 7, she remembers "games" that involved disrobing and, more clearly, genital stroking and cunnilingus. She does not remember other sexual acts although she assumes that they may have happened. She does not think there was any penetration. She remembers being uneasy and telling her parents, who did not believe her. They both emphasized that John was a friend who wouldn't hurt her and that she must have misunderstood a game or sign of affection. She insisted that they confront John and they invited him to the house for a discussion. He denied all the allegations with "smiling sincerity" and the parents believed him, although her mother did suggest not going to his house any more. Her father chastised Debra. For the rest of her childhood and adolescence she remembered being both angry and afraid. She had heard rumors that John had engaged in similar sexual games with his daughter and, later, a granddaughter and other children. Even though these were rumors, they certainly seemed to fit the pattern of a pedophile. She remembered confronting him at age 16 and asking him why he did it. He smiled and said, "Because I loved you." She continued to hate him but was able to avoid him for most of her adult life until the recent incident when she saw her father wave to him. She "blew up" at her father and, since then, has been preoccupied with anger and rage toward John, her father, and, to a lesser extent, her mother. She feels vulnerable, unsupported and unprotected by everyone except her lover.

Debra cried throughout the discussion of the history. She said she understood the rage but didn't understand her confusion. Most of the first two sessions were devoted to this history, positive support, and information that her reactions were, indeed, appropriate. In the third session, she agreed to a suggestion for anger work. An "empty chair" technique was used to encourage expression of anger. She quickly "confronted" John with her hurt and anger but seemed rather controlled in doing it. She did not respond to any suggestion of striking out at him or hurting him. When confronted with her rather mild reactions and reluctance to "let him have it" verbally or physically, she stopped talking and crying for several minutes and then sobbed uncontrollably when she said that she couldn't really hurt him because she had loved him. Later in that session, she acknowledged that it was the first time she had ever dealt with the ambivalence and with the double hurt that comes from being violated by someone one trusts and not being protected by someone who should have been a protector.

Ongoing Treatment

Continuing treatment focused on ways that she could feel safe and be in positive control both within her sexual relationship and within the family. Conjoint sessions were held with her lover to discuss ways that she could better express her needs for safety. Debra and her friend were able to develop new sexual and nonsexual (stroking) patterns to reinforce their mutual control over their own pleasuring. Eventually, they were able to desensitize the cunnilingus behavior through relaxation and gradual increase in the duration of the behavior from a few seconds to several minutes to the point where Debra reported again being orgasmic with that stimulation.

Regarding her family, Debra was able to ask for support regarding her current feelings rather than, again, introducing the debate over what had happened 20 years ago. Her mother was willing and able to be supportive and listened to Debra's feelings about the protection and vulnerability issues. Her father acknowledged her pain but refused to deal with it, insisting that she forget it and get on with her life. Presumably because of this position, her parents refused Debra's invitation to family sessions.

Debra benefited greatly from writing about her feelings and composing letters and poems to John and her parents and then, for the most part, destroying them. She also gained support from an adult survivors' group, receiving considerable validation for the feelings of rage, and ambivalence, and confusion.

During the 8-month treatment period, she earned a promotion at work and reported improved self-esteem, assertiveness, and sense of control over her life. She also moved in with her lover.

Termination

Individual counseling was terminated after approximately 8 months. Debra reported greatly improved control and only occasional outbursts of rage regarding John. She was encouraged to continue these outbursts in a safe setting. Debra continued her involvement with the adult survivors' group for 2 years, becoming a peer facilitator during the last year. She also developed two strong friendships with women in the group. A year after termination from the group, these friends reported that she continued to be doing well.

No substantive evidence was ever gathered against John. He has never been arrested or reported for sexual abuse. It should be noted that this lack of "proof" did not significantly hamper the treatment, and the accuracy of Debra's recollections was not an issue.

Case Study H
Ado/Adu, I, L, S—Female Offender

Presenting Problem

Richard, age 15, called the community information service to find out how his stepmother could be "forced into someplace to get help for her drug problem when she doesn't want to go." During the discussion, he talked about her heavy use of cocaine and alcohol and the "the final straw" was that she had approached him sexually. He specified that she had performed fellatio on him the night before. He was directed to call Child Protective Services.

Investigators interviewed Richard and his parents, Roger (age 48) and Allison (age 29) 2 days later. Allison admitted that she had been "stoned" for most of a 4-day period ending the night of the alleged offense. Roger had been out of town on business at the time. She remembered being in Richard's room and acknowledged that she "could have done it." She said that she had a "very serious problem" and accepted her husband's demand that she enter a treatment facility immediately. She was admitted to an inpatient chemical dependency program that day.

Descriptive Information

Roger was an insurance and financial planning consultant. His first marriage, to Richard's mother, ended in divorce 5 years ago when she left the state to "marry another man" after "years of arguments and hassles." He married Allison 2 years ago, describing her a "gorgeous young thing who wanted to be taken care of." He described their marriage as "amicable and pleasant" until she started drinking heavily 6 months ago. He hadn't been aware of her cocaine use until he recently noticed how much money was being spent out of her checking account. He noted that he worked long hours and spent quite a bit of time out of town on business.

Allison had not been married before. She had been working as a topless dancer for 2 years before marrying Roger and had not worked out of the home since then. She reported that she married him because he was a "kind man who could give me a way out of that life." She acknowledged a long history of polydrug use before she met Roger, which she had kept hidden from him.

Richard was an only child who was in the 10th grade of a private high school. He had had an excellent behavioral and academic record and was described as mature and responsible. He reported feeling good about his parents' divorce because of their arguments but missed his mother. He reported liking Allison but "not as a mother."

Crisis Intervention

Allison completed a 28-day detoxification and treatment program. She was seen as having both alcohol and cocaine dependence along with major depression and evidence of eating-disordered behavior at points of her life. During and after the inpatient treatment, she was also seen by a counselor to focus on sexuality issues.

Allison reported her history, focusing on her physical attractiveness in contrast to a perceived lack of affection and nurturance for most of her life. She remembered being entered in beauty contests and modeling from age 6 through adolescence. She also reported almost constant dieting throughout adolescence. She was the youngest of three children but always felt that her siblings, peers, and even parents were "jealous," and she never felt close to any of them. She described herself as having been "an obnoxious snob" during her young adult years. She dated little because "all the boys were just after sex." She later learned that she could "use sex and my looks to get what I want." During this same time, however, she also became depressed and began her polydrug use at age 18. She then reported a cycle of drug use, short-term relationships, depression, and employment instability. She became a topless dancer because it was "easy work and great money" but quickly used the money to develop a strong cocaine addiction, using alcohol as a way to "mellow" herself. After 6 months, she reported hating the dancing but felt like she had no alternative. She began to look for a man with whom she could change her lifestyle and found Roger, a business associate of her employer. She "straightened up" to make a positive impression and after 2 or 3 months of dating, married him. She continued a low-level use of cocaine surreptitiously throughout their marriage. She felt that Roger gave her more caring and nurturing than she had ever felt and reported feeling "very satisfied" with a warm and intimate sexual relationship. She increased her use of cocaine as "part of the nurturing feeling—that I really deserved to feel good" but acknowledged that it quickly got out of control.

During crisis intervention, after discharge from the substance abuse facility, Allison was seen in individual counseling, marital dyads, triad apology sessions, and Cocaine Anonymous. During individual sessions, she accepted responsibility for the pedosexual contact, saying that she did, in fact, remember going into Richard's room "to talk" but after a few minutes pulled back the sheets and began licking and stroking his penis until he told her to stop. She did not remember any feelings at the time, whether he was aroused, or what happened afterwards. She repeated the same details to Roger in a marital session and Richard in a triad apology session, clearly accepting the responsibility for the sexual contact as well as the drug use. Both Roger and Richard expressed their support and committed to treatment.

Roger was seen individually and in the marital dyads. He reported feeling "disgusted and ashamed" about the incident but also concerned about Allison's drug use. After talking with Richard, Roger thought Richard had done the right thing and thought he "was not traumatized" and was continuing to "handle it well." He spoke with considerable pride about his son's achievements and maturity, after which he tearfully expressed shame that he had not taken any action sooner regarding Allison's drug dependence. In marital sessions, he provided support for Allison and acknowledged his share of the responsibility for treating her "as a beautiful possession" rather than a partner.

Richard was seen individually and in the apology sessions. He declined the invitation for group counseling. Richard remembered being "shocked" by the sexual incident and denied arousal at that time or since. He remembered being irritated by Allison's presence in his room and frustrated by her "drinking and drugs which I was trying to keep secret from Dad so his feelings wouldn't get hurt." He was tolerating her that night because she said she wanted to "make friends" and then suddenly pulled back the sheets and said "this will make you feel good" and began licking his penis. He told her to stop and she left the room without saying anything else. He remembered not being able to sleep that night and "checking" on Allison twice to find her passed out on her bed. He expressed anger and resentment over "the way she takes advantage of my Dad" but said that he did not want them to divorce as long as "my Dad wants to stay with her." He reported no trauma or adjustment problems as a result of the contact and indicated his support of Allison "as long as she never does drugs again."

Allison was charged with attempted sexual conduct with a minor (under 18, but over 15) and received a plea-bargain sentence of 3 years probation with mandated treatment for the sexual issues as well as chemical dependency. She was ordered to abstain from all drug use, including alcohol. She was permitted to continue to live in the family home.

Ongoing Treatment

Allison's individual treatment focused on her responsibility for self-control and appropriate expression of needs and feelings. She gained insight into her needs for nurturance and acceptance as a whole person and began setting priorities on ways that she could appropriately take care of herself (especially, the "lost child" within her). Individual treatment paralleled her work in the 12-step program of Cocaine Anonymous. She was specifically encouraged to be aware of, and express, her own affective and sexual needs rather than relying on "pleasing behaviors." She reported particular success with an increase to nonsexual touching and stroking, leading to more relaxed sexual contacts and "more orgasms than I've ever had." As confirmed by random testing, she remained drug-free throughout treatment.

Marital sessions focused on these same issues along with a variety of ways that power, communication, and responsibility could be shared more equally. Allison became more involved in Roger's business and learned basic computer skills to assist both in his business and in household financial management. Roger, in turn, reduced his workload and spent more time with Allison on business and family matters. He, too, reported a great improvement in their sexual relationship.

Family sessions replaced the individual sessions for Roger and Richard. Expanding on the marital sessions, responsibility and control issues were addressed, with some shifting of tasks and expectations. Allison expressed her desire to be in more of a "mother role" for Richard, and they agreed on some areas where she could provide support without trying to "be friends."

Termination

Allison and the family were successfully terminated from treatment, with the permission of the probation department, after 19 months.

Her risk of recidivism regarding the sexual contact was seen as minimal and Richard, age 17 by then, was seen as clearly able to protect himself. Her risk of relapse into the chemical dependency was seen as higher and she was mandated to continue Cocaine Anonymous and random testing for the remainder of her probation. She obtained a part-time job working for the facility where she had been treated as an outreach coordinator.

Two years after termination, follow-up indicated that Richard was attending college away from home and that the marital relationship continued "with a few problems." Allison was employed full-time at the treatment facility. She reported remaining drug-free.

Case Study I
C/Adu, I, H, Unknown—Isolated Treatment of Victim/Youthful Offender

Adapted from Rencken, R. (1996). Body violation: Physical and sexual abuse. In D. Capuzzi & D. Gross (Eds.), *Youth at risk* (2nd ed., pp. 59–80). Alexandria, VA: American Counseling Association.

Presenting Problem

Jason was a 9-year-old who was voluntarily turned over to Child Protective Services by his father and stepmother on grounds that he was dangerous to his younger sisters (ages 5 and 2) because of physical attacks, one alleged attempt at setting fire to the 5-year-old's bed, and fondling and attempting oral sex with both younger sisters. The father and stepmother had previously relinquished custody of Jason's 11-year-old sister after she had apparently initiated sexual contact with him, the 5-year-old, and at least two children in a daycare center. The father and stepmother had reluctantly assumed custody of the three oldest children about 18 months previously after the children were removed from the mother's custody in another state. In that investigation, it was alleged that the mother had performed mutual oral and manual sex with Jason and his older sister and forced these two children to perform oral sex and coitus with each other in front of a group of adults. She would severely spank Jason (more intensely than the others) and afterwards "make up" for the spanking by performing fellatio on him. The mother was charged with sexual abuse but fled the state to avoid prosecution.

The father and stepmother acknowledged increasingly severe physical punishment of Jason but denied sexual abuse. The children corroborated this. The parents refused participation in treatment and eventually permanently relinquished custody of all three children to the state.

Jason was placed in foster care, and individual therapy was initiated. He was in five foster placements in 4 months because of his behavior, which included fondling younger children, urinating and defecating in corners, and stealing. Individual therapy included attempts at appropriate expression of feelings (verbal and through art and play), trust building, and limit setting. The individual therapist also provided supportive counseling to the foster parents. Jason was placed in a self-contained class for the seriously emotionally disabled.

Ongoing Treatment

Jason was finally stabilized in a foster home after the multiple changes. Two years after the natural father relinquished custody, the parental rights were severed and the foster parents adopted him.

Individual therapy continued to focus on appropriate self-control and dealing with limits, as well as positive expression of feelings and needs. He also was given medication (Imipramine, 25 mg per day), which seemed to have a positive effect on his ability to attend and remain on task. His play in and out of therapy sessions became more focused; for example, he completed jigsaw puzzles for the first time. Although he sometimes expressed "missing" his sisters, he focused more on the foster family and was particularly enthusiastic about family activities. He seemed to remember little about events that happened with his mother, but frequently described his father and stepmother as "mean" because they "hit us all the time." He used the foam bat to hit the adult doll figures that he had labeled as "them." He also built elaborate castles of blocks with the dolls of the foster family inside and "them" outside. Gradually, he began building the castles without "them" and then moved to using the doll house for family play. He made great progress in his issues of anxiety and rejection and seemed to bond with the foster parents.

The foster parents were seen regularly and also completed a parenting skills course in a community program. They received support and encouragement along with specific problem-solving techniques. They reported that the aggressive and sexual behavior continued for several months but then subsided, although Jason still tested limits and got into more power struggles than their other (natural) child. They also had consistent problems with lies, although that also decreased in frequency.

Jason remained in the self-contained Emotionally Disturbed placement for 3 years, with increased mainstreaming during the last year. During this time, he improved from pre-readiness skills to 3rd-grade level achievement (still 3 years behind age peers). His impulse control and attention improved dramatically.

Sexual issues were specifically addressed through the use of age-appropriate sex education media jointly used by counselor and foster parents. He role-played protection skills, with the situation also reversed so he could experience how it "must feel" when he touched other children. Anatomically correct dolls seemed to be helpful in dealing with these issues.

Termination

Individual and family treatment continued for 1 year after the adoption (3 years after referral), with a focus on communication, control, and self-esteem issues. Behavioral issues remained a concern but the parents seemed to deal with these adequately and appropriately. There were no indications of sexual acting-out. Follow-up 1 year after termination indicated continued good adjustment and functioning.

Case Study J
No Contact, E, P—Hebephilia; Brief Intervention

Presenting Problem

Ted, age 40, called at the urging of his girlfriend to explore whether he was a "nonoffending pedophile," apparently because he was aroused by pubescent girls with early breast development and recently admitted that to his girlfriend, who assumed that meant that he was a pedophile. Both she and Ted were confused about how he could be aroused by these girls and also attracted to her (or other adults). He insisted that he had never taken any action on these arousal patterns and had not really wanted to. The girlfriend was also concerned about the welfare of her 3-year-old granddaughter and risk of offense.

Crisis Intervention

Ted was seen the next day after his call. He was in extreme distress over the possibility of losing this relationship, although he denied unusual depression or suicidal ideation. He described a nonexclusive arousal to pubescent girls since he was in high school, where he was also attracted to small-breasted girls. He was a writer and therefore worked by himself most of the time. He had had a few relationships in his adult years but mostly had lived by himself until this current relationship. He described most of his sexual history as centered around masturbation to these pubescent fantasy themes. He denied extensive use of pornography, although he noted that there are many "normal" sources of these girls from movies to magazines. He described a very positive sexual relationship with his current girlfriend, although he had difficulty early in the relationship with literally sleeping together, because he was not used to sharing a bed. He denied any interest or arousal in prepubescent children, including unusual general interest. He denied any history of physical or sexual abuse.

In the first two sessions, this history was taken and Ted was informed of the probability that he was a hebephile, rather than a pedophile. He was also given reassurance that his control over his behavior up to this point had been an optimistic factor in treatment and risk reduction. He acknowledged some obsessive behaviors in the past, including binge alcohol consumption, which he had under control for the last year. He had shown high motivation and was convinced that the relationship would be the key factor in keeping his arousal under control. He was cautioned about taking too large of a leap in addressing the problem and urged to focus on one day at a time.

The girlfriend was seen individually. Although Susan was 48 years old, somewhat older than Ted, she was quite youthful in appearance, with a petite, almost adolescent figure. She was informed that Ted did, indeed, have a compulsive arousal pattern of long duration but that it was unlikely that he would be attracted to young children. She was discouraged from thinking that he would be able to change these patterns easily but that he had done an acceptable job of keeping the pattern under control. She acknowledged that she was jealous over his attraction to younger girls and wanted to have his full attention.

The couple was seen conjointly to set up agreements regarding communication and sexual relationships, including discussion of feelings and emphasis on nonsexual touch, intimate contact, and verbal discussion of needs. They also agreed to a response code, with Ted saying that he "had a good day," which would indicate that he was not aroused by any pubescent girl. This prevented her from checking into his arousal patterns everyday, setting up more hostility in the relationship.

In the fourth session, Ted was given techniques for helping to stop the compulsive patterns, including snapping a rubber band on his wrist and verbally saying "NO!" in order to help shift the pattern and bring it into his awareness.

Ongoing Treatment

Ted was seen in five monthly sessions, with the goal of monitoring the arousal patterns and behaviors and keeping the awareness of these patterns in the forefront. He acknowledged that he was still attracted to the pubescent body type but that he had not fantasized about any girls or had any contact with them. He reported that his relationship with Susan was consistently improving and that he was feeling very positive about that.

Termination

This brief intervention focused on gaining control over arousal patterns that are, like it or not, closer to that of most adults than is pedophilia. The presence of these patterns will probably continue for some time, but it is doubtful that long-term treatment would be more effective. Both Ted and Susan agreed to resume treatment if any new problems arose, and follow-up at 6 months time confirmed that their relationship was continually improving.

Case Study K
C/Adu, I, L, R,—Adult Survivor; Brief Intervention

Presenting Problem

Rosemary, age 52, was referred by her primary physician to a counselor who was seen as an "expert" in sexual abuse issues. She reported multiple problems, including financial concerns, relationship problems, and increasing depression. She had reinitiated antidepressant medication, but it was too early to see results from this. She reported that she had been sexually abused by her father as a young child. She had been in weekly therapy for 9 years in another city.

She was significantly late to her first three sessions and demanded longer sessions than usual because she was such an unusually needy client. She sobbed incoherently for most of each session, repeating her history at every opportunity and tangentially discussing her recent financial problems (over which she clearly had lost control). She gave multiple indications of a Borderline Personality Disorder.

Ongoing Treatment

After the initial three sessions, the counselor informed Rosemary that she would be seen no more frequently than once a month and that she could not call unless there were a true emergency and, in that case, would need to go to a hospital emergency room. After initial reluctance to this plan, pleading that she needed several sessions a week, she agreed to this plan as an alternative to the extensive therapy she had in the past.

After six of these monthly sessions, she reported continued problems but these were normalized, as opposed to being in any way related to her history of sexual abuse. Although the counselor had some suspicion of falsely recovered memories, the validity of the allegations was not confronted; instead, they focused on her current behaviors and concerns. Her medication was also seen as being effective in adding an improved sense of control and focus.

Termination

Rosemary agreed to termination of therapy, with the understanding that she could reinitiate treatment in no less than 6 months, in order to accent her positive skills and ability to adjust, a true empowerment process. She would continue to be followed by her psychiatrist regarding the medication issues. The psychiatrist also agreed to the plan and agreed to notify the counselor if he observed any extremely unusual behavior.

She has not initiated any further contact. Telephonic follow-up indicated that she continued to recognize problems but felt better able to gain control over them.

CHAPTER 6

The Road Ahead

Prevention and Education

"All right," you say, "let's get to the roots of this problem. Let's stop this Band-Aid approach and deal with prevention."

"Where do we start?"

"Why, we start with the children, of course. We teach the children that sexual touching is bad, you can't trust adults even within your own family, and that it's their responsibility to 'just say no' and run away screaming."

"Wait a minute. I thought we were supposed to teach kids that their sexuality is good, that trust is essential, and that abuse is the adult's responsibility."

"Well, that's true too. We'll teach them that good touching like hugs is OK unless they're too close and kissing is OK unless it's too long and washing is OK unless it's in the private parts. We can't talk about sex because of district policy so we'll tell them not to trust anyone they don't feel comfortable with and we'll tell them that if they report a bad touch from their father, he'll go to prison for a long, long time and then they won't have any more scary feelings."

I hope my colleagues who are struggling with the creation and implementation of prevention programs will forgive me. I truly do empathize with the task of translating this incredibly complex problem into programs that are helpful, understandable, and accurate for children, adolescents, and adults. We question our success in prevention programs for substance abusers and dropouts (which are far more tangible and less complex), yet we expect to put together a successful prevention program targeted for the victims rather than the perpetrators of a behavior.

Here I focus attention on prevention programs within school systems although some other programs (church and community youth groups) are being put into effect using similar approaches. Since the previous edition of this book, there has not been a significant shift in this direction and schools, when they do anything, stand pretty much alone. This is similar to our societal relegation of sexuality education to the schools, even when we say we don't want that. I also look at educational programs and related societal issues.

School prevention programs typically focus on identification of abuse (signs, symptoms, and reporting), body ownership, trust issues, and saying no (the latter three sometimes grouped under "empowerment"; Tennant, 1988; Tharinger et al., 1988). Curricula that are aimed at children frequently use books in conjunction with movies, puppet play, drawing/coloring pages, or behavioral role-playing. Typical messages include the following:

- the right to safety of the child's own body and nobody else's right to touch it;
- saying no to unwanted or uncomfortable touches;
- assertiveness;
- good versus bad secrets; and
- reporting abuse.

Handled correctly, these messages make sense. We certainly want our children to have the ability to protect themselves, or at least provide a layer of protection. Having our children memorize phone numbers helps when they are lost but doesn't alleviate our responsibility to see that they don't get lost. To extend the analogy, most of us tell our children that it will be OK if they get lost, that an adult will help them; the message in these prevention programs is that, somehow, the kids should be worried about abuse, building their anxiety, if they hear the message at all.

Two surveys of prevention programs (Finkelhor & Dzuiba-Lederman, 1994; General Accounting Office, 1996) have concluded that there remains no evidence of any true prevention from any of the school programs. In fact, there is some thought that the lack of effectiveness has added to a sense of "backlash" against the reporting and treatment of sexual abuse (Finkelhor, 1994).

Tharinger et al. (1988) reviewed prevention programs, and their cogent observations are still true some 10 years later. I summarize two empirical and two philosophical concerns that they raised.

The first empirical concern is whether children, particularly young children, understand the messages that are intended for them. The confusion that was described at the beginning of this section is probably magnified in the mind of a young child without the developmental ability to abstract, generalize, and apply the information. One example, from my experience, is that children are unable to explain what "private parts" are or else they repeat a definition given to them like "parts covered by a bathing suit" without any idea that these adults are talking about their "pee-pee." Likewise, although "good touch-bad touch" concepts seem to make sense to us as adults, children have difficulty conceptualizing discomfort and questionable touches—in their mind, bad touch hurts but we know that most pedosexual contact does not, in fact, physically hurt. Hindman (1989) specifically noted the same objection, that children do not understand the concept of "bad touch." Despite our best efforts, many children simply "don't get it," and there is essentially no empirical evidence that they do understand.

The second empirical criticism is that there is little or no evidence that even if children "get it," there will be any lasting effect. The latest available national survey (General Accounting Office, 1996) indicates that children retained knowledge and skills from these programs for only 3 months to a year, with 3 months being more typical. The layer of protection may be too thin against the other complex and powerful variables that create sexual abuse. The research is, unfortunately, in the position of trying to prove the negative (sexual abuse did *not* happen), which ironically, is the goal of most prevention programs. As educators, we should have long ago learned the lesson that positive focus, encouragement, and reinforcement are far more effective than negative messages, to the point that these messages become negatively reinforcing, potentially increasing the behavior we don't want.

There have been some statistics that may point to an increase in reporting of abuse after some programs that focus on that aspect *and* provide the mechanisms for reports (Freeman-Longo & Blanchard, 1998). This does not appear to have increased the substantiated reports. Do prevention programs prevent? It does not seem likely.

With my training in sexology as well as counseling, I was delighted that Tharinger et al. (1988) asked the philosophical question, How can we teach about sexual abuse without dealing with sex? With the continuing, and perhaps even growing, resistance to sexuality education, many programs have to emphasize safety instead of sex and use euphemisms (e.g., private parts) or indirect references.

It's like discussing the concept of "quacking" without being able to talk about ducks. The programs may even add to sex-negativity because "bad touch" and "say no" certainly receive more emphasis than "sex is a wonderful thing between consenting adults." If sex-negativity has to be mentioned, it should be balanced by developmentally appropriate sex-positive messages. Freeman-Longo and Blanchard (1998) also pointed out that the child (if they "get it") may actually become oversensitized to even appropriate touching and, therefore, become more sex-negative.

The other major philosophical question is whether the potential (or actual) victims should bear the responsibility for solving this problem. Some critics have pointed out the unfairness, ineffectiveness, and negative effects of placing that burden on the child rather than on the perpetrator, specifically, or societal issues more generally (Conte, Rosen, & Saperstein, 1986; Crewdson, 1988; Krazier, 1986; Prendergast, 1996). These authors have suggested that this may take the focus off the true and complex causes of pedosexual behavior. It may even create an increased level of generalized anxiety in some children (Freeman-Longo & Blanchard, 1998).

Although school-based prevention programs may be necessary, their effectiveness is, at best, limited. Has the school lunch program solved the hunger problem in America? No. Why? Because despite the help, it does not deal with the larger economic, employment, and societal issues. And, besides, the kids don't eat the lunches!

The need for broader based education is clear. That's what this book is all about. The professions directly involved with the problem as well as the general public need to understand, in at least a basic way, that this is a problem rooted in many societal issues that we have chosen to ignore, resist, and deny.

We can educate toward the concept of sex positivism, the notion that sexuality is a positive, vital force within each of us—a force of caring, love and concern, a force of intimacy and vulnerability, a force of pleasure, awareness, and spirituality. Sex becomes negative only when we, as a society, allow it to be.

We can educate toward the concept of gender equity. Russell (1986) effectively articulated that two of the most neglected causes of incest, rape, extrafamilial sexual abuse, and sexual harassment are "the way males are socialized to behave sexually and the power structure within which they act out this sexuality" (p. 15). Sexual abuse cannot exist in a society of sexual equality. Almost by definition, it is an offense of the stronger (usually men) against the weak, created out of a lack of true personal power and self-control. Gender equity must not only be pursued at the societal level by truly addressing issues of equal opportunity and rights, but it also must be pursued in the next generation, teaching children that they are valued equally, treated equitably, and encouraged enthusiastically, regardless of their biological sex (and, by extension, regardless of their sexual orientation). Children must feel that they can line up together; learn about reading, math, and sexuality together; and play together. This should be a basic assumption rather than a constant struggle. This is *real* empowerment.

We can educate toward the concept of sexual literacy (Reinisch, 1990). As a society, we can acknowledge that children and adults need and are entitled to accurate, developmentally appropriate, and nonjudgmental information about sexuality, intimacy, and relationships. We now even have a wonderfully clear set of developmental guidelines for the provision of sexuality education, whether in or out of the school system (National Guidelines Task Force, 1991). In my experience, these guidelines have almost completely been ignored by educators.

We can educate toward the concept of positive self-esteem. When each of us feels good about ourselves—our body, our feelings, our successes and failures—the need for controlling and exploiting others simply does not exist. Despite some negative reactions to self-esteem programs in schools and communities, the importance cannot be minimized and has to be an ongoing, developmental, and positive approach throughout the whole educational system.

We can educate toward the concept of healthy family functioning. The basic foundation of our society need not be left to chance. We can learn how to be more responsible, responsive, affective and effective family members and appreciate the full depth in the diversity of families.

The Challenge

Sexual abuse (and the concept of pedosexual behavior) is one of the most complex problems that we as counselors and other helping professionals face in our careers. The issues are societal and yet dramatically affect the lives of individuals. We are faced, as we have been before, with healing the effects of sexism, family dysfunction, exploitation of power, sexual ignorance, and our continuing failure to protect and support our children.

It is heartening that we can *immeasurably* help the healing process in many cases with offenders and in most cases with victims and survivors. The word *immeasurably* is used with two meanings; we know as we see families reunited or children functioning well that we have done a great job, but the results are difficult to measure and quantify. This difficulty in substantiation is critical within the political arena when we try to make a case for treatment rather than warehousing in prison. It also damages our credibility within the criminal justice system.

Research, then, becomes a vital need, but research design seems impossible. How do we control the innumerable variables? What is our consensus regarding treatment goals? What exactly is "good versus bad touch"? What is the true repeat offense rate? By whom? Against whom? Is there a uniform notion of severity? How accurate are our arousal measures? Almost all the research that I reviewed cautions that more research and more systematic approaches are needed. Research still, primarily, comes from the clinical arena.

As counselors, we are in an almost untenable position, but we will continue to face the challenge. The counselor working with pedosexual behavior may need more and better skills than most others. This work demands expertise in individual counseling with men, women, and children; group approaches; dealing with the criminal justice and child protection systems; marital and family therapy; sex education and therapy; substance abuse; and the ability to work in integrated treatment teams over the long haul.

How can we plan for the future? We have to recognize that our tremendous effort is barely scratching the surface. Remember the metaphor of the snow-covered volcano introduced in chapter 1? We are handling the volcano with snow shovels. There are more of us involved in the struggle and we know more about what we're doing, so that we can identify the crevices and the obstacles and maybe even escape from the lava flow, but we can neither stop it nor accurately predict it. We have to face the challenge for precisely as long as society tolerates the problems noted above.

How can we keep going? How can we continue to face the challenge? The answer is easy and, yet, frustrating. We get our reward and encouragement from the teary-eyed offender hugging his daughter for the first time in a year; from the confident smile of a mother at reunification; from the pride of a young survivor graduating from high school; and from the almost embarrassing elation of an adult survivor reporting her first orgasm.

The challenge is for everyone to face, like it or not. Some of us can and will do more than others in directly tackling the tasks, but the challenge is clearly societal and professional.

The challenge is ours. For the children!

GLOSSARY

Anilingus—Oral stimulation of anal area.

Chemical castration—The use of hormonal treatment to reduce sex drive in men.

Child Protective Services—Division of county or state government that is responsible for child welfare (usually the primary agency for reporting any child abuse or neglect). In some states, this agency may be called Children's Services or Family Services.

Coercion—The power tool used to affect another person's behavior; specifically, in the field of sexual abuse, the power used by an offender against a victim, varying from persuasion to physical violence.

Coitus—Genital intercourse; penetration of penis into vagina.

Cunnilingus—Oral (literally, tongue) stimulation of the female genital area.

Deviate/deviant behavior—Behavior that is different from the statistical (or societal) norm. Criteria are usually relativistic and nonscientific. Frequently used in a pejorative manner but seldom used for research or clinical practice. See also *Paraphilia.*

Digital penetration—Insertion of the finger(s) into the anus or vagina.

DSM-IV—The 4th edition of the *Diagnostic and Statistical Manual of Mental Disorders,* published by the American Psychiatric Association.

Dyad (triad) therapy—Conjoint therapy with two (three) people. Sometimes used as a "bridge" from individual to family therapy.

Ejaculation—Flow of semen from the penis; for some females, the release of similar fluid from the vagina.

Ephebophilia—Compulsive arousal to male adolescents.

Exploitation—Sexual abuse of children that may not involve physical contact; for example, nude or sexually explicit photography. In some jurisdictions it is a criminal offense separate from sexual abuse or molestation.

False allegations—allegations of abuse by a child or adult that seem to be inaccurate or untrue.

Fellatio—Oral stimulation of the penis.

Fondling—In general use, touching affectionately. In sexual offense, touching or stroking breast, genital, anal, or buttock areas.

Gender dysphoria—Discomfort with one's gender role, that is, one's masculinity or femininity; sometimes described as being in the body of the wrong sex.

Genital apposition—Rubbing genitals together without penetration, either while clothed or not. This is a frequently reported behavior that may not be illegal in some jurisdictions.

Hebephilia—Compulsive arousal to female adolescents.

Homosexuality—Sexual behavior or orientation directed toward the same sex. Same-sex behavior in pedosexual contact may not be indicative of true homosexual orientation in either partner. Homophobia, the fear of homosexuality, is frequently present in offenders, victims, and adult survivors.

Hymen—Membrane that may wholly or partially cover the vaginal opening. Its absence does not necessarily indicate sexual penetration, although certain patterns of tearing may be used as evidence of penetration if appropriately documented in a medical examination.

Incest—Nonspousal sexual contact within the nuclear family. Definitions vary from one jurisdiction to another and from one researcher to another, making the term ambiguous. It has been replaced by the more accurate term *intrafamilial sexual abuse.* Although sibling contact is incestuous, it may or may not be abusive and is generally excluded.

Intercourse—Contact involving the genitals of at least one person. Although frequently used synonymously with *coitus,* it is a more general term that may not be accurately descriptive. The term may be defined differently by various legal jurisdictions to include coitus, oral contact, anal penetration, digital penetration, or penile-femoral contact.

Intergenerational boundary—The theoretical boundary that exists between adults and children within a family.

Intrafamilial sexual abuse (contact)—Sexual contact within the family or family living unit as opposed to extrafamilial contact.

Labia—The lips or rolls of tissue external to the vaginal opening (often incorrectly referred to as the *vagina*).

Mandatory reporting—The law, in all states, requiring the reporting of any child abuse. Jurisdictions vary as to whether knowledge has to be direct (from the child) or whether suspicion of abuse has to be reported. The "good faith" reporter is usually shielded from liability.

Mandatory sentencing—The law, in some jurisdictions, requiring a specific minimal sentence for a crime without judicial discretion. In Arizona, for example, first-time sexual abuse offenders are required to spend a minimum of 12 years in prison with no probation available. If convicted on two counts, the minimum is 42 years. Preliminary evidence indicates that this has reduced convictions and, certainly, reduced treatment options.

Masturbation—Sexual manual self-stimulation. Although also often used to mean genital stroking of another person, as in *mutual masturbation*, this seems less clear than a more behavioral description, such as *genital stroking/rubbing* or *manual clitoral stimulation.*

Molestation—Any sexually abusive contact between an adult and child. The term is not useful because of its vague and judgmental usage.

Paraphilia—The diagnostic classification for behaviors or arousal patterns that deviate from the societal norm. Pedophilia is included in this classification. Researchers are still struggling with the classification and nomenclature of the paraphilias. Paraphilias may or may not have legal sanctions.

Parentification—The family dynamic that places the child into an inappropriate parenting role.

Parole—Postimprisonment supervision. Jurisdictions vary on the length of parole and extent of supervision.

Pederasty—Classically, men's love of boys, with or without sexual behavior. It has also come to be used for man-to-boy sex, particularly anal contact, making the term vague and unhelpful. Pederasty may still be considered a criminal offense in some jurisdictions but typically is an archaic term.

Pedophilia—Diagnosis in the *DSM-IV* (coded as 302.20 on Axis I) indicating a consistent sexual preference for, or arousal to, prepubertal children. It is generally compulsive and frequently exclusive, with high-frequency behavior.

Pedosexual—Used in this book to describe any sexual contact involving a child; no value judgment or diagnostic or prognostic implications are associated with the use of this term in this book.

Penetration—Insertion of finger, penis, or object into the anus, vagina, or mouth.

Penile transducer—(also known as plethysmograph)—Instrument used to measure minute penile erection/arousal for either diagnostic or treatment monitoring purposes.

Plea bargain—Agreement between the defense and prosecution that calls for the defendant to plead guilty (or no contest) to one or more charges in return for dismissal or reduction of other charges. Also referred to as *copping* (change of plea).

Pornography—Media, typically sexually explicit, that are judged by society to be unacceptable. The term is virtually meaningless and vague. Behavioral descriptors again seem more helpful (e.g., nudity, sexual explicitness, simulated rape). Children may become objects of media known collectively as *kiddie porn*, whose consumers are likely to be pedophiles. Access to the Internet and videotaping equipment has apparently increased the amount of sexually explicit media available. Distinctions between "hard-core" and "soft-core" or between "erotica" and "exploitation" have not been helpful.

Probation—Supervised alternative to prison with varying conditions and restrictions. Typically, violation of probation results in a revocation process and possible incarceration.

Rape—Coitus (or in some jurisdictions, any sexual penetration or attempted penetration) with an unwilling person, typically involving force or physical violence.

Rebonding—The process of rebuilding the affectional and nurturance bond between parent (usually mother) and child.

Recovered memories—The controversy of whether repressed or forgotten memories can be recalled in adulthood.

Repressed memories—The psychodynamic principle that traumatic memories or experiences are repressed into the unconscious.

Ritual abuse—Physical or sexual abuse that is performed in a highly ritualistic and repetitive manner, including modes of dress, specific verbage, and prescribed behaviors.

Satanic cult abuse—A specific case of ritual abuse, in which the devil (or equivalent) is worshiped and celebrated. Sexual contact and human sacrifice are reported to be associated with satanic cults, but there is little substantiation of this.

Sexual abuse—Sexual contact between an adult and child with damaging or potentially damaging consequences. In some jurisdictions, this may also apply to adult-adult contact that does not meet other criteria of sexual assault or rape.

Sexual addiction—Sexually compulsive (nonspecific) behavior that produces an addictive drive for sexual activity. The behavior may be consensual adult activity, multiple or serial partners, masturbation, exhibitionism, or voyeurism, frequently in combination. Children may be objects for an outlet for the sexual addict. Some clinicians and researchers prefer the term *sexually compulsive individuals.*

Sexually transmitted disease (STD)— Any disease that can be transmitted through sexual contact. Includes the traditional "venereal diseases" such as gonorrhea, syphilis, chancroid, and also human immunodeficient virus (HIV), the probable vehicle for AIDS.

Children are, of course, at risk of contracting these, and an STD screen normally is done as part of an initial medical evaluation. There have been very few documented cases of children being infected by HIV as a result of sexual abuse, although caution is still essential.

"Skin-to-skin" contact—Terminology used by law enforcement or prosecutors to indicate touch or other contact without clothing as a barrier.

Taboo, incest—The essentially universal cultural proscription against adult-child sexual contact within the family.

Vagina—The birth canal. The space (or more accurately, the potential space) to contain the penis during coitus. Frequently misused to refer to the external genitalia (labia or vulva).

Vulva—Generic term for the external female genitalia.

Work furlough/release—A program that allows a convicted offender time to work at a regular job and serve "jail time" in the evenings or weekends.

References

Abel, G., & Becker, J. (1984). *The treatment of child molesters.* New York: Columbia University Press.

Abel, G., Huffman, J., Warberg, B., & Holland, C. (1998). Visual reaction time and plethysmography as measures of sexual interest in child molesters. *Sexual Abuse: A Journal of Research and Treatment, 10,* 81–85.

Alexander, M. (1999). Sexual offender treatment efficacy revisited. *Sexual Abuse: A Journal of Research and Treatment, 11,* 101–116.

Alexander, P., & Lupfer, S. (1987). Family characteristics and long-term consequences associated with sexual abuse. *Archives of Sexual Behavior, 16,* 235–245.

Allen, C. (1990). *A comparative analysis of women who sexually abuse children.* Des Moines: University of Iowa Press.

Allen, C. (1991). *Women and men who sexually abuse children: A comparative analysis.* Brandon, VT: Safer Society Press.

Althof, S. (1994). A therapist's perspective on the false memory controversy. *Journal of Sex Education & Therapy, 20,* 246–254.

American Psychiatric Association. (1980). *Diagnostic and statistical manual of mental disorders* (3rd ed.). Washington, DC: Author.

American Psychiatric Association. (1987). *Diagnostic and statistical manual of mental disorders* (3rd ed., rev.). Washington, DC: Author.

American Psychiatric Association. (1994). *Diagnostic and statistical manual of mental disorders* (4th ed.). Washington, DC: Author.

Armsworth, M., & Stronck, K. (1999). Intergenerational effects of incest on parenting: Skills, abilities, and attitudes. *Journal of Counseling & Development, 77,* 303–314.

Baldwin K., & Roys, D. (1998). Factors associated with denial in a sample of alleged adult sexual offenders. *Sexual Abuse: A Journal of Research and Treatment, 10,* 211–226.

Barbach, L. (1975). *For yourself.* Garden City, NY: Anchor Press.

Barbach, L. (1982). *For each other.* New York: Anchor Press.

Bass, E., & Davis, L. (1988). *The courage to heal.* New York: Harper & Row.

Bass, E., & Thornton, L. (1983). *I never told anyone.* New York: Harper & Row.

Bauserman, R., & Davis, C. (1996). Perceptions of early sexual experiences and adult sexual adjustment. *Journal of Psychology & Human Sexuality, 8*(1), 37–59.

Bear, E. (1988). *Adults molested as children: A survivor's manual for women and men.* Brandon, VT: Safer Society Press.

Bell, A., & Weinberg, M. (1978). *Homosexualities.* New York: Simon & Schuster.

Bera, W. (1990). The systemic/attributional model: Victim-sensitive offender therapy. In W. Bera (Ed.), *The use of victim–offender communication in the treatment of sexual abuse* (pp. 45–67). Brandon, VT: Safer Society Press.

Berliner, L., & New, M. (1999). The impact of health care reform: A survey of victim and offender treatment providers. *Sexual Abuse: A Journal of Research and Treatment, 11*(1), 5–16.

Blanchard, G. (1995). *The difficult connection.* Brandon, VT: Safer Society Press.

Blanchard, R., & Dickey, R. (1998). Pubertal age in homosexual and heterosexual sexual offenders against children, pubescents, and adults. *Sexual Abuse: A Journal of Research and Treatment, 10,* 273–282.

Blanchard, R., Watson, M., Choy, A., Dickey, R., Klassen, P., Kuban, M., & Ferren, D. (1999). Pedophiles: Mental retardation, maternal age, and sexual orientation. *Archives of Sexual Behavior, 28,* 111–128.

Blasingame, G. (1998). Suggested clinical uses of polygraphy in community-based sexual offender treatment programs. *Sexual Abuse: A Journal of Research and Treatment, 10,* 37–46.

Bradford, J., & Greenberg, J. (1996). Pharmacological treatment of deviant sexual behavior. *Annual Review of Sex Research, 7,* 283–306.

Brady, K. (1979). *Father's days: A true story.* New York: Dell.

Brislin, R. (Ed.). (1990). *Applied cross-cultural psychology.* Newbury Park, CA: Sage.

Butcher, J., Dahlstrom, W., Graham, J., Tallegen, A., & Kremmer, B. (1989). *The MMPI-2 manual for administration and scoring.* Minneapolis: University of Minnesota Press.

Butz, C., & Spaccarelli, S. (1999). Use of physical force as an offense characteristic in subtyping juvenile sexual offenders. *Sexual Abuse: A Journal of Research and Treatment, 11,* 217–232.

Capuzzi, D., & Gross, D. (1996). "I don't want to live": The adolescent at risk for suicidal behavior. In D. Capuzzi & D. Gross (Eds.),

Youth at risk (2nd ed., pp. 253–283). Alexandria, VA: American Counseling Association.

Carnes, P. (1983). *The sexual addiction.* Minneapolis, MN: CompCare.

Carnes, P. (1985). *Out of the shadows: Understanding sexual addiction.* Minneapolis, MN: CompCare.

Carnes, P. (1988). *Contrary to love: Helping the sexual addict.* Minneapolis, MN: CompCare.

Carnes, P. (1991). *Don't call it love: Recovering from sexual addiction.* New York: Bantam.

Comas-Diaz, L., & Griffith, E. (Eds.). (1988). *Clinical guidelines in cross cultural mental health.* New York: Wiley.

Conte, J., Rosen, C., & Saperstein, L. (1986). An analysis of programs to prevent the sexual victimization of children. *Journal of Primary Prevention, 6,* 141–155.

Courtois, C. (1988). *Healing the incest wound.* New York: Norton.

Crewdson, J. (1988). *By silence betrayed: Sexual abuse of children in America.* Boston: Little, Brown.

Daleiden, E., Kaufman, K., Hilliker, D., & O'Neil, J. (1998). The sexual histories and fantasies of youthful males: A comparison of sexual offending, nonsexual offending, and nonoffending groups. *Sexual Abuse: A Journal of Research and Treatment, 10,* 195–210.

Damon, L., & Waterman, J. (1986). Parallel group treatment of children and their mothers. In K. MacFarlane & J. Waterman (Eds.), *Sexual abuse of young children* (pp. 244–298). New York: Guilford Press.

Davin, P. (1999). Secrets revealed: A study of female sex offenders. In E. Bear (Ed.), *Female sexual abusers* (pp. 9–134). Brandon, VT: Safer Society Press.

Davin, P., Hislop, J., & Dunbar, T. (1999). *Female sexual abusers.* Brandon, VT: Safer Society Press.

Davis, L. (1990). *The courage to heal workbook: For women and men survivors of child sexual abuse.* New York: Harper & Row.

Davis, L. (1991). *Allies in healing: When the person you love was sexually abused as a child.* New York: HarperCollins.

Derogatis, L. (1978). *Derogatis Sexual Functioning Inventory.* Baltimore: Clinical Psychometrics Research.

Dobson, J. (1970). *Dare to discipline.* Wheaton, IL: Tyndale.

Dunbar, T. (1999). Women who sexually molest female children. In E. Bear (Ed.), *The female sexual abuser: Three views* (pp. 311–393). Brandon, VT: Safer Society Press.

Earle, R., & Crow, G. (1989). *Lonely all the time.* New York: Simon & Schuster.

Elkind, D. (1967). Egocentrism in adolescence. *Child Development, 38,* 1025–1035.

Elliott, M. (1993). What survivors tell us—an overview. In M. Elliott (Ed.), *Female sexual abuse of children* (pp. 5–13). New York: Guilford Press.

Erikson, E. (1968). *Identity: Youth and crisis.* New York: Norton.

Finkelhor, D. (1979). *Sexually victimized children.* New York: Free Press.

Finkelhor, D. (1984). *Child sexual abuse.* New York: Free Press.

Finkelhor, D. (1990). Early and long-term effects of child sexual abuse: An update. *Professional Psychology: Research and Practice, 21,* 325–330.

Finkelhor, D. (1994). The backlash and the future of child protection advocacy. In J. Myers (Ed.), *The backlash: Child protection under fire* (pp. 1–16). Thousand Oaks, CA: Sage.

Finkelhor, D., & Dziuba-Leaterman, J. (1994). Victimization of children. *American Psychologist, 49,* 173–183.

Finkelhor, D., Williams, L., & Burns, N. (1988). *Nursery crimes: Sexual abuse in day care.* Newbury Park, CA: Sage.

Fischer, L., & Smith, G. (1999). Statistical adequacy of the Abel Assessment for Interest in Paraphilias. *Sexual Abuse: A Journal of Research and Treatment, 11,* 195–206.

Fleming, J., & Rickord, B. (1997). Solution-focused brief therapy: One answer to managed mental health care. *The Family Journal: Counseling and Therapy for Couples and Families, 5,* 286–294.

Fraser, S. (1988). *My father's house.* New York: Ticknor & Fields.

Freeman-Longo, R., & Blanchard, G. (1998). *Sexual abusers in America: Epidemic of the 21st century.* Brandon, VT: Safer Society Press.

Freeman-Longo, R., Bird, S., Stevenson, W., & Fiske, J. (1995). *1994 Nationwide survey of treatment programs and models serving abuse-reactive children and adolescent and adult sex offenders.* Brandon: VT: Safer Society Press.

Freund, K., & Blanchard, R. (1989). Phallometric diagnosis of pedophilia. *Journal of Consulting and Clinical Psychology, 57,* 100–105.

Freund, K., & Kuban, M. (1994). The basis of the abused abuser theory of pedophilia: A further elaboration on an earlier study. *Archives of Sexual Behavior, 23,* 553–564.

Freund, K., Watson, R., & Dickey, R. (1990). Does sexual abuse in childhood cause pedophilia: An exploratory study. *Archives of Sexual Behavior, 19,* 557–568.

Friedman, S. (1988). A family systems approach to treatment. In L. Walker (Ed.), *Handbook on sexual abuse of children* (pp. 326–349). New York: Springer.

Fuller, A., & Bartucci, R. (1991). Sexual abuse and HIV transmission. *Journal of Sex Education and Therapy, 17,* 46–52.

Gardner, R. (1987). *The parental alienation syndrome and the differenti-*

ation between fabricated and genuine child sex abuse. Cresskill, NJ: Creative Therapeutic.

General Accounting Office. (1996). *Preventing child sexual abuse: Research inconclusive about effectiveness of child education programs* (GAO/GCD-96-156). Washington, DC: U.S. Government Printing Office.

Giaretto, H. (1982). *Integrated treatment of child sexual abuse.* Palo Alto, CA: Science & Behavior Books.

Gordon, B., & Schroeder, C. (1995). *Sexuality: A developmental approach to problems.* New York: Plenum Press.

Groth, A. (1979). *Men who rape: The psychology of the offender.* New York: Plenum Press.

Groth, A., & Birnbaum, H. (1978). *Adult sexual orientation and attraction to underage persons. Archives* of Sexual Behavior, 7, 175–181.

Hanson, R. (1997). How to know what works with sexual offenders. *Sexual Abuse: A Journal of Research and Treatment, 9,* 129–145.

Hathaway, S., & McKinley, J. (1943). *Manual for the Minnesota Multiphasic Personality Inventory.* Minneapolis: University of Minnesota Press.

Heiman, J., & LoPiccolo, J. (1988). *Becoming orgasmic: A sexual and personal growth program for women.* New York: Prentice Hall.

Herman, J. (1981). *Father/daughter incest.* Cambridge, MA: Harvard University Press.

Hindman, J. (1989). *Just before dawn: From the shadows of tradition to new reflections in trauma assessment and treatment of sexual victimization.* Ontario, OR: AlexAndria Associates.

Hindman, J., & Hutchens, L. (1990). The restitution model: The restitution treatment and training program. In J. Yokley (Ed.), *The use of victim-offender communication in the treatment of sexual abuse* (pp. 23–44). Brandon, VT: Safer Society Press.

Hislop, J. (1999). Female child molesters. In E. Bear (Ed.), *Female sexual abusers* (pp. 135–310). Brandon, VT: Safer Society Press.

Howes, R. (1998). Plethysmographic assessment of incarcerated nonsexual offenders: A comparison with rapists. *Sexual Abuse: Research and Treatment, 10,* 183–194.

Huber, C. (1997). Time-limited counseling: Invisible rationing and informed consent. *The Family Journal: Counseling and Therapy for Couples and Families, 5,* 325–327.

Hunter, M. (1990). *Abused boys: The neglected victims of sexual abuse.* New York: Fawcett Columbine.

Iglehart, J. (1996). Managed care and mental health. *New England Journal of Medicine, 334,* 131–135.

Indart, G. (1999). The experience and effect of sexual abuse and trauma. In G. Ryan (Ed.), *Web of meaning: A developmental-contex-*

tual approach in sexual abuse treatment. Brandon, VT: Safer Society Press.

Johanek, M. (1988). Treatment of male victims of child sexual abuse in military service. In S. Sgroi (Ed.), *Vulnerable populations* (Vol. 1, pp. 103–114). Lexington, MA: Lexington Books.

Johnson, S., & Cuestas-Thompson, E. (1999). Summary and future directions. In A. Lewis (Ed.), *Cultural diversity in sexual abuser treatment* (pp. 215–222). Brandon, VT: Safer Society Press.

Jones, R., Loredo, C., Johnson, S., & McFarlane-Nathan, G. (1999). A paradigm for culturally relevant sexual abuser treatment. In A. Lewis (Ed.), *Cultural diversity in sexual abuser treatment* (pp. 3–44). Brandon, VT: Safer Society Press.

Jones, W., & Emerson, S. (1994). Sexual abuse and binge eating in a nonclinical population. *Journal of Sex Education and Therapy, 20,* 47–55.

Kaplan, M., Becker, J., & Tenke, C. (1991). Assessment of sexual knowledge and attitudes in an adolescent sex offender population. *Journal of Sex Education & Therapy, 17,* 217–225.

Kaufman, A., & Kaufman, N. (1993). *Manual—Kaufman Adolescent & Adult Intelligence Test.* Circle Pines, MN: American Guidance Services.

Klein, M., & Tiefor, L. (Speaker). (1997). *How sexology limits it's own effectiveness clinically, academically, and in public policy* (Cassette Recording No. 19A–9725). Arlington, VA: American Association of Sex Educators, Counselors and Therapists.

Knopp, F., & Benson, A. (1996). *A primer on the complexities of traumatic memory of childhood sexual abuse: A psychobiological approach.* Brandon, VT: Safer Society Press.

Kosky, R. (1983). Child suicidal behavior. *Journal of Child Psychology and Psychiatry and Allied Disciplines, 24,* 457–468.

Krazier, S. (1986). Rethinking prevention. *Child Abuse and Neglect, 10,* 259–261.

Lalumiere, M., & Harris, G. (1998). Common questions regarding the use of phallometric testing with sexual offenders. *Sexual Abuse: A Journal of Research and Treatment, 10,* 227–238.

Lee, C. (Ed.). (1997). *Multicultural issues in counseling: New approaches to diversity* (2nd ed.). Alexandria, VA: American Counseling Association.

Leitenberg, H., Greenwald, E., & Tarran, M. (1989). The relation between sexual activity among children during preadolescence and/or early adolescence and sexual behavior and sexual adjustment in young adulthood. *Archives of Sexual Behavior, 18,* 299–314.

Levin, S., & Stava, L. (1987). Personality characteristics of sex offenders: A review. *Archives of Sexual Behavior, 16,* 57–79.

Lew, M. (1988). *Victims no longer.* New York: Ruby Street Press.
Lewis, A. (1999a). *Cultural diversity in sexual abuser treatment: Issues and answers.* Brandon, VT: Safer Society Press.
Lewis, A. (1999b). Working with culturally diverse populations. In A. Lewis (Ed.), *Cultural diversity in sexual abuser treatment: Issues and approaches* (pp. 45–67). Brandon, VT: Safer Society Press.
Li, C., West, D., & Woodhouse, T. (1993). *Children's sexual encounters with adults: A scientific study.* Buffalo, NY: Prometheus.
Lindstrom, B. (1999). Attachment, separation, and abuse outcomes: Influence of early life experience and the family of origin. In G. Ryan (Ed.), *Web of meaning: A developmental-contextual approach in sexual abuse treatment* (pp. 32–48). Brandon, VT: Safer Society Press.
Loftus, E., & Ketcham, K. (1994). *The myth of repressed memory: False memories and allegations of sexual abuse.* New York: St. Martin's Press.
Long, S. (1986). Guidelines for treating young children. In K. MacFarlane & J. Waterman (Eds.), *Sexual abuse of young children* (pp. 220–243). New York: Guilford Press.
MacFarlane, K. (1986). Child sexual abuse allegations in divorce proceedings. In K. MacFarlane & J. Waterman (Eds.), *Sexual abuse of young children* (pp. 121–150). New York: Guilford Press.
MacFarlane, K., & Waterman, J. (1986). *Sexual abuse of young children.* New York: Guilford Press.
Maletsky, B. (1996). Denial of treatment or treatment of denial? *Sexual Abuse: Research and Treatment, 8*(1), 1–5.
Maletsky, B. (1998). Science, technology, and sexual offending. *Sexual Abuse: Research and Treatment, 10,* 169–173.
Maltz, W. (1991). *The sexual healing journey: A guide for survivors of sexual abuse.* New York: Harper.
Maltz, W., & Holman, B. (1987). *Incest and sexuality: A guide to understanding and healing.* Lexington, MA: Lexington Books.
Marotta, S., & Asner, K. (1999). Group psychotherapy for women with a history of incest: The research base. *Journal of Counseling & Development, 77,* 315–323.
Marshall, W., & Anderson, D. (1996). An evaluation of the benefits of relapse prevention programs with sex offenders. *Sexual Abuse: A Journal of Research and Treatment, 8,* 209–221.
Marshall, W., & Barbaree, H. (1990). An integrated theory of the etiology of sexual offending. In W. Marshall, D. Laws, & H. Barbaree (Eds.), *Handbook of sexual assault: Issues, theories, and treatment* (pp. 257–275). New York: Plenum Press.
Mathews, R., Mathews, L., & Speltz, K. (1989). *Female sexual offenders: An exploratory study.* Brandon, VT: Safer Society Press.

Matthews, J. (1993). Working with female sexual abusers. In M. Elliott (Ed.), *Female sexual abuse of children* (pp. 57–73). New York: Guilford Press.

Maurer, A. (1972–1994). Various articles. *The Last Resort?* The Newsletter of the Committee to End Violence Against the Next Generation.

McCann, S., & Petrich-Kelly, B. (1999). Learning to feel good about yourself: Puberty education reconsidered. *SIECUS Report, 27*(6), 24–27.

McCarthy, B. (1990). Treatment of incest families: A cognitive-behavioral model. *Journal of Sex Education and Therapy, 16,* 101–114.

McConaghy, N., Blaszczynski, A., Armstrong, M., & Kidson, W. (1989). Resistance to treatment of adolescent sex offenders. *Archives of Sexual Behavior, 18,* 97–108.

McCormack, A. (1986). Runaway youths and sexual victimization: Gender differences in an adolescent runaway population. *Child Abuse and Neglect, 10,* 387–395.

McFadden, J. (Ed.). (1999). *Transcultural counseling* (2nd ed.). Alexandria, VA: American Counseling Association.

McGovern, K., & Peters, J. (1988). Guidelines for assessing sex offenders. In L. Walker (Ed.), *Handbook on sexual abuse of children* (pp. 350–370). New York: Springer.

McGrath, M., Cann, S., & Konopasky, R. (1998). New measures of defensiveness, empathy, and cognitive distortion for sexual offenders against children. *Sexual Abuse: A Journal of Research and Treatment, 10,* 25–36.

McKenry, P., Fishler, C., & Kelly, C. (1982). Adolescent suicide. *Clinical Pediatrics, 21,* 266–270.

McNaron, T., & Morgan, Y. (1982). *Voices in the night.* Pittsburgh: Cleis Press.

Miletski, H. (1995). *Mother–son incest: The unthinkable broken taboo: An overview of findings.* Brandon, VT: Safer Society Press.

Millon, T. (1984). *Millon Clinical Multiaxial Inventory* (2nd ed.). Minneapolis, MN: National Computer Systems.

Monto, M., Zgourides, G., & Harris, R. (1998). Empathy, self-esteem, and the adolescent sexual offender. *Sexual Abuse: A Journal of Research and Treatment, 10,* 127–140.

Morfit, S. (1994). Challenge to psychotherapy: Through the lens of the "recovered" or "false memory" debate. *Journal of Sex Education and Therapy, 20,* 234–245.

Morris, M. (1982). *If I should die before I wake.* New York: Dell.

Murrey, G., Bolen, J., Miller, N., Simensted, K., Robbins, M., & Truskowski, F. (1993). History of childhood sexual abuse in women with depressive and anxiety disorders: A comparative study. *Journal of Sex Education and Therapy, 19,* 13–19.

Nagayama-Hall, G. (1995). Sexual offender recidivism revisited: A meta-analysis of recent treatment studies. *Journal of Counseling and Clinical Psychology, 63,* 802–809.

National Guidelines Task Force. (1991). *Guidelines for comprehensive sexuality education.* New York: Sexuality Information and Education Council of the U.S.

Nichols, H., & Molinder, I. (1984). Multiphasic Sex Inventory: Manual. Tacoma, WA: Authors. (Available at 437 Bowles Drive, Tacoma, WA 98466)

Nyman, A., & Svensson, B. (1997). *Boys sexual abuse and treatment.* Bristol, PA: Kingsley.

Okami, P., Olmstead, R., & Abramson, P. (1997). Sexual experiences in early childhood: 18-year longitudinal data from the UCLA Family Lifestyles Project. *Journal of Sex Research, 34,* 339–347.

Pawlak, A., Boulet, J., & Bradford, J. (1991). Discriminant analysis of a sexual functioning inventory with intrafamilial and extrafamilial child molesters. *Archives of Sexual Behavior, 20,* 27–34.

Perry, G., & Orchard, J. (1992). *Assessment and treatment of adolescent sex offenders.* Sarasota, FL: Professional Resource Press.

Porter, F., Blick, L., & Sgroi, S. (1982). Treatment of the sexually abused child. In S. Sgroi (Ed.), *Handbook of clinical intervention in child sexual abuse* (pp. 115–130). Lexington, MA: Lexington Books.

Prendergast, W. (1996). *Sexual abuse of children and adolescents.* New York: Continuum.

Rasmussen, L. (1999). Factors related to recidivism among juvenile sexual offenders. *Sexual Abuse: A Journal of Research and Treatment, 11,* 69–85.

Reinisch, J. (1990). *The Kinsey Institute new report on sex: What you must know to be sexually literate.* New York: St. Martin's Press.

Rencken, R. (1996a). Body violation: Physical and sexual abuse. In D. Capuzzi & D. Gross (Eds.), *Youth at risk: A prevention resource for counselors, teachers, and parents* (2nd ed., pp. 59–80). Alexandria, VA: American Counseling Association.

Rencken, R. (1996b). Sex positivism for mental health counselors. In W. Weikel & A. Palmo (Eds.), *Foundations of mental health counseling* (2nd ed., pp. 105–107). Springfield, IL: Thomas.

Rosencrans, B. (1997). *The last secret.* Brandon, VT: Safer Society Press.

Rush, F. (1980). *The best kept secret.* Englewood Cliffs, NJ: Prentice-Hall.

Russell, D. (1986). *The secret trauma.* New York: Basic Books.

Ryan, G. (1999a). Victim to victimizer: Rethinking victim treatment. In G. Ryan (Ed.), *Web of meaning; A developmental-contextual approach in sexual abuse treatment* (pp. 1–18). Brandon, VT: Safer Society Press.

Ryan, G. (1999b). *Web of meaning: A developmental-contextual approach in sexual abuse treatment.* Brandon, VT: Safer Society Press.

Salkind, N., & Ambron, S. (1987). *Child development* (5th ed.). New York: Holt, Rinehart & Winston.

Schlank, A., & Shaw, P. (1996). Treating offenders who deny their guilt: A pilot study. *Sexual Abuse: A Journal of Research and Treatment, 8,* 17–23.

Schneider, J. (1988). *Back from betrayal: Surviving his affairs.* New York: Harper & Row.

Schwartz, M. (1992). Sexual compulsivity as post-traumatic stress disorder: Treatment perspectives. *Psychiatric Annals, 22*(5), 333–338.

Sgroi, S., & Sargent, N. (1993). Impact and treatment issues for victims of childhood sexual abuse by female perpetrators. In M. Elliott (Ed.), *Female sexual abuse of children* (pp. 14–36). New York: Guilford Press.

Smith, G., & Fischer, L. (1999). Assessment of juvenile sexual offenders: Reliability and validity of the Abel Assessment for Interest in Paraphilias. *Sexual Abuse: A Journal of Research and Treatment, 11,* 207–216.

Spiegel, L. (1988). Child abuse hysteria and the elementary school counselor. *Elementary School Guidance and Counseling, 23,* 275–283.

Stevenson, M., & Gajarsky, W. (1991). Unwanted childhood sexual experiences relate to later revictimization and male perpetration. *Journal of Psychology & Human Sexuality, 4,* 57–70.

Stroud, D. (1999). Familial support as perceived by adult victims of childhood sexual abuse. *Sexual Abuse: A Journal of Research and Treatment, 11,* 159–176.

Studer, L., & Reddon, J. (1998). Treatment may change risk prediction for sexual offenders. *Sexual Abuse: A Journal of Research and Treatment, 10,* 175–181.

Sue, D. W., & Sue, D. (Eds.). (1990). *Counseling the culturally different: Theory and practice* (2nd ed.). New York: Wiley.

Summit, R. (1983). The child sexual abuse accommodation syndrome. *Child Abuse and Neglect, 7,* 177–193.

Tennant, C. (1988). Preventive sexual abuse programs: Problems and possibilities. *Elementary School Guidance and Counseling, 23,* 48–53.

Tharinger, D., Krivacska, J., Laye-McDonough, M., Jamison, L., Vincent, G., & Hedlund, A. (1988). Prevention of child sexual abuse: An analysis of issues, educational programs, and research findings. *School Psychology Review, 17,* 614–634.

Timms, R., & Connors, P. (1992). *Embodying healing: Integrating bodywork and psychotherapy in recovery from childhood sexual abuse.* Brandon, VT: Safer Society Press.

Turner, M., & Turner, T. (1994). *Female adolescent sexual abusers: An exploratory study of mother–daughter dynamics with implications for treatment.* Brandon, VT: Safer Society Press.

Vargas, L., & Koss-Chioino, L. (Eds). (1992). *Working with culture.* San Francisco: Jossey-Bass.

Vontress, C., & Epp, L. (1997). Historical hostility and the African American client: Implications for counseling. *Journal of Multicultural Counseling and Development, 25,* 170–184.

Ward, T., & Hudson, S. (1998). The construction and development of theory in the sexual offending area: A metatheoretical framework. *Sexual Abuse: A Journal of Research and Treatment, 10,* 47–64.

Ward, T., Hudson, S., & Keenan, T. (1998). A self-regulation model of the sexual offense process. *Sexual Abuse: A Journal of Research and Treatment, 10,* 141–165.

Waterman, J. (1986). Developmental considerations. In K. MacFarlane & J. Waterman (Eds.), *Sexual abuse of young children* (pp. 15–29). New York: Guilford Press.

Waterman, J., & Lusk, R. (1986). Scope of the problem. In K. MacFarlane & J. Waterman (Eds.), *Sexual abuse of young children* (pp. 3–14). New York: Guilford Press.

Wechsler, D. (1981). *Wechsler Adult Intelligence Scale Revised Manual.* New York: The Psychological Corporation.

Wernik, U. (1993). The role of the traumatic component in the etiology of sexual dysfunctions and its treatment with Eye Movement Desensitization Procedure. *Journal of Sex Education & Therapy, 19,* 212–222.

Wieckowski, E., Hartsoe, P., Mayer, A., & Shortz, J. (1998). Deviant sexual behavior in children and young adolescents: Frequency and patterns. *Sexual Abuse: A Journal of Research and Treatment, 10,* 293–303.

Wiehe, V. (1990). *Sibling abuse: Hidden physical, emotional, and sexual trauma.* Lexington, MA: Lexington Books.

Williams, S. (1999). Alcohol's possible covert role: Brain dysfunction, paraphilias, and sexually aggressive behaviors. *Sexual Abuse: A Journal of Research and Treatment, 11,* 147–158.

Wilson, R. (1999). Emotional congruence in sexual offenders against children. *Sexual Abuse: A Journal of Research and Treatment, 11,* 33–47.

Wolf, S., Conte, J., & Engel-Meinig, K. (1988). Assessment and treatment of sex offenders in a community setting. In L. Walker (Ed.), *Handbook for sexual abuse of children* (pp. 371–390). New York: Springer.

Wyatt, G. (1991). Child sexual abuse and its effects on sexual functioning. *Annual Review of Sex Research: An Integrative and Interdisciplinary Review, 2,* 249–266.

Wylie, M. (1993, September–October). The shadow of a doubt. *Family Therapy Networker,* 18–73.

Yates, A. (1978). *Sex without shame.* New York: Morrow.

Yokley, J., & McGuire, D. (1990). Introduction to the therapeutic use of victim–offender communication. In J. Yokley (Ed.), *The use of victim–offender communication in the treatment of sexual abuse* (pp. 7–21). Brandon, VT: Safer Society Press.

Zilbergeld, B. (1978). *Male sexuality.* New York: Bantam Books.

INDEX